Industrial Landscapes
of the
East Midlands

Kimberley Brewery: a sketch showing the tower and private railway sidings (by courtesy of Hardys and Hansons plc).

Industrial Landscapes
of the
East Midlands

Marilyn Palmer
&
Peter Neaverson

Phillimore

1992

Published by
PHILLIMORE & CO. LTD.,
Shopwyke Hall, Chichester, Sussex

ISBN 0 85033 829 8

Printed and bound in Great Britain by
BIDDLES LTD.,
Guildford, Surrey

CONTENTS

LIST OF ILLUSTRATIONS

Frontispiece: Kimberley Tower Brewery and private railway sidings

FOREWORD

The series, *The Making of the English Landscape*, initiated by W. G. Hoskins in 1955, was a milestone in the study of the historical evolution of the landscape. The fourth of the series dealt with Leicestershire but Hoskins, who was to become the Professor of English Local History at the University of Leicester, disliked that county's industrial landscape. He claimed, probably rightly, that it 'nowhere attained the dramatic and demented ugliness of the Potteries or the Black Country. It is profoundly dull, as one might expect from industries making such prosaic things as vests and pants, boots and shoes, biscuits and bricks.' He failed to appreciate the solid prosperity which characterised the Victorian landscape of the East Midland counties. The series has included a volume on Northamptonshire, but not, as yet, on Derbyshire and Nottinghamshire. The series generally pays little attention to the industrial landscape.

The term 'industrial archaeology' was also born in 1955 and its study, together with a growing appreciation of the Victorian built environment and concern for its conservation, has created the concept of 'industrial heritage' which now plays a major role in environmental considerations. This present book is aimed both at the serious student of the landscape and the interested tourist, enabling them to interpret the field evidence of two hundred years of industrial change in the four East Midland counties. The first two chapters examine the visual evidence for manufacturing and extractive industry within the region, together with a brief account of their historical development. These two themes are explored in more detail in the next two chapters as a series of area studies, chosen to illustrate the wide diversity of the industrial landscapes of the East Midlands. Each area study concludes with a gazetteer of sites which is not limited to the main theme but illustrates the inter-relationship between industry and transport in any one area. The final chapter looks at the landscapes of selected East Midland towns, which attained the height of their prosperity during the Victorian era.

The East Midlands has witnessed the beginnings of the powered cotton spinning and hosiery industries, mass production of boots and shoes and the invention of machine-made lace. The diverse mineral resources created the need for early railway and canal systems. The 'dramatic and demented ugliness of the Potteries and the Black Country' has now largely been swept away, but the evidence for the more prosaic industries of the East Midlands remains and may be found and interpreted by the interested visitor.

This book is the result of many years of fieldwork and documentary research in the East Midlands. It is impossible to acknowledge all the sources consulted, but the reader is referred to the Bibliography at the end of the book. Particular thanks are due to the various County Record Offices and Local Studies Libraries who have made us welcome. The county industrial archaeology and history societies of the East Midlands meet regularly at Conferences and these, along with society publications, have provided us with information. Among many individuals, we would especially like to thank Ron Greenall and Geoffrey Starmer from Northamptonshire, Don Morley from Nottinghamshire, Mark Higginson and Brian Walden from Derbyshire and members of the Leicestershire Industrial History Society Research Group. We would also like to thank Janet Neaverson for her company on field trips and her forbearance during long hours spent at the word processor and John Fletcher for his assistance in preparing the manuscript. We gratefully acknowledge financial assistance in publication from Redland Aggregates Ltd. and Hardys and Hansons PLC.

1. The East Midlands Region, showing the areas covered in the Gazetteers in Chapters Three, Four and Five.

3.1 The Bassetlaw Area of Nottinghamshire

3.2 The Trent Valley and Rural East Nottinghamshire

3.3 The Derwent and Wye Valleys of Derbyshire

3.4 The Soar Valley and the Grand Union Canal Line

3.5 The Nene Valley of Northamptonshire

4.1 The East Derbyshire and Nottinghamshire Coalfield

4.2 The South Derbyshire and North-west Leicestershire Coalfield

4.3 Rural East Northamptonshire and Leicestershire

5.1 Nottingham and its Satellites

5.2 Newark-on-Trent

5.3 Derby

5.4 Leicester

5.5 Leicestershire Market Towns

5.6 Northampton and the Shoe Towns, Kettering, Desborough and Rothwell

INTRODUCTION

Industrial Archaeology and the Study of the East Midlands Landscape

The purpose of archaeology is to utilise the tangible evidence of past human activity as part of our attempt to understand the development of human society. Such tangible evidence includes artefacts like tools and pottery, humps and bumps in the landscape which indicate the presence of demolished buildings or burial places and standing buildings which survive, often in altered form. Archaeology is generally taken to mean the knowledge of times long past, but the excavation of a Roman villa and the recorded survey of a row of late 18th-century workers' cottages make equal contributions towards the understanding of past human society. The nearer one comes to the present day, the more likely it is that maps and documents can tell much of the story but these are selective in their coverage: written evidence was more often produced by the masters rather than the men. It is the task of the industrial archaeologist to record the surviving physical evidence of the industrial past, whether in the form of standing buildings, surviving machinery, changes to the landscape or below-ground remains, and to interpret them in their topographical, technological and human environment. Industry has been the dynamic force which has shaped human development over at least the past two centuries and change in the landscape has largely been conditioned by the human response to industrial activity. The industrial archaeologist is, in fact, the archaeologist of industrial society.

At first sight, the mosaic pavements, Roman forts and Norman churches seem a far more attractive aspect of our past heritage than the remains of blast furnaces, lead smelt mills, textile workers' houses or disused canals. But man at work in the past is to many people more relevant and approachable than our Roman conquerors and Norman clerics. Most of our lives are spent in a working environment, and the reasons why a miller, struggling to grind corn in a water-powered mill subject to the freezing and drying up of his power supply, welcomed the steam engine or the potter, attempting to transport his wares by packhorse over unmade roads, invested in the building of a canal are immediately understandable. Much that was unattractive about the industrial past was also ephemeral: the tin roofs on mining sites or the smoke and grime of the Potteries have largely disappeared, leaving a heritage of well-built stone and brick buildings, often converted to other uses but whose original function is discernable to the knowledgeable eye. The purpose of this book is to develop that knowledgeable eye in the reader, showing him how to recognise in both landscape and buildings the evidence of man at work in the past.

The East Midlands may at first sight seem an unlikely area for the study of industrial archaeology, not having experienced immense industrial development like that of Lancashire or the Potteries. But 20th-century redevelopment has equally not been on a large scale, and so buildings associated with its 18th- and 19th-century food processing, textile, boot and shoe and mining industries have survived to be of interest to the investigator. In 1965 David Smith produced his book on *The Industrial Archaeology of the East Midlands*, one of the best in the David and Charles series. His main interest was in the textile industries, and he omitted the major food processing industries of the East Midlands, such as malting and brewing, and dealt only briefly with the extractive industries. The photographic surveys he made of buildings were deposited with the National Monuments Record and now form an invaluable archive, since some of them have been either demolished or altered, and so his work as an industrial archaeologist is a continuing example to all of us in the field. But the study of industrial archaeology has grown during the last 25 years: listing and scheduling procedures now include industrial monuments, and conservation areas have been established which involve important groups of industrial buildings, such as the Lace Market in Nottingham. Local authorities have seen the value of preservation as opposed to demolition of industrial structures and many local trusts have been set up to encourage visitors to industrial sites and museums. The time is ripe for a re-assessment of the development of the industrial landscape of the East Midlands.

The East Midlands as a Region

There are no clear boundaries either geographically or historically to define the East Midlands. Derbyshire, Nottinghamshire and Leicestershire, including Rutland, are generally accepted as part of the area and we have chosen to include Northamptonshire, whose transport and industrial developments were closely linked with those of Leicestershire. On the other hand, we have excluded Lincolnshire, since the River Trent in its lower reaches was a formidable barrier with neighbouring Nottinghamshire and led to Lincolnshire's separate and distinctive industrial development. Only 19th-century railway growth, particularly that associated with the exploitation of ironstone in the east of the region, integrated Lincolnshire with Northamptonshire and the eastern part of Leicestershire. We have also excluded the north-western area of the Derbyshire Peak District, which has obvious transport and industrial links with Lancashire and Cheshire rather than the East Midlands.

The lack of a coastline had an important effect on the industrial development of the region, encouraging self-sufficiency since access to distant markets, particularly London, was troublesome. All major East Midland rivers drain eastwards and northwards into either the Humber or the Wash while the Trent, the Welland and the Nene were all improved for navigation during the 17th and 18th centuries. This encouraged eastward export of processed products such as lead and wool but failed to create easy access to large centres of population which might have stimulated manufacturing industry. On the roads, long distance carriers did operate between East Midland towns and London by the mid-17th century, for example along Watling Street from Northamptonshire, but the Great North Road only touched the extreme north-eastern corner of the region. Most major routes in the four counties were turnpiked by the mid-18th century but this strengthened local trading links rather than encouraged the exploitation of distant markets. Not until canals were constructed in the late 18th century did the East Midlands as a whole have reasonable links with the west and north-west, and these did benefit the coal and textile trades. But it was the building of railways in the 19th century which was the single most important development in breaking the pattern of self-sufficiency in East Midlands industry, enabling mechanisation and greatly increased output in the textile and leather industries and wider markets for Derbyshire

2. The East Midlands Region, showing the principal rivers and land over 400 feet (122m) above sea level. Towns are marked as in number one.

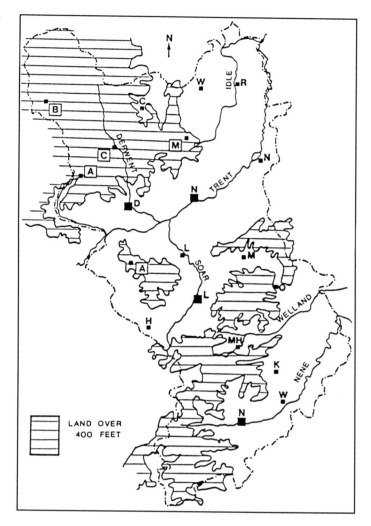

and Nottinghamshire coal and iron. It has been argued that the breakthrough into modern industry in the East Midlands only occurred after 1850 and, although this ignores the considerable technological innovation which took place in the late 18th century, it cannot be denied that the railways were the major factor in enabling East Midlands industry to break free of restraints imposed by its geographical position.

The region has few well-defined natural boundaries. In the north-west, the Derbyshire gritstone moors and limestone plateaux rise to over 1,000 feet, providing good water-powered sites for an early textile industry. The east of the region is bounded by the broad Jurassic limestone belt, exploited for building stone and then for ironstone in the 19th century. The south

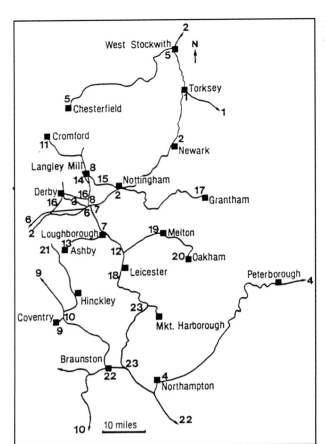

3. The East Midlands Region, showing the navigable rivers and canals. The dates of opening are shown.

1.	Roman	Foss Dyke, from the River Trent at Torksey to Lincoln
2.	1699	River Trent, passable to Burton, subsequent improvements
3.	1721	River Derwent, from River Trent at Wilne to Derby
4.	1761	River Nene, from the Wash to Northampton
5.	1777	Chesterfield Canal, from the River Trent at West Stockwith to Chesterfield, via Retford and Worksop
6.	1777	Trent and Mersey Canal, from the River Trent at Wilne to Preston Brook, via Shardlow, Burton and Fradley Junction
7.	1778	River Soar Navigation, from the River Trent to Loughborough
8.	1779	Erewash Canal, from the River Trent to Langley Mill
9.	1790	Coventry Canal, from Coventry to the Trent and Mersey Canal at Fradley Junction.
10.	1790	Oxford Canal, from the River Thames at Oxford to the Coventry Canal at Hawkesbury Junction, via Braunston
11.	1794	Cromford Canal, from Langley Mill to Cromford, with branches to Pinxton and Lea Wood
12.	1794	Leicester Navigation, from Loughborough to Leciester, using sections of the River Soar
13.	1794	Charnwood Forest Canal, from Nanpantan, near Loughborough to Thringstone
14.	1795	Nutbrook Canal, from the Erewash Canal to Shipley
15.	1796	Nottingham Canal, from Nottingham to Langley Mill
16.	1796	Derby Canal, from the Trent and Mersey Canal at Swarkestone to Sandiacre, via Derby with branch to Little Eaton
17.	1797	Grantham Canal, from the River Trent at Nottingham to Grantham
18.	1797	Leicester and Northampton Union Canal, from Leicester to Debdale wharf, extended in 1809 to Market Harborough via Foxton
19.	1797	Melton Mowbray or River Wreake Navigation, from the Leicester Navigation at Syston to Melton Mowbray
20.	1803	Oakham Canal, from Melton Mowbray to Oakham
21.	1804	Ashby Canal, from the Coventry Canal at Marston to Moira, via Hinckley and Measham
22.	1805	Grand Junction Canal, from the River Thames at Brentford to the Oxford Canal at Braunston with link opened to the River Nene at Northampton in 1815
23.	1814	Grand Union Canal (old) from Foxton to the Grand Junction Canal at Norton Junction, with arm to Welford

and south-west have no clear limits, the rolling country of Northamptonshire passing imperceptibly into Buckinghamshire and Oxfordshire. In Leicestershire, high ground is limited to the pre-Cambrian inliers and igneous intrusions, valuable sources of building and road materials. From an industrial point of view, the most important geological features are the two coalfields: the Nottinghamshire and Derbyshire coalfield extends southwards from Yorkshire as far as Nottingham, while a smaller coalfield has been worked further south across the Derbyshire and Leicestershire border. Both coalfields contain resources of ironstone and clay as well as coal.

The settlement pattern of the region is one of market towns and nucleated villages rather than scattered farms and hamlets, since open field farming survived longer in the East Midlands than elsewhere in the country and a relic of this can still be found at Laxton in Nottinghamshire. Isolated farms date from the period of parliamentary enclosure in the late 18th and early 19th centuries, when some farmers chose to build their homes on their newly acquired consolidated holdings. Some villages, particularly those in the Vale of Belvoir and parts of Northamptonshire, were dominated by major landowners who prevented the development of rural industry since it did not boost estate incomes and its practitioners could become a charge on the parish. Other villages, especially those on the fringes of towns or on poor agricultural land, remained open to immigration and their inhabitants supplemented their incomes by spinning or framework knitting. This distinction between the open and closed village has had a considerable effect on the East Midland industrial landscape.

Population growth in the region remained below the national average until late in the 19th century, when the simultaneous development of railways and the coalfields broke up the self-sufficiency of the region and encouraged the growth of a national market. Leicestershire and Northamptonshire did not, on the whole, share in this development and remained below the national average in the rate of population growth. The region has no obvious urban centre in the way that Birmingham dominates the West Midlands. Each county has its county town, and only Derby, Nottingham and Leicester had a population of over 10,000 in 1801. A century later there were 16 towns of over 20,000 and a spectacular growth of urban centres in the 5,000 to 10,000 range on the Nottinghamshire and Derbyshire coalfields. In Leicestershire, only Loughborough approached Leicester in size, while in Northamptonshire, Kettering and Wellingborough, both centres of iron production as well as boot and shoe manufacture, and Peterborough were, with Northampton itself, over 15,000 in 1901. Elsewhere in these two counties, the market town rather than the urban industrial centre continued to dominate the scene.

Industrial Development

There are two clear strands in the industrial development of the East Midlands. The first derives from the region's comparative isolation from national markets until the 19th century and therefore its self-sufficiency. The characteristic industries of the East Midlands grew from a rural base, processing the products of agriculture for either food or clothing. This is the image promoted by incentives to visit the Shires, the fox-hunting centre of 19th-century England. But it ignores the immense diversity of mineral resources possessed by the East Midlands, the exploitation of which has on the whole succeeded in integrating into the rural landscape. The first two chapters of this book will give a brief historical account of these two strands of development but, since it is a book about landscapes, will lay more emphasis on the kinds of visual evidence which still indicate past industrial activity in the region.

1

MANUFACTURING INDUSTRIES

Agriculture was the mainstay of the East Midlands economy until at least the end of the 18th century. In this area and the south Midlands, the open field system was retained longer than in any other part of England but there was considerable variation within it. The temporary conversion of arable strips to pasture enabled farmers in suitable areas like the eastern uplands of the region to keep larger flocks of sheep than normal, and in Northamptonshire and southern Leicestershire cattle were fattened for beef production. Both Celia Fiennes in the late 17th and Daniel Defoe in the early 18th century commented on the quality of livestock to be found in the region. Consequently, following the final phase of enclosure of the open fields by Act of Parliament in the second half of the 18th century, a considerable proportion of previously arable land was converted to pasture. This had two major effects on the industrial development of the East Midlands. Firstly, there was a decline in the output of barley for the traditional industries of brewing and malting, although the import of grain from East Anglia was greatly eased by improvements to river navigation. Secondly, conversion of arable to pasture led to a decline in the amount of agricultural labour needed and many farm workers were forced to seek alternative employment. The traditional by-employment of Leicestershire and Nottingham-shire had been hand-knitting of worsted thread into caps and hose from at least the 15th century, followed by machine knitting in the 17th, and the influx of surplus rural labour turned this from a by-employment into a full-scale industry. Hand-made lace was an alternative by-employment in Northamptonshire, particularly near its southern borders.

Worsted thread had been produced in the East Midlands from the late Middle Ages, but with the exception of parts of Northamptonshire the area had not developed a tradition of weaving: spun thread was sent from Leicester, Nottingham and other towns to the well-established weaving centres like Norwich and West Yorkshire. Consequently, when the need arose to satisfy demand for thread from the hosiery industry, the spinning industry was able to diversify and produce silk and cotton thread as well as worsted, even though the raw materials for these had a long way to travel, at first from London and later from Liverpool. The initiative came from inventors and entrepreneurs such as Thomas Lombe, Richard Arkwright and Jedediah Strutt, who recognised the market for thread in the hosiery industry and made use of new technology to meet it. The first successful water-powered textile mill was pioneered in Derby by Thomas Lombe early in the 18th century, while in the cotton spinning industry the first application of both water and steam power was carried out in the East Midlands. The region's early technological lead did not last, largely because of the communication difficulties already discussed, but for a brief period at the end of the 18th century, the East Midlands possessed the most innovative textile industry in the world.

Agricultural change stimulated other industries as well. For example, the enclosure of previously uncultivated areas of waste and common at a time of unprecedented demand, particularly during the Napoleonic Wars, led to a great demand for burnt lime to dress the land. Once holdings were consolidated rather than held in scattered strips, farmers built new houses and outbuildings on their own land rather than remaining in the village and these isolated farms are a conspicuous feature of the East Midlands landscape. Arable land which became permanent pasture retained its characteristic ridge and furrow, now permanently fossilised under grass and still easily seen, particularly in east Leicestershire and in Northamptonshire. Agriculture remained the dominant industry of the East Midlands until well into the 19th century.

Food processing

The long survival of the open field system in the East Midlands encouraged the establishment of large numbers of small, water-powered cornmills, each usually only serving a particular manor or village. Generally, mills were small and unpretentious, built of stone in much of Derbyshire and in the east of the region and in red brick elsewhere. Large steam mills were only built as transport improved. With little high ground except in the north-west of the region, waterwheels tended to be breast-shot rather than overshot and considerable effort was devoted to the construction of storage ponds and long leats to raise the head of water. On the River Sence in Leicestershire, for example, which is a small river with a reasonable fall of over 20 feet per mile in its 13.5-mile length, the use of leats and storage ponds enabled ten mills to last into the 20th century. Two of these, Sheepy Magna and Odstone, were large enough to afford the installation of turbines to replace water-wheels in the early 1900s. In some cases, rather than a leat being built, the whole stream was diverted and now contours around a hill rather than flowing in the valley bottom, as is the case at Anstey, Leire and Newtown Linford in Leicestershire.

When rivers were improved for navigation, battles raged with millers anxious to keep their head of water and most river navigations incorporated locks by-passing the weirs which diverted water to the mills. The Nene in Northamptonshire was made navigable in the first half of the 18th century but had 33 watermills along its sinuous course between Northampton and Peterborough. These mills were by-passed by staunches and pound locks; the staunches have been replaced and the locks are now conspicuous by their bottom guillotine-type gates. The River Soar had 20 mills throughout its length and its tributary, the Wreake, improved for navigation in the 1790s, nine mills in its 13.5-mile length, each needing a by-pass lock and weir. The landscape effect of this dual use of water for both power and navigation can be particularly well seen along these three rivers since many of the mills survive, albeit converted to alternative use.

Two other alternative uses of water could affect the livelihood of millers. The building of public reservoirs for water supply for growing towns deprived mills of their water resources: the miller at Quorndon in Leicestershire was paid £2,750 in 1893 when the construction of Swithland Reservoir impounded his water supply. Late 19th-century flood prevention schemes were the death knell for several mills in Leicester and Loughborough.

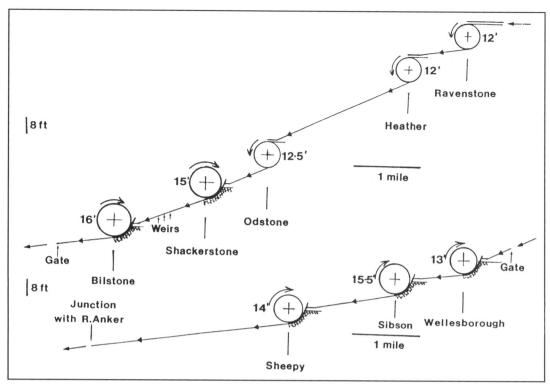

4. Watermills on River Sence in West Leicestershire, a schematic river profile with wheel sections.
(Redrawn from *The Plan and Section of the Rivers Anker and Sence* by John Sinclair, 1845, in Leicestershire Record Office).

5. Titchmarsh watermill and lock on the River Nene in Northamptonshire.

6. South Luffenham wind and steam mills in the Rutland District of Leicestershire.

7. Eland Street Maltings in Nottingham.

Lacking the steady wind of East Anglia, windmills are less common but are more frequently found on the high ground in the north-west and east of the region, where they tend to be stone built with several brick courses below the cap. Some post-mills survive, like the Cat and Fiddle mill in Derbyshire, but many were replaced by tower mills in the early 19th century. In several cases where the terrain permitted, a watermill and windmill worked in conjunction, 'helping out' when conditions were better suited to one or the other. At South Luffenham in Rutland, a stone-built watermill operated on its Domesday site until 1948, working during the 19th century in conjunction with a brick tower mill until this was replaced by a steam-powered roller mill built alongside the railway. There are many other examples of this kind of economic interaction in the East Midlands.

Barley had figured in open field crop rotations in the East Midlands, particularly in the eastern part of the region. This was converted into malt by a widely dispersed rural malting industry until the end of the 19th century, when malting became concentrated in a few urban centres such as Newark and Nottingham or alongside railways, as at Langwith in Derbyshire. The traditional process of floor malting created numerous distinctive buildings which can still be recognised despite their conversion to other uses. Barley was steeped in water and then allowed to germinate for a week or two, depending on conditions. During this time it was spread four to eight inches deep on the floor and turned frequently by the maltsters. Consequently, maltings were usually buildings of two or three low storeys, since height was unnecessary on the malting floors, and had small windows fitted with louvres to exclude light and allow ventilation. Once the barley had germinated, it was dried in a kiln and the pyramidal roof, crowned with a vent, is a further characteristic feature of maltings. They can be found in villages, as at Stathern in Leicestershire or Ranskill in Nottinghamshire: along the Trent, as at Fiskerton, Laneham and later the great concentration in Newark: in market towns like Oundle,

Southwell or Market Harborough: and later large malting complexes in urban centres like East Retford and Nottingham.

Breweries were less widely distributed than maltings, but rural examples can still be found, although large breweries in towns superseded them by the end of the 19th century. Ground malt was mixed with water to form wort, boiled with hops and then fermented with yeast. Since liquids were involved, use was made of gravity to ease the flow of materials throughout the process and breweries are often characterised by tall narrow buildings and even towers. Since brewers distributed their own products, there were numerous ancillary buildings often grouped round a yard, including coopers' workshops for the production of barrels, stables for dray horses and office accommodation. Two splendid 19th-century tower breweries survive in Nottingham, while smaller ones can be detected in large villages like Sileby in Leicestershire and towns such as Oundle and Worksop. Rather more unusual in this part of the world was an extensive hop-growing industry centred around Tuxford and Ollerton in the Bassetlaw district of Nottinghamshire, which declined once the railways enabled easy transport of hops grown in southern England to East Midlands breweries.

Textiles

The evidence for the widespread hand worsted-spinning industry of the East Midlands is largely documentary in the form of inventories, although some 15th-century churches such as Loughborough benefited from the wealth generated by wool staplers and worsted merchants. In Northamptonshire worsted thread had been woven into cloth in Northampton, Kettering and surrounding villages like Corby as an outpost of the East Anglian cloth industry, but, as in Norwich, the industry was hit by competition from West Yorkshire towards the end of the 18th century. Worsted thread was in great demand for hosiery by the 18th century, but remained hand-spun until Arkwright's water-frame was adapted for worsted spinning in the 1780s. Some water-powered mills were built in Nottinghamshire but none lasted for very long, possibly because they were divorced from the main centre of worsted hosiery. This had always been the specialisation of Leicestershire but, because of its lack of good water power resources, it was not until steam power was applied to the worsted spinning process that the industry could become established in Leicester, its natural home. But industrial unrest prevented its early adoption and powered spinning was established first in the West Midlands rather than the East. It was not until the 1820s that Leicester began to reassert its leadership in this field and Loughborough, too, became an important centre. The steam-powered mills were often situated alongside canals to enable easy transport of coal, like Cartwright and Warner's pedimented building in Loughborough and the even more impressive Friar's Mill and West Bridge Mills in Leicester. They were multi-storey and wider than the early cotton spinning mills as many made immediate use of gas lighting rather than being forced to rely on daylight and candles or oil lamps. It is impossible to tell a worsted spinning mill from a hosiery factory from its external appearance, and many of the spinning mills were utilised for hosiery manufacture from the 1880s.

Silk throwing was an industry entirely generated by the demand for silk yarn by the hosiery industry, since the raw silk had to be imported from France and Italy through London and transported to the East Midlands. The first water-powered silk mill was set up in Derby in 1702 by Thomas Cotchett, a local barrister, really the first powered textile mill of any description.

8. Gorsey Bank cotton spinning mill at Wirksworth in Derbyshire.

9. Cressbrook cotton spinning mill on the River Wye in Derbyshire.

This failed, but Thomas Lombe's mill was a more successful experiment and provided silk thread for an expanding hosiery industry in both Derby and Nottingham. Further silk mills were built in the East Midlands, mostly in Derby but also in isolated villages with good water power sites like Tideswell or Pentrich and in larger centres like Sutton-in-Ashfield and Chesterfield. The introduction of steam power for silk throwing towards the end of the 18th century enabled big mills to be built in Nottingham, some of which still survive. Most mills went over to steam, apart from the very isolated ones; one of the best survivals is the silk throwing community at Maythorne in north-east Nottinghamshire, grouped around the water-powered mill.

In the middle of the 19th century there were nearly 6,000 people employed in the silk industry in Derbyshire and Nottinghamshire, comprising nearly 14 per cent of silk workers in England. These figures include those producing silk hose or gloves on the knitting frame. But changes in fashion, particularly the abandonment by men of knee breeches in favour of long trousers, initiated a decline in the silk industry which was made worse by a free trade treaty with France in 1860. This exposed the local silk industry to direct competition from France, and the number of mills in Derbyshire fell from 42 to 14 by 1890. By the second decade of the 20th century, silk manufacture had practically disappeared from Derby, although it survived further west around Leek and Macclesfield. There are few remains of the industry in Derby itself, although the foundations of Lombe's mill do survive as part of the Industrial Museum.

The silk-throwing process involves twisting thread already spun by the silkworm into usable thread. Spinning cotton requires steady motion to stretch and twist cotton fibres into thread and is a more complex process than silk throwing. It was in fact in Birmingham that the first steps towards mechanising the cotton spinning process were taken, by John Wyatt and his partner Lewis Paul in the 1730s. They experimented with the idea of using rollers to draw out the cotton fibres, a process later successfully exploited by Richard Arkwright. They opened a small factory in Birmingham, but this impinged on the East Midlands when in 1742 Edward

Cave opened a small water-powered mill in Northampton using the Wyatt and Paul method. This failed, but engravings do still exist of this pioneer factory in an area not really suited to water-powered textile manufacture.

The Derby silk mill revealed both the potential of the application of water power to textile processes and the existence of an expanding market for thread by the East Midlands hosiery industry. It is not, therefore, surprising that both James Hargreaves and Richard Arkwright brought their cotton spinning inventions to this area when driven out of Lancashire by riots. Both arrived in Nottingham in 1768. Hargreaves' spinning jenny was still hand-powered and produced soft, rather coarse, threads more suitable for wefts in weaving than for hosiery. However, its installation demanded considerably less capital than the Arkwright machine and jennies were used in small workshops, particularly in the western parts of Derbyshire. Several of the later mills in this area, notably Edale, Tideswell and Bamford, evolved from a small workshop of this kind rather than from the better known factory system generated by Richard Arkwright.

Arkwright had adapted the Wyatt and Paul roller spinning principle to produce a strong thread suitable both for warps and for knitting. He drove his machine first by horse-power at Hockley in Nottingham but the quest for water power took him to Cromford on the River Derwent in Derbyshire, where his machine became known as the water frame. In partnership with Samuel Need, the wealthiest hosier in Nottingham, and the banker Ichabod Wright, he built his first water-powered factory at Cromford in 1771. This was driven not by the powerful Derwent but by a small stream known as the Bonsall Brook and a lead mining drainage sough. The story of Arkwright is too well known to need repetition here, but he was responsible for building ten cotton mills in the East Midlands and his partners and other entrepreneurs, like Jedediah Strutt, Samuel Unwin, George and James Robinson and Thomas Evans, for the construction of many more. By 1788 there were 56 'Arkwright-type' mills in the East Midlands, although this was only one quarter of the total as the industry had already begun to shift northwards to Lancashire and Yorkshire. The archetypal water-powered cotton mill was a three- or even four-storey stone or brick building about 70 feet long but only 30 feet wide to allow maximum penetration of daylight. The interior beams supporting the various floors were of wood, and there were large numbers of comparatively small windows giving the building a domestic look: some of the early mills, like those in Wirksworth in Derbyshire, resemble a row of substantially built two-storey cottages. The early mills were entirely functional in design, but Masson Mill, begun in 1783, initiated a trend towards architectural pretension with its pediment, Venetian windows and central cupola: this trend was echoed in Cressbrook Mill in the Wye Valley, built by William Newton in 1815 to replace an earlier Arkwright mill.

Water-power resources were the paramount consideration in siting the mills. Some were constructed alongside major rivers, particularly in the Derwent Valley and a little later along the Rivers Maun, Meden and Poulter in the north-east of the region. Others made use of smaller rivers and streams, since over 2,000 spindles could be driven from a 16-feet diameter wheel. Substantial storage ponds are a feature of many of these mills, since water supplies were unreliable. Good examples can still be found at Pleasley, Cuckney and in association with the Robinson's mills at Papplewick and Linby, all in Nottinghamshire. The need for good water-power sites resulted in the isolation of many of the mills, which created a problem of labour supply, and some mill owners made use of pauper apprentice labour until prevented from doing

10. The *Prince of Wales* Brewery at Basford, Nottingham.
11. Laneham Maltings, beside the River Trent in Nottinghamshire.

12. Friars' Mill, built for wool combing and worsted spinning, by the River Soar in Leicester.

13. Sectional drawing of
North Mill, Belper, in
Derbyshire, powered by
the River Derwent.
(Abraham Rees, *The
Cyclopaedia; or
Universal Dictionary of
Arts, Sciences and
Literature, 1819-20.*)

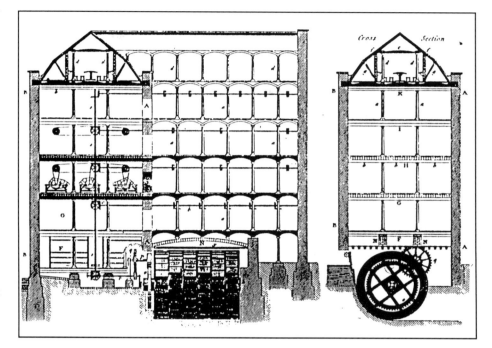

14. The North and East
Mills by the River
Derwent at Belper in
Derbyshire.

so by early 19th-century legislation. A good example of an apprentice house survives at Cressbrook Mill, where 200 to 300 apprentices worked, and there were others associated with the Robinson mills at Linby in Nottinghamshire. From the beginning, however, Arkwright had encouraged whole families to reside near his Cromford mills, employing the women and children in the mill and the men either as overlookers or on knitting and weaving as outwork. Whole new communities were added to existing settlements, such as Darley Abbey just north of Derby. Arkwright, Strutt and Evans included community buildings such as churches, chapels and schools in their model communities.

The contents of a cotton mill -- raw cotton, oil from machinery, candle and later gas-lighting -- made the timber-framed buildings a very high fire risk, as is indicated by insurance premiums in the later years of the 18th century. Arkwright's first mill in Nottingham was destroyed by fire in 1781, and there are many other examples. The first improvement in construction was to protect the wooden beams by iron sheeting underneath and by a tiled floor above, a system tried by Jedediah Strutt in a four-storey warehouse built in Milford in 1792-3 and shortly afterwards in his calico mill in Derby. These buildings utilised cast iron columns to support the floors, and when one of his Belper mills burnt down in 1803, Strutt decided to replace the transverse timber beams by cast iron as well. This had already been tried by Charles Bage at the Ditherington flax mill near Shrewsbury and Strutt was acquainted with Bage. The North Mill at Belper, constructed in 1804, made use of cast iron beams and columns together with brick vaulted arches supporting a tiled floor on each storey. It was the third of its kind to be erected and set a pattern which was reproduced in numerous textile mills in other parts of the country. For the

15. A house on Alfreton Road in Nottingham with top floor workshop for framework knitting.

16. A framework knitter's house in Calverton, Nottinghamshire, dated 1857 in the brickwork.

East Midlands had already begun to lose its early lead in the cotton spinning industry. The first direct application of steam power to cotton spinning took place in a mill belonging to the Robinsons of Papplewick in 1786: they were experiencing problems with water supply and made use of a Boulton and Watt engine with sun and planet gearing to provide rotary motion, which had only been patented in 1782. Their engine was not particularly successful, but once the principle had been established other mill owners followed suit. Lancashire possessed both a coalfield and the port of Liverpool through which most of the raw cotton was now coming, and the cotton spinning industry naturally began to gravitate northwards. Few new mills were built in the East Midlands although some were added to existing structures like the impressive brick-built East Mill of 1912 in Belper. Some mills on the coalfield, like those in Pleasley and Mansfield, went over to steam and sprouted imposing chimneys, but on the whole steam was more common in the urban worsted mills and some of the water-powered cotton mills continued into the 20th century.

Hosiery and Knitwear

Silk and cotton spinning came into existence in the East Midlands to provide yarn for its most important textile industry, the manufacture of hosiery. An important handknitting industry was mechanised as early as 1589 by William Lee's invention of the stocking frame, probably at Calverton in Nottinghamshire. Since it was silk hose which were in demand at the time, he took his machine to London and then to France and it was not until the middle of the 17th century that framework knitting became well established in the East Midlands. During the 18th century the region began to dominate the British hosiery industry, reaching a position shortly after 1800 when over 90 per cent of the industry was centred in the East Midlands. At the time of a Government Commission set up in 1844 to examine the condition of the framework knitters, there were nearly 48,500 knitting frames in Great Britain and only 4,500 of those were located elsewhere, mainly in the important knitwear industry of the Scottish Borders. By this time, because of the location of the yarn spinning industry, Leicestershire dominated the worsted branch of the industry, Nottingham the cotton and Derbyshire the silk, although there was some interchange of the two latter fibres across the county borders.

The industry was organised on a putting-out system, knitters being dependent on yarn spinners situated in the major towns for their supplies. Consequently, the main knitting centres were usually located six miles or less from the spinning centres of Mansfield, Sutton-in-Ashfield, Nottingham, Derby, Loughborough, Leicester and Hinckley. This resulted in the concentration of the industry in the river valleys of the Leen, Erewash, Derwent and Soar. There was little framework knitting in West Derbyshire, where lead mining provided alternative employment, or in the east of the region. This was largely due to the social structure of the settlements. Framework knitting tended to become established in the 'open' villages of the area, not subject to domination by aristocratic landowners, often on marginal agricultural land and where immigration was freely allowed. The 'closed' villages of the east of the region, under the domination of the Duke of Rutland and other major landowners, did not welcome immigrants or the intrusion of rural industry and remained largely agricultural in their occupational structure.

The knitting frame remained hand-powered for almost three centuries after its invention and so the hosiery industry remained home-based until well into the 19th century. This late survival

17. A framework knitter's workshop at Bonsall in Derbyshire with external access steps to upper floor.

18. The interior of the Framework Knitters' Museum at Ruddington in Nottinghamshire.

19. A typical late 19th-century hosiery factory at Duke Street in Leicester (*Leicester Chamber of Commerce Year Book*, 1921).

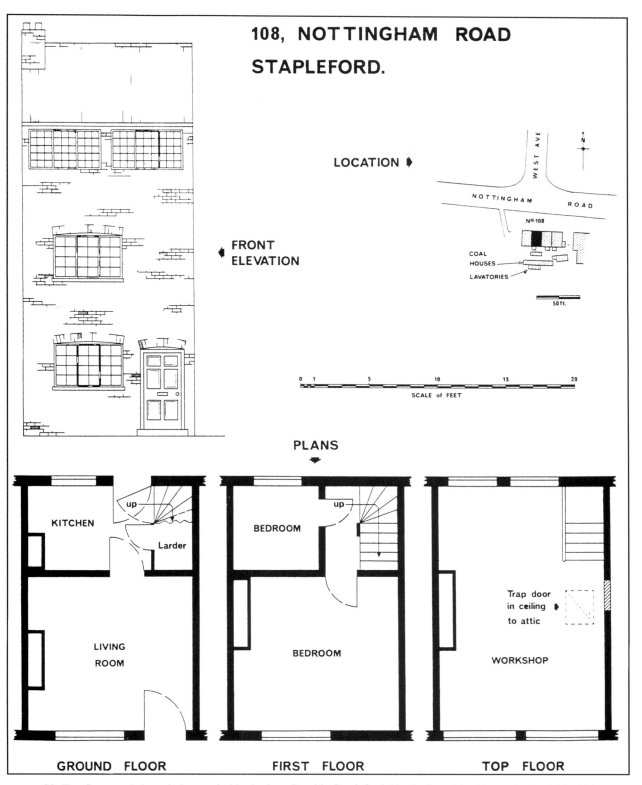

20. Top floor workshops in houses in Nottingham Road in Stapleford, Nottinghamshire (drawn by David Smith).

21. A tenement lace factory: Clyde Works in Radford, Nottingham.

of a domestic industry means it is possible to utilise the visual evidence provided by buildings in a way that is rare in other branches of the textile industry. The buildings in fact reveal four phases of development. In the first place, when the stocking frame began to be used in the East Midlands in the late 17th century, knitters inserted long windows into their homes to allow maximum light to fall on its rather complex mechanism. These can be recognised in some timber-framed buildings in the region, notably in Hinckley and Shepshed in Leicestershire and Sutton Bonington in Nottinghamshire. As the industry grew during the 18th century, speculative builders began to take advantage of the knitters' need for houses with a workshop large enough to contain their frames and so rows of houses were built incorporating workshops. If these were placed on the first or second storey, the light was better than on the ground floor but strengthening was needed to support the weight of the frame. Maximum light was also achieved by the omission of interior partition walls. It has been suggested that there is a regional pattern in this phase of building, with top-shops preferred in some areas and ground floor workshops in others, but survival is not sufficiently comprehensive to test this theory. Houses of this kind continued to be built until well into the 19th century, as an example dated 1857 in Calverton demonstrates. But by then wide stocking frames were being built to knit fabric rather than single hose and it was difficult to find room for these large machines in the home. The third phase of building is that of small workshops where hand-powered machines were operated. These were usually of one or two storeys and characterised by windows on several sides of the building. Two good examples have become museums of the industry at Ruddington in Nottinghamshire and Bushloe End in Wigston, Leicestershire.

The hosiers dominated the industry, being responsible both for the provision of yarn and the finishing and marketing of knitted goods. The knitters themselves paid rent both for their homes to landlords and their frames to the hosiers and other middlemen in the industry. They also often rented the space in which their frames stood, whether in the home or workshop. This system suited the hosiers so well that little notice was taken of various early experiments to power the knitting frame. William Cotton of Loughborough patented a machine in 1864 which automatically narrowed and widened knitted fabric by steam power, but the industry did not break out of its antiquated system of production until frame rent was abolished in 1874 and the Education Acts of 1870 and 1876 broke up the family unit. The use of powered machines increased during the 1870s and 1880s and the last three decades of the 19th century witnessed the building of a vast number of hosiery factories, with adjacent boiler houses and chimneys attesting to their use of steam power. Gas or oil engines provided alternative sources of power. The whole urban landscape of Leicester, Loughborough and, to a lesser extent, Nottingham changed during this period and small factories were also built in market towns and even villages like Countesthorpe and Fleckney south of Leicester, where labour was cheaper than in the towns. Alongside the factories grew up dyeing houses, easily detected because of their long louvred roofs, and bleachworks. A stream or riverside site was important for these, as can be seen at Frog Island on the River Soar in Leicester. This sudden urbanisation of the hosiery industry resulted in rapid town expansion, and row upon row of well-built brick terraced houses sprang up: the back-to-backs, common in the Leeds textile and clothing industries, were never a prominent feature in East Midland towns.

One exception to this was Nottingham, where the open fields limiting the town's expansion were not enclosed until the mid-19th century and some of the worst basement and court housing in England could be found there. Nottingham had been more prominent than Leicester in the hosiery industry at one time, but the adaptation of the stocking frame for lace manufacture at the end of the 18th century transformed the industrial development of the town. The first major development was the warp machine, whose 20th-century descendant is the Raschel machine: on these machines a lacy pattern is knitted on to a warp similar to that found on a loom. The point net frame of 1778 was an adaptation of the stocking frame to produce net rather than knitted fabric. This was greatly improved upon by John Heathcoat's bobbin or twist net machine, developed in the first decade of the 19th century, producing a regular mesh which could then be embroidered. Leaver's lace machine, first patented in 1813 to produce mesh but later modified to use a jacquard attachment, could by the 1840s produce patterned lace rivalling that produced on the lace pillow. The Victorian passion for lace curtains and antimacassars as well as lace on clothing stimulated both the lace industry and the cotton spinning industry which provided much of the yarn.

Purpose-built housing incorporating workshops characterised the early years of the lace industry much as it did the hosiery industry, as can be seen in surviving examples at Stapleford; it is impossible to distinguish between buildings for the two industries by visual evidence alone. Lace machines, which were considerably larger than hosiery frames, were being installed in workshops by the 1830s. The application of steam power soon followed so that by 1850 there were few hand-powered machines remaining, in contrast to the hosiery industry. The high cost of powered lace machines led to the creation of a system whereby a small business could be set up in the lace industry with little capital outlay by renting machines and factory space and sharing power sources with other firms in the same building. A number of speculative builders, often themselves involved in lace machine manufacture, built huge tenement factories for this purpose, usually in the satellite towns and villages of Nottingham where land was cheaper. Good examples survive, still in multiple occupation but not all now concerned with lace, in Radford, Beeston and Sandiacre. There were few hosiery factories built on the scale of the lace tenement factories, and so there is an interesting contrast between the late 19th-century urban landscape of Leicester and the Nottingham area. Heavier and larger lace machinery required single storey buildings, which intruded on the urban scene in the early 20th century.

The finishing processes, dyeing and trimming, were carried out in separate premises by lace dressers whilst mending and packaging took place in the warehouse. Marketing was previously London-based but transferred to Nottingham in the 1850s, resulting in the creation of the Lace Market. The elaborate architectural style of these warehouses contrasts sharply with the stark utilitarian facades of the tenement factories, although the attic mending windows in the warehouses indicate their role in lace finishing.

Leather and Rural Crafts

Further south in Northamptonshire and parts of Leicestershire, the rural setting of the East Midlands provided the raw materials for another clothing industry, the processing of leather into boots, shoes and other goods. Like the textile and hosiery industries, its presence in the region is not easy to account for, but by 1960 Northamptonshire and Leicestershire combined produced 45 per cent of the total output with 66 million pairs of leather footwear. It is well known that in 1642 Thomas Pendleton, a Northampton boot maker, obtained a large order for footwear for the army bound for Ireland, which was the first of many orders placed in the area for army boots. Northamptonshire certainly had a pastoral economy, producing suitable hides, and oak forests providing tannin but so did other areas in Britain, notably the Lake District, which did develop a considerable footwear industry. It was the county's central position in Britain which was important. Watling Street provided easy communication with London, at once both the major market for footwear and an important source of hides. London's own footwear industry, like its hosiery industry, was hedged around with the restrictive practices insisted upon by the guilds and Livery Companies of the city, and so expansion for large scale production was impossible. The worsted industry of Northamptonshire declined in the face of

22. Back garden workshops at Wood Street, Earl Shilton, in Leicestershire.

23. An early boot and shoe factory at Long Buckby, in Northamptonshire.

24. Barratt's Footshape Boot Works in Northampton.

competition from Yorkshire, but left a legacy of capital and labour which could be utilised for the footwear industry. Finally, as in the textile industry, the initiative of individual entrepreneurs like Thomas Pendleton, and later the Gotch family and Thomas Crick in Leicester, was responsible for both technological and organisational development in the industry.

The tanning industry was mainly located in rural areas and the outskirts of towns because of the noxious fumes generated by the process. Tanning by means of oak bark meant that the hides had to be soaked for a lengthy period in a series of pits, which were situated in single storey buildings with ventilation louvres. The process was accelerated by the introduction in the 19th century of mechanically driven drums and later by the faster chrome tanning process. These innovations enabled tanners to dispense with the open pits and the tannery could be accommodated in factory-type buildings, although usually still with ventilation louvres. At the same time the great increase in demand meant that hides had to be imported and these were usually tanned at the ports. The final dressing processes, however, still took place in the East Midlands, often in more elegant buildings than those normally associated with the industry.

The footwear industry remained home-based even longer than the hosiery industry and so its development can be traced through a study of its buildings. Production was split into separate processes which were carried out by different operatives, usually in separate premises. Consequently, partly-finished goods were transferred from one place to another by what became known as the basket-work system. Cutting out the leather, or clicking, was a highly skilled job if waste of the hides was to be avoided. This process was the first to be removed from the home into warehouses, multi-storey buildings with wall-mounted cranes for lifting the raw leather and containing clicking rooms where a degree of quality control could be exercised. Closing, or assembling the components together, was generally carried out in backyard workshops, often purpose built and included in the rent of the house like the top shops of the hosiery industry. These did not need to be more than single storey and many were built as lean-tos against the garden wall, as can be seen very well in Rushden, Rothwell and in the areas of Kettering and Northampton developed in the second half of the 19th and even in the early 20th century. The use of the Singer sewing machine from the 1850s did not alter the organisation of the industry, since early machines were treadle-powered and could be used in home workshops. It was mechanisation of the processes of cutting out heavy leather for soles and attaching these to the upper, a process known as lasting, which brought domestic workers into a factory environment. Thomas Crick patented his method for riveting boots, establishing a factory in Leicester. The heavy Blake sole-stitching machine, introduced from America in the 1860s, required power operation and was usually driven by line-shafting from a steam or gas engine: like hosiery, the footwear industry never passed through a water-powered phase. Once power was available, closing processes could also be done more quickly in a factory environment although the basket-work system persisted well into the 20th century. Small footwear firms occasionally took over the workshop premises of hosiery firms in south Leicestershire when these were vacated for factory production, indicating the persistence of the domestic system within the footwear industry.

The typical footwear factory of the late 19th century was generally of three storeys and a basement, where leather was stored in dark and cool conditions. Clicking and closing took place on the top floor, where there was maximum light, with lasting on the second floor and packaging and despatch on the ground floor. As shoe machinery became heavier, firms were obliged to move some processes into single storey units. It is possible in some Northamptonshire towns and villages to study all the phases of development of the industry on a single site, a multi-storey factory with north-light single storey additions being situated in the midst of an area of terraced housing with back yard workshops for closing and finishing. Northamptonshire and south Leicestershire towns and villages expanded dramatically in the last three decades of the 19th century because of the expansion of the footwear industry, and have left a landscape of well-built brick houses interspersed with small factories. Only a few firms expanded into vast premises, like Barratts and Manfields in Northampton or the CWS Wheatsheaf Works in Leicester, which are comparable with lace factories in Nottinghamshire. Wholesale warehouses were also built, some to service their own shop chains and others of more elaborate style to impress retail customers.

Like textiles and hosiery, the footwear industry brought ancillary industries in its wake. Packaging was required, both in the form of small wheeled baskets or skeps for use in the industry and boxes for packing the finished goods. Waste leather was ground and used for the manufacture of leatherboard, several corn mills switching to its production. The fashion for elastic-sided boots in the mid-19th century created another industry, the production of elastic web. This was a knitted fabric with a cotton warp and rubberised weft which was also used for corsets, hence the large corset factories in south Leicestershire and Northamptonshire.

The boot and shoe industry is an excellent example of the value of surviving visual evidence in demonstrating the effect of a particular industry on the built environment. The same cannot be said for the widespread rural crafts of the East Midlands, which did not on the whole take place in buildings whose function can be determined from their external appearance. One exception is rope-making, where the long low buildings seen more frequently in dockyards and fishing ports do still survive. Ropes were in considerable demand for agricultural purposes and also for canal use, and small rural roperies did exist, as at Shardlow close to the Trent and Mersey Canal. Basket-making was extremely important in the valleys of the River Trent and its tributaries well into the 20th century, using locally grown osiers and even surpassing the production of the Somerset Levels. Baskets were in great demand for both agricultural use and general packaging until replaced by non-returnable containers. Skeps were in extensive use in both hosiery and footwear factories as well as in the textile mills. The work was carried out in small workshops and factories which are difficult to identify in the field. Cooperages formed an important adjunct to breweries, while wheelwright's shops and smithies provided essential equipment for agriculture. The successors to these were the engineering works of the late 19th century, usually situated in towns to take advantage of transport links. They developed partly to manufacture the machinery required for the rural based industries described in this chapter but also to service the extensive extractive industries which are an equally important adjunct of the East Midlands scene.

Engineering

Engineering was a new industry which emerged as a result of the advances in industrialisation towards the end of the 18th century. There were three main groups of people in the new industry. The first group evolved from the village craftsmen: the skills of the blacksmith, wheelwright and carpenter, who were used to working in wrought iron and wood, were combined in the craft of the millwright, whose traditional work in watermills and windmills was greatly extended by the new demands from textile mills and factories. As William Fairbairn said in 1861, the millwright 'was the engineer of the district in which he lived, a kind of jack-of-all-trades who could with equal facility work at the lathe, the anvil, or the carpenter's bench'. For example, the first rotative steam engine supplied by Boulton and Watt to the Papplewick cotton mill was installed by Thomas Lowe, a millwright from Nottingham, who was also responsible for the supply of the drive shaft system. Precision craftsmen, such as the clockmaker, gunsmith and maker of optical instruments, formed the second group who applied their skills to making both the early machines for the mills and also machine tools for the manufacture of components for the later, more complex, machines. In 1771 Richard Arkwright advertised in the *Derby Mercury* for workers to build the water frames for his new mill at Cromford: 'Wanted immediately, two journey men Clock-Makers or others that understand tooth and pinion well: Also a smith that can forge and file'. The third group of engineers evolved from the builder in wood, stone and brick who had to learn to apply new materials like iron to the construction of multi-storey mills, canal aqueducts and railway bridges. The first group of professional engineers to receive public recognition were the Civil Engineers by the foundation of their own Institution in 1818. The three groups did not remain distinct, as a glance at a 19th-century trades directory will show: one business could be listed as ironfounder, millwright, machinist and structural engineer.

Within the East Midlands, the clothing industries, with their demands for lace, hosiery and boot and shoe machinery, created their own machine building specialists. The hand craft of the framesmith was later applied to the mass-production of machines for hosiery and lace but their machine tools could also be applied to other products. The East Midlands lost its innovatory lead to the USA and Germany in particular, who captured much of the market for boot and shoe machinery and knitwear and lace machines in the last three decades of the 19th century. This encouraged East Midland engineering firms to diversify. For example, Manlove and Alliott, established as framesmiths in 1838 in Nottingham, were by the 1880s employing over 500 men making steam laundry plant, refuse destructors and sugar machinery as well as acting as millwrights. Other textile machinists took advantage of the demand for bicycles, such as the firm bought by Frank Bowden which became the Raleigh Cycle Company in Nottingham in 1889. A blacksmith from Manlove and Alliott, William Humber, founded a cycle making business in Nottingham in 1868 which eventually moved to Beeston, where it employed 500 men with a large export market. The firm later moved to Coventry and switched to motor car manufacture.

25 & 26. The purpose-built iron foundry and engineering works of Gimsons on Vulcan Road in Leicester. (R. Read, *Modern Leicester*, 1880.)

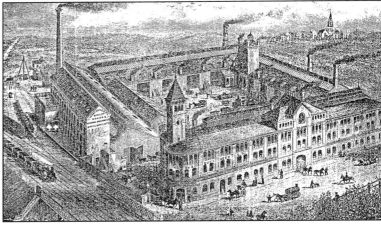

27. A detail of the ironwork on the 1871 Trent Bridge in Nottingham.

The extensive East Midlands iron industry had created a large number of foundries which entered all branches of engineering, providing millwrights, machinists and structural engineers. As early as the 1770s, Francis Thompson of Ashover was producing atmospheric pumping and winding engines for mines and Ebenezer Smith of the Griffin Foundry in Chesterfield supplied and machined cylinders for them. A better known maker of steam engines was Gimson & Company of Leicester, whose beam engines may still be seen at Clay Mills in Staffordshire and the Abbey Pumping Station in Leicester. The founder, Josiah Gimson, had been apprenticed to a Leicester ironfounder, James Cort, and by the 1870s had set up the integrated Vulcan Works alongside the Midland Railway in Leicester. By 1900 they advertised boilers, steam engines, shafts and gears, lifts and hoists and boot and shoe machinery among their products as well as acting as jobbing ironfounders. In Derby, Andrew Handyside acquired the Britannia Foundry in 1848 and produced, as well as engine castings, a whole range of structural ironwork from window frames to bridges for a national market. Richards of Leicester also produced structural castings, many of which may still be found on London's railways. The position of Derby as a railway junction in an important iron producing area encouraged the Midland Railway Company to set up its locomotive works there in 1840 and a new foundry, carriage and wagon works were added later.

Towards the end of the 19th century, the mechanisation of the hosiery industry had freed a resource of skilled male labour and this, coupled with available building land and good transport connections, encouraged the foundation of a diverse engineering industry. In Loughborough, the Anglo American Brush Electric Light Corporation and Herbert Morris, crane manufacturers, were attracted to the town by its canal and railway system. Rather than expand in Manchester, Rolls Royce chose Derby to build a new car factory in 1908 because of cheapness of labour and land and the established foundry and engineering trades there as well as proximity to suppliers in Birmingham and Sheffield.

One of the leading engineering companies in the East Midlands was the Butterley Company, founded in 1790 as Benjamin Outram and Company, a partnership which also included William Jessop, the canal builder. By 1827 the Company was employing 1,500 men. They had their own blast furnaces as well as foundries and produced rails for several horse-drawn waggonways surveyed by Outram and Jessop, including those for the Ashby Canal Company, the Grantham Canal Company and the Cromford and High Peak Railway. For the latter, the Butterley engineering shops also produced the nine twin beam steam winding engines for the inclines.

The engineering industry developed partly to manufacture the machinery required for the rural-based industries described in this chapter but also to service the extensive extractive industries which have been an equally important adjunct to the East Midlands scene. The industry has created a skilled labour force which, in its turn, has attracted further specialised manufactures to the area, including chemical, electronic and electrical engineering. This diversity of employment in the East Midlands has cushioned the effect of the decline of its extractive industries, whose development will be described in the next chapter.

2

EXTRACTIVE INDUSTRIES

The image of the East Midlands promoted by its Tourist Board is that of the Shires, a peaceful rural retreat where famous hunts pursue the fox on the eastern uplands, and the forest areas of Sherwood and the Dukeries provide pleasant leafy walks. It is remarkable that the region has managed to retain this image despite a wide range of extractive industries. The iron beams supporting the roof of St Pancras station and the decks of H.M.S Warrior came from Derbyshire: bricks for the construction of Heathrow Airport and granite setts to pave London streets were sent from Leicestershire: Nottinghamshire's alabaster has been extensively used for church monuments, while her output of gypsum has always accounted for one third of the country's total production. From Northamptonshire, even more unexpectedly, came the steel tube used to supply fuel to Northern France in Operation Pluto. Perhaps it is the very variety of extractive industries in the East Midlands which accounts for their comparative unobtrusiveness. There are still large limestone and granite quarries together with a few sizeable coal mines, but they are distant from one another and leave much undisturbed land in between.

The geological trend of the region is from south-west to north-east, most marked in the Jurassic Ridge running from Northamptonshire through east Leicestershire and Rutland. This was a rich source of limestone for building material as well as marlstone for iron production. The trend is echoed in a belt of Magnesian Limestone running along the Nottinghamshire border with Derbyshire between Mansfield and Worksop, while in the west of the region is the Carboniferous Limestone of Derbyshire in which most of its lead ore is found. Millstone Grit, source of many grindstones for the Sheffield steel industry as well as millstones, makes up much of the rest of Derbyshire, with the Coal Measures sandwiched between this and the limestone of the east. Sandstone figures prominently in Nottinghamshire, most marked in the bluff crowned by Nottingham castle, and extends into south Derbyshire and west Leicestershire. Geologically, the oldest rocks in the region are the pre-Cambrian inliers found in Leicestershire.

The extraction of minerals affects the landscape in various ways. Early working of shallow coal seams and veins of lead was by bell-pits, which leave small bumps with a hollow in the centre where the shaft used to be. In Derbyshire, these follow the length of the lead vein, resembling a string of beads, and are known as rakes. Later mines both for lead and coal went deeper, the latter leaving a legacy of spoil heaps which are now being landscaped and replanted: some have even been given a new lease of life as dry ski slopes! Open-cast mining for coal and clay in the 20th century has had the most drastic effect of all on the landscape, destroying all evidence of previous working and leaving barren moonscapes which take years to recover. Quarries can be equally harsh on the landscape, particularly the vast limestone quarries in Derbyshire, but elsewhere they either revert to tranquil lakes and ponds or are infilled with

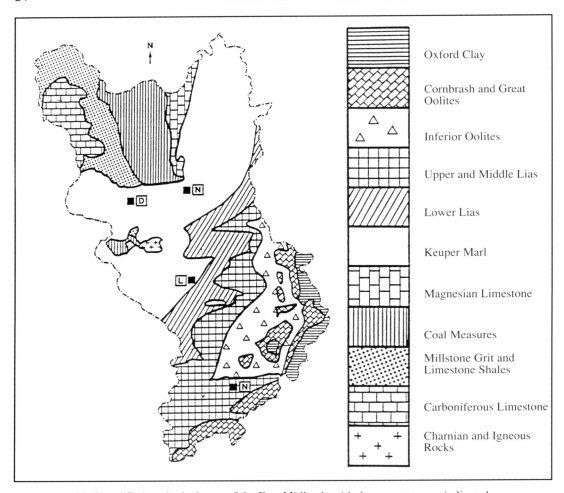

Oxford Clay

Cornbrash and Great
Oolites

Inferior Oolites

Upper and Middle Lias

Lower Lias

Keuper Marl

Magnesian Limestone

Coal Measures

Millstone Grit and
Limestone Shales

Carboniferous Limestone

Charnian and Igneous
Rocks

28. Simplified geological map of the East Midlands with the county towns indicated.

rubbish and the land eventually re-utilised. The ironstone workings which dominated the scene in the east of the region earlier in the 20th century are now barely visible, the only evidence being the lowered landscape, with roads standing proud of fields from beneath which several feet of stone have been removed. The railways which once served the quarries can only be detected by grassed-over cuttings passing beneath isolated bridges carrying farm tracks and roads. Only old photographs, particularly the aerial shots taken in the 1940s, indicate the extent to which the East Midlands landscape has been affected by extractive industry.

More permanent are the settlements which grew as a result of mining and quarrying and have survived because new industries have been introduced when extractive industry ceased. In Derbyshire, the combination of lead-mining and farming meant that settlement remained scattered, although the periods of prosperity in the industry are reflected in substantial stone houses in villages like Wirksworth and Winster. On the coalfields, early settlement was

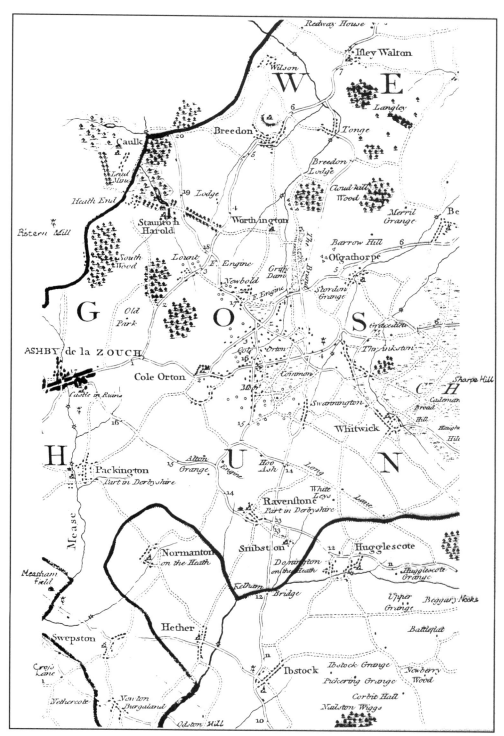

29. A section of John Prior's map of Leicestershire, surveyed 1775-7 at the scale of 1" to 1 mile; 'o' represents a coal pit and 'F. Engine' indicates a steam pumping engine: water and wind mills are shown by conventional symbols.

scattered for the same reason as can be seen near Coleorton in Leicestershire and Cossall in Nottinghamshire. By the 19th century, red brick terraces encroached on previously untouched countryside, although miners' housing was usually substantially built. These were superseded in their turn as the coalfield developed eastwards by planned settlements incorporating community buildings and open spaces. There is a tremendous contrast within the East Midlands between the small, integrated villages found in the rich agricultural areas in the east and south of the region and the large, sprawling settlements which grew to service extractive industries but came to incorporate manufacturing industry as well.

Lead Mining

Lead ore, or galena, is found in veins in the Carboniferous limestone which have been mined down to depths of over 500 feet. This occurs largely in Derbyshire, but lead has also been mined in a small area of north-west Leicestershire around Staunton Harold and Shepshed. The Derbyshire lead mining area is one of the most ancient as well as interesting industrial landscapes in the East Midlands. Its Roman origin is attested by numerous lead pigs with Latin inscriptions while in Domesday Book of 1086, Derbyshire was the only county with a recorded lead output. The mining customs and laws devised by Derbyshire miners were first written down in the Quo Warranto, a document resulting from an Inquisition at Ashbourne in 1288. Upon payment of various royalties to the landowners, mining could take place without hindrance although strictly controlled by the Barmote Court. This resulted in a wide spread of shallow workings along the rakes, using primitive methods of haulage and drainage. The small stone-built coes which provided shelter can still be found, but may well conceal a shaft in one corner.

The landscape changed with the arrival of large mining concerns who possessed the capital for large scale working. The depth of mines had been limited by the fact that only hand- or horse-driven machines were available to drain mines and raise the ore. An important feature of the lead mining area was its position on a plateau bounded by deep river valleys, which meant that drainage by underground channels or soughs was possible. These are found on other ore fields, but nowhere are they so numerous as in Derbyshire. Two hundred or so soughs were built between the mid 17th and late 19th centuries, some of them still discharging into the rivers Derwent and Wye. They took years to excavate and were usually undertaken by specialist groups rather than the miners themselves. They remained the chief method of mine drainage in Derbyshire, assisted by hydraulic engines underground, until the end of the 19th century. The landscape of the Derbyshire lead field is therefore different from that of Shropshire, with its numerous steam engine houses, or Cardiganshire, with powerful waterwheels. There is little surface water on the Derbyshire limestone and coal is only found some distance away: given the terrain, soughs were the cheapest and most efficient method of drainage.

Some steam engines were introduced onto the lead field, first Newcomen engines in the Winster area and later Cornish engines on the Magpie and Millclose Mines. But they were never very common nor lasted for long: John Farey, the author of the Board of Agriculture's *General View* for Derbyshire, reported that in 1810 there was only one steam pumping engine at work on a Derbyshire lead mine. Winding, too, made little use of steam and the horse gin remained common in Derbyshire. Horse power was also used for crushing the ore, as can be seen from the surviving crushing circles at Odin, Eldon Hill and Watts Grove. Water-driven crushing rolls

30. Ore crushing circle near the lead mine at Eldon Hill in Derbyshire.

31. A rectangular buddle for ore separation on Bonsall Leys moor in Derbyshire.

32. Magpie lead mine, near Sheldon in Derbyshire, showing the Cornish-style pumping engine house with later pit head gear.

and circular buddles, common on other lead fields, are rare in Derbyshire where earlier methods of crushing and dressing the ore survived. It is this which makes the landscape of Derbyshire lead mining unique. The small scale workings still visible near Brassington and Winster are more in keeping with local mining tradition than the somewhat alien, Cornish-inspired engine houses of Magpie and Millclose, which are the more noticeable landscape features.

Derbyshire has less to offer on the smelting side of the lead industry than, for example, the Yorkshire Dales. The term 'bolehill' is commonly found on maps, signifying the previous existence of a smelting hollow where wind provided a natural draught. Water-powered ore hearths were constructed, but the best survivals in Derbyshire are of the reverberatory furnaces or cupolas, introduced into the area in the 1730s. These used coal as fuel and a chimney to induce a draught: the oldest surviving free-standing industrial chimney in Britain is that at the Stone Edge Cupola, which dates from 1770. The maze of flues connected to it can still be seen.

Lead mining was not a labour-intensive industry like coal mining, except at Millclose Mine in the 1930s when over 800 men were employed. At its peak in about 1750, the mines employed about 4,000 individuals which a century later had fallen to half that number. Until the 19th century, mining was combined with farming and no really large mining settlements developed as they were to do on the coalfield. Wirksworth was perhaps the centre of the industry, but other villages like Brassington had their own Barmote Courts and so remained in control of their own affairs. Women and children washed and dressed the ore brought up by their menfolk and so, apart from the few large mines, the lead industry of Derbyshire remained a local affair that integrated with rather than disfigured the landscape.

Coal Mining

The mining of coal in the two East Midland coalfields is not of such proven antiquity as lead mining, although Nottinghamshire coal has been found in a Roman context in the Fens. It was certainly well established by the 13th century but served only a small local market. Coal was not a popular fuel for domestic purposes until chimneys became common on houses: wood smoke was more acceptable than coal fumes. It was used for industrial purposes such as limeburning and brewing but not until the 17th century did it become widely used as a domestic fuel. Output certainly increased in the East Midlands at this time, but the coalfields could only serve a limited regional market because of the distance either from navigable rivers or the coast. Even as late as 1830, the East Midlands coalfields produced only just over 5 per cent of the national coal output, compared with 10 per cent 60 years later. The coal was there for the getting, but high transport costs reduced its market. Railway transport totally transformed the outlook for the industry in the second half of the 19th century, and the East Midland coalfields remained productive until the 1980s, with the prospect even then of new pits being opened.

Early mining was by bellpits to shallow seams, good examples of which can still be seen at Strelley in Nottinghamshire. Open-cast coal extraction reveals older workings for a brief period before totally destroying evidence of past activity. In 1991 late medieval timber-lined shafts were revealed at the Lounge open-cast site in north-west Leicestershire. The outline of bellpits can occasionally be seen in ploughed fields: these often show up well near Coleorton in Leicestershire, where coal was worked by the Beaumonts in the 15th century. The shape of pillar and stall working are also preserved here in an area of pasture. Longwall working became fairly general by the 19th century, characterised by the greater amount of spoil which found its

33. Miners' housing at Rawdon Terrace in Moira, Leicestershire.

34. The 1806 Newcomen pumping engine house at Furnace Pit, Moira, in north west Leicestershire.

way to the surface. But generally it is more difficult to reconstruct previous mining landscapes in the coal industry as opposed to the lead industry because continuation into the 20th century has meant considerable modernisation, with consequent destruction of the evidence of earlier methods of working.

As mines became deeper during the 16th century, drainage became a major problem and generally the mines were situated in basins where sough drainage was not so effective as in the Derbyshire lead field. Soughs were built, but often drained into underground sumps from which the water had to be raised by hand or horse power. Despite ingenious machines for this purpose invented by Huntingdon Beaumont, who managed mines for both his own family in Leicestershire and the Willoughbys of Nottinghamshire in the late 16th century, it was the Newcomen atmospheric engine patented in 1712 which was the most important single innovation. Some of the Leicestershire coal proprietors had business connections with Griff Colliery in Warwickshire, where a Newcomen engine was installed in 1715. Engines followed quickly in the Measham and Swannington collieries and were soon adopted elsewhere in the East Midland coalfields. Replacement by Watt engines was less crucial than on metalliferous mines where the Newcomen engine's vast coal consumption greatly increased pumping costs. Atmospheric engines continued to be used on East Midland coal mines well into the 19th century, leaving us with an important industrial monument at Moira in Leicestershire where a Newcomen engine house of 1806 survives. An atmospheric engine built at Moira in 1821 worked on into the 20th century, to end its days at the Henry Ford Museum in Dearborn, Michigan in the USA.

Haulage was a greater problem in coal mines than it was in lead mines because of the bulky nature of the material extracted and the greater depths involved. Steam power was used for winding both materials and men, although horse gins did survive into the 19th century and an example from Pinxton in Nottinghamshire has found its way into the Industrial Museum in Wollaton Park. Vertical and horizontal winding engines replaced the beam engine: a rare example of the former is preserved at Bestwood in Nottinghamshire. Engine houses survive in isolated spots, like the curiously named Who'd 'a Thought It and Seldom Seen pits in Leicestershire and Derbyshire respectively.

Both the organisation and scale of the coal mining industry was different from that of lead mining and this is reflected in the nature of settlements on the coalfield. Such free mining customs as existed disappeared with the need for greater production from the 16th century onwards. Landowners were responsible for the development of many of the mines and occasionally provided housing, like the Earl of Moira's Stone Rows in the Leicestershire village named after him, built in 1811. During the 19th century, mines were generally leased from the landowners by partnerships of mining entrepreneurs, who raised the necessary capital for development. New settlements were grafted on to existing villages like Hucknall and Bulwell in the Leen Valley, where other occupations like framework knitting already existed, resulting in a diverse industrial conurbation rather than a total mining community. New settlements were created early in the 19th century, such as George Stephenson's new town of Coalville which grew up around Long Lane and Snibston pits along the Leicester and Swannington Railway. Men came to work here both from other Leicestershire pits and those in adjoining counties: some were housed in tenement blocks known as Barrack Row and Deputies Row, which were uncommon on the East Midland coalfields where terraced houses predominated. Other new settlements, like the Bestwood Iron and Coal Company's village in Nottinghamshire, were close to older centres of population and integrated with them. Not until the exploitation of the concealed coalfield in Nottinghamshire in the later 19th century were planned mining communities created in areas of previously sparse settlement, such as Creswell near Bolsover, where 280 two-storey houses were built around a large green and a variety of public buildings were provided. Creswell is a far cry from the scattered houses and farms around Coleorton, and the two settlements illustrate the transition of coal mining from a part-time to a full-time occupation over a period of several hundred years.

Clay

Brick and pottery manufacture has been widespread throughout the East Midlands because of the varied nature of the regional geology. Suitable raw material is found in the Liassic clays and the Oxford clay in Northamptonshire, the Keuper marls in Leicestershire and Nottinghamshire and the Coal Measures in the two major coalfields. The latter was often highly siliceous clay, which was very suitable for refractory wares. The industry is certainly Roman in origin and continues to the present day, probably reaching its height in the middle of the 19th century when between three and four hundred brickworks were functioning in the four counties.

Roman and medieval potteries have been excavated in the area, and their products can be seen in local museums. The market for domestic pottery expanded as population grew in the 16th century and new potteries were opened, particularly in Derbyshire. John Farey listed 14 potteries in the county in the first decade of the 19th century, including Chesterfield, where brown ware had been produced since the 15th century, and Belper, where clay from Denby was being sent. The latter closed shortly after Farey's survey but Denby itself continued to produce the stoneware for which it is still famous. Farey also lists a group on the south Derbyshire coalfield including Ticknall, where red ware continued to be manufactured until late in the 19th century and Church Gresley, where the highly decorated Measham teapots beloved of canal boatmen were made. At Smalley, where a pot kiln now forms part of a teashop and garden centre, the hollow pots first used by William Strutt to lighten the roof construction in fireproof textile mills were produced. Farey also noted the existence of small quantities of china clay in Derbyshire and the Derby China works had begun about 1750, being given the right to mark their products as 'Crown' Derby by George III in 1773. The firm was re-established as the

35. Beehive brick kilns at Coalville in Leicestershire, two remaining out of an original eleven.

36. Decorative brickwork on terraced housing in Halkin Street in the Belgrave district of Leicester.

37. The distinctive outlines of pottery kilns at Swadlincote in Derbyshire.

38. The Morley Park blast furnaces in Derbyshire, now in the care of Derbyshire Archaeological Society.

39. The ironstone railway incline at Eastwell in Leicestershire.

Crown Derby Porcelain Company in 1878, moving to the former workhouse in Osmaston Road, Derby, from which it continues to operate. Both domestic stoneware and fine china were, then, produced in Derbyshire for a national market, while a small quantity of pipe clay in the north of the county was used for the manufacture of tobacco pipes.

Brick clay had a far wider distribution than pot clay and brickworks were often set up on small pockets of clay to meet local needs: these can now often only be traced from old maps and place names such as Brick Pit spinney or close. The first bricks were fired in clamps, clay covered circles on which green bricks were piled, covered with turves and fired. These continued to be used where large quantities of bricks were needed quickly, as in the construction of railway tunnels, canal locks and bridges. More permanent structures were built for use on estates, such as the rectangular Scotch kiln on the Calke Abbey estate in Derbyshire. This was an intermittent kiln, into which bricks dried in the open-sided shed alongside were placed, fired for several days, allowed to cool and then unloaded. Scotch kilns and downdraught round kilns were also constructed at brickworks and their outlines can be traced on large scale maps of the 19th century, although few actual structures now survive. These intermittent kilns were gradually replaced from the 1860s by the continuous multi-chamber or Hoffman kiln, a good example of which still survives in Ilkeston. In these, twelve or more chambers were set into an annular gallery around a central chimney: the surplus heat from the chamber being fired was fed into the adjacent chamber, thus pre-heating it and saving on fuel costs. The firing zone was advanced round the kiln by opening dampers and the fired chambers left to cool before unloading and re-stacking with green bricks. An early use of Hoffman kilns in the region was by the Nottingham Patent Brick Company, formed by the amalgamation of two brickyards at Mapperley and Carlton in Nottinghamshire, who supplied 60 million bricks for the building of St Pancras Station from their 'patent' Hoffman kilns. The first experiments with tunnel kilns, where bricks travel slowly on special cars through pre-heating, firing and cooling zones in a tunnel, were carried out in the 1750s but few were built for bricks before the 20th century. The Ibstock brickworks in Leicestershire still possesses one built in 1934.

Brickmaking expanded rapidly in the late 18th century since they were needed for lock and bridge construction on canals as well as for fireproof mills and housing. This encouraged the government to include bricks, along with window glass, in a list of goods subject to taxation at a time of financial crisis following the end of the War of American Independence in 1782. Various forms of tax avoidance were practised, such as the increased use of tiles for cladding until they too were taxed in 1803, but one of the most interesting evasions was the production by Joseph Wilkes of Measham in Leicestershire of double-size bricks which cut down by a half the number of bricks needed for a building project. The drying shed for his brickworks and many of his 'Jumbie'-built houses with characteristic blind arcading survive in the village, dating from the last two decades of the 18th century before a double tax was imposed on double-size bricks in 1803.

The 19th-century expansion of the coalfields caused a dramatic growth in the brick industry, since brick clay was mined along with coal and unsaleable slack coal was a cheap fuel for the kilns. Many colliery companies set up brick and tile works, such as the Whitwick Colliery Brick and Tile Company in Coalville, founded in 1827. This gained national notoriety through its manager, George Smith, who campaigned in the middle decades of the century for the application of the Factory Acts to the brickyards. He finally wrote in 1871 *The Cry of the*

Children from the Brickyards of England, which was widely circulated and achieved its objective the same year, when labour by women and boys under 12 was prohibited in the brickyards. In Northamptonshire, the expansion of railways and housing associated with the ironstone industry led to an equally rapid growth of brick manufacture, with large works being set up on the Upper Lias clays. The well-built houses with elaborately carved and moulded brick decoration which proliferated in the towns and industrial villages of the East Midlands in the late 19th century are lasting evidence of the quality of product from the region's brickyards.

The rapid urban expansion caused a spate of Public Health Acts from 1848 onwards, which benefited the pottery industry of south Derbyshire. Fireclay deposits mined alongside coal proved ideal for the manufacture of sanitary pottery and salt-glazed drainpipes, and the construction of railways for cheap transport of a bulky product enabled the Swadlincote area to become one of the major suppliers of these goods to the towns of Britain. Firms already making domestic stoneware switched to sanitary ware and new firms were founded, so that by the Public Health Act of 1875 ten firms in the area were producing sanitary ware and pipes, the best known being Ensors of Church Gresley, John Knowles of Woodville and Thomas Wragg of Swadlincote. The characteristic shape of the pot kilns can still be seen in the midst of a lunar landscape caused by more recent open-cast mining of coal and clay.

Iron

As in the coal industry, the extraction and processing of iron ore in the East Midlands moved from west to east during the 19th century and has consequently had a major impact on the landscape of much of the region. In the west, the iron ore, like fireclay, was associated with the Coal Measures as nodules intermixed in the coal or blackband ironstone. These have been extracted by mining, since the iron industry in this area ceased before modern open-cast methods were used. In the east, ironstone has generally been quarried rather than mined since it occurs in beds under a relatively shallow overburden and could be worked as quarry faces. Iron ore is found in two strata of the Jurassic series. The Marlstone beds of the Middle Lias outcrop from Caythorpe in Lincolnshire to Wartnaby in Leicestershire, most notably in the wooded ridge crowned by Belvoir Castle. There are other isolated outcrops, for example near Tilton. The Northampton Sand bed occurs in the Lower Oolitic outcrop which extends from the Humber to Wilbarston in Northamptonshire, flattening out towards the Oxfordshire border. Neither form of ore is as rich as, for example, the haematite of West Cumberland, being only about 30 per cent iron, and suffers from a high phosphorus content. The Coal Measure ironstone provided ore for both charcoal and early coke furnaces in Derbyshire and north-west Leicestershire, whereas the Jurassic ores were not exploited until the second half of the 19th century. Railway development enabled the transport of fuel for ironworks to the ironstone area and also the carriage of ore to furnaces elsewhere, particularly Derbyshire and South Wales. The adoption of the Gilchrist-Thomas process in the 1870s also made it possible to utilise high phosphoric ores for steel manufacture.

Iron manufacture before the middle of the 18th century was dependent on resources of charcoal and water power, and traces of early ironworking sites in the East Midlands are generally found in hilly, forested areas such as Rockingham Forest and parts of Derbyshire. Ironstone was extracted from bellpits similar to those used for coal and lead, and smelted in

40. Butlin's blast furnaces at Wellingborough in Northamptonshire, now demolished. (Reproduced by permission of Mr. and Mrs. M. Palmer.)

41. An extract from the 25" Ordnance Survey map showing the Cransley Iron Works near Kettering in Northamptonshire. (Sheet XXV.13 1926 edition.)

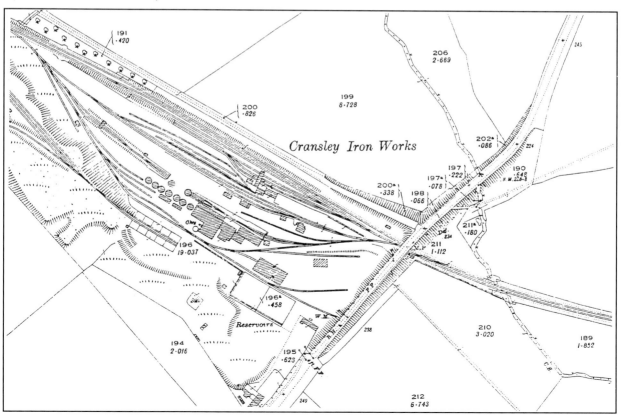

bloomeries, primitive furnaces using water-powered bellows: these are only traceable from quantities of slag and scattered documentary references. The iron bloom was worked into wrought iron in water-powered forges, which are more often referred to in documents since they continued to work well into the 18th century, long after the bloomery had been replaced by the blast furnace. This, using charcoal as a fuel, was introduced into this country in the early 16th century. It was a square stone structure probably twenty feet or less in height, with an adjacent house for water-powered bellows and a casting area in front of the furnace, probably covered with a roof. The erection of a furnace needed more capital than the older bloomeries, and the furnaces were built by landowners such as the Sitwells of Renishaw Hall. They operated furnaces at Foxbrooke and South Wingfield during the 17th century, together with forges and rolling and slitting mills, and produced a variety of iron goods, many of which were exported to the West Indies for use in the sugar industry. No charcoal furnace survives in the East Midlands, although the remains of a furnace at Melbourne in south Derbyshire was excavated in the 1960s before the site disappeared under Staunton Harold reservoir.

Woods were coppiced and cut in rotation to provide fuel for the ironmasters, but since it took about 8,000 acres of coppice per year to maintain a furnace in full production, ironmasters had to seek far afield for their fuel and many local furnaces had closed by the early 18th century, the sites often being re-used for other purposes such as corn mills. Coke-fuelled furnaces were slowly beginning to replace charcoal furnaces, and the application of steam power to drive bellows by the end of the 18th century freed the iron industry from its dependence on water power and charcoal. It is possible that Alderwasley Furnace in Derbyshire, built in 1764, was intended to be fuelled by charcoal — in which case it would have been the last charcoal furnace to be built in Britain — but used coke from the beginning, making it the first East Midlands coke furnace. This was followed by 11 other furnaces before the end of the century, mainly situated alongside the Chesterfield and Cromford canals. One of these survives, that at Morley Park, built in the early 1780s and refurbished in 1818, together with a second furnace added about 1825. These are both stone stacks, but the surviving furnace at Moira in Leicestershire, built between 1804 and 1806 alongside the Ashby Canal, is a massive brick structure. The East Midlands is thus fortunate in possessing two of the earliest surviving coke furnaces in Britain but the remains of its later iron industry are less well conserved.

The expansion of the Derbyshire industry began to exhaust local supplies of ore by the middle of the 19th century, and the ironmasters turned to Northamptonshire for alternative sources. Although there is archaeological evidence of early working, the bedded ores in east Leicestershire and Northamptonshire were not rediscovered until exposed in railway cuttings from the 1840s onwards. Samples of Northamptonshire ore were shown at the Great Exhibition in 1851 and furnaces erected in Northamptonshire shortly afterwards. This encouraged Derbyshire iron companies to lease iron-bearing land, and both the Stanton and Staveley companies did so, eventually themselves opening new furnaces in the ironstone area, as at Holwell in 1878.

The first quarries were situated alongside existing railway lines, like Hardingstone and Manor Farm on the LNWR Blisworth to Peterborough branch. As the railway network expanded, further quarries were opened and eventually mineral loop lines were built specifically to serve the quarries. The ironstone was worked by removing the overburden, taking out the ironstone beneath and then replacing the topsoil, a process which could restore the land to cultivation within five years or so. Only after 1951 was restoration compulsory, financed by a levy on the stone extracted. The overburden was dug out by hand in the early years of the industry and wheeled precariously along plank barrow-runs over the top of the working face. Mechanical excavators and draglines first appeared in the 1890s. The ore was transported in waggons on railway lines laid temporarily along the face, which could be moved as the face progressed. Mineral railways connected the quarries to the main lines, often making use of inclines to take the waggons to loading bays. All that remains of the industry in the landscape are abandoned quarry faces several feet high and now covered with scrub, together with cuttings, embankments and bridges from the mineral lines. In some places the separate heaps of topsoil and subsoil have not been levelled, resulting in a hill and dale formation. Otherwise, the roads stand proud of the surrounding fields by several feet, indicating the depth of ironstone removed from alongside.

Even less survives of the massive furnaces built to utilise the Jurassic ores in Derbyshire, Leicestershire and Northamptonshire, all alongside railway lines, much as their predecessors had sought the banks of canals. These were vertical steel-cased cylindrical structures with loading hoists alongside and ancillary buildings including blast engine houses. When compared with Moira and Morley Park, these furnaces indicate the transformation in scale of the iron industry in the first half of the 19th century. In Leicestershire, there were short-lived furnaces at Nevill Holt in the south of the county, where a quarry was opened beside the LNWR Rugby to Peterborough line, and the Holwell Ironworks near Asfordby in the east of the county: the latter remained in use from 1878 until 1958. In Northamptonshire the first ironworks was opened at Wellingborough in 1852, the second was at Upper Heyford in 1857, followed by three in the 1860s and five more in the 1870s. By 1880, the number of furnaces in blast had reached their maximum at 20, at which date they were producing about 2 per cent of the national output of pig iron. Five sites had ceased ironmaking by 1900 and the rest of the 19th-century works had closed by the 1960s. The one survivor, until 1980, was the massive Corby plant which was opened by the Lloyds in the first decade of the 20th century and transformed for steel and tube production by Stewarts and Lloyds in the 1930s. The Company built over 2,000 houses for its employees, turning a small village into a flourishing town which was designated as a New Town in 1950. By the 1970s, however, it was proving more economic to import higher grade ore from overseas than to use the low grade local ores. Corby, therefore, along with other inland ironworks such as Consett, was closed and the British iron and steel industry was concentrated in large plants close to the coast in Lincolnshire and South Wales. It was the end of an era for an East Midlands industry which had a considerable impact on the national economy as well as on the local landscape.

Stone Quarrying and Processing

Rocks of all geological ages from the Pre-Cambrian to the Pleistocene occur in the East Midlands, which consequently has developed a bewildering variety of industries based on quarrying. The oldest rocks used commercially are found in Leicestershire, a small county which nevertheless has, from the late 19th century onwards, supplied at least a quarter of the country's roadstone. The attractive area of Charnwood Forest is an outcrop of Pre-Cambrian volcanic sediments, around which occur several dioritic intrusions of different geological age and it is these which have been quarried for what is commonly, although incorrectly, known

42. An excavated lime kiln at Margaret's Close on the Calke Abbey estate at Ticknall in Derbyshire. The kiln had been abandoned in a partially rebuilt condition.

43. A sett maker at the Mountsorrel granite quarries in Leicestershire. (Reproduced by permission of Redland Aggregates Ltd.)

as granite. An outcrop in the Forest itself near Markfield was utilised in Neolithic times for stone axes, which have been found in locations as far afield as East Anglia, indicating that these were traded like those from better known quarries in the Lake District and North Wales. Medieval use is displayed in churches like Quorn and, despite its hardness, local granite was used locally as a building stone during the 18th and 19th centuries. Systematic quarrying at Mountsorrel began in the second half of the 18th century, when granite setts were first used on the turnpike roads and then on the streets of Leicester. Production was greatly increased after the Leicester Navigation was opened in 1794, enabling setts to be sent further afield. Scotsmen from Aberdeen, familiar with working their own granite, were brought to Mountsorrel in the 1820s to show Leicestershire men better methods of cutting the hard rock. Rail links to both the Midland and Great Central Railways were constructed there in the second half of the 19th century, coinciding with the tremendous urban expansion of that period and consequent demand for setts and kerbstones in London and other cities. Sett manufacture created vast quantities of chippings, which found a use in road surfacing and railway ballast, eventually superseding the use of the setts themselves. New quarries were opened at Bardon Hill and further south in Leicestershire which, like Mountsorrel, used steam powered crushers to produce the chippings. Housing was built for quarry workers, such as Granitethorpe near Sapcote in south Leicestershire and Bardon Hill cottages near Coalville, recently demolished. Environmental considerations now limit the expansion of quarrying, but Leicestershire still produces a considerable proportion of the country's supply of road stone.

Charnwood Forest also produces an ancient slate, technically known as greywacke but generally referred to as Swithland slate after the location of its principal quarries. This is green or purple in colour and does not split as finely as the geologically younger slates of Wales. It has been quarried since Roman times, when slates were used for roofing Roman buildings both in the county and in nearby Lincolnshire. Documentary evidence indicates its continuing use, both for roofing and later for articles such as troughs, fireplaces and cheese presses. By the early 18th century, Swithland slate was also being extensively used for gravestones. Primitive quarrying methods seem to have remained in use in the quarries, with horse-driven engines for pumping out water and manually operated cranes. The slates were also transported on horse-drawn waggons, there being no evidence for any mineral railway lines. The repeal in 1831 of William Pitt's tax on the carriage of slate by sea exposed the local industry to competition from cheaper Welsh slate, which grew more serious once a rail network was established. There was a brief revival in the 1860s, but by 1900 only small scale slate working was continuing at Groby. It was Welsh slate, needing lighter roof timbers, which benefited from the urban development in the East Midlands in the late 19th century and rows of terraced houses gain further monotony from its uniform greyness. The more attractive and expensive local product was reserved for mansions and public buildings, and is still carefully re-used in building projects.

Limestone occurs extensively in the East Midlands and has been widely used both for building and, when burnt, for mortar and agricultural purposes. There are three major formations which have been exploited. The most extensive is the Jurassic limestone and marlstone in the east of the region, whose value as a building and roofing material is shown in the numerous attractive stone villages found in east Leicestershire and Northamptonshire which present the classic picture of 'The Shires'. Collyweston in Northamptonshire produced excellent roofing slats which were widely used, providing a contrast with the warmer-tinged marlstone. This limestone has also been used for the production of lime, for example at a small kiln at Pickworth in east Leicestershire which was worked by the 19th-century poet, John Clare, and more recently at huge works near Ketton, opened in 1928, for the production of cement. Generally, however, it was more valued as a building stone. On the western edge of the Jurassic formation is a belt of limestone belonging to the Lower Lias, often covered with boulder clay but quarried where it was exposed since it provided hydraulic lime cement which would harden under water. In Leicestershire, lime has been produced at Barrow-on-Soar since the Roman period, later being used for mortar to build the 14th-century brick castle at Kirby Muxloe. The construction of the Soar Navigation nearby greatly increased output enabling Derbyshire coal to reach the Barrow kilns and burnt lime to be exported for use in the construction of piers and harbours. Kilns were established in the same Jurassic limestone at Kilby Bridge, close to the Grand Junction Canal south of Leicester.

The second of the limestone formations in the East Midlands is the belt of Magnesian limestone or dolomite of Permian age on the Nottinghamshire-Derbyshire border. Quarries at Mansfield Woodhouse and Steetley yielded a grey or honey-coloured stone which can be seen in buildings such as Worksop and Blyth priories. This limestone ceased to have merely a local importance when, in 1878, it was found that the stone made an excellent lining for Bessemer steel-making furnaces and the Steetley Lime and Building Stone Company was established to supply this need. More extensive is the Carboniferous limestone, which makes up much of Derbyshire with inliers in the northern part of Leicestershire. Burnt lime from this type of

44. Lime kilns beside the former Midland Railway at Millers Dale in Derbyshire.

45. Millstones abandoned alongside the Bole Hill quarry railway in Derbyshire.

limestone was greatly in demand for agricultural use, particularly in the latter half of the 18th century when previously waste land was being taken into cultivation. William Pitt, author of the Leicestershire *General View*, and John Farey indicate how much lime was in demand: Pitt reported that 40 loads of lime were being put on the land where only one load would have been used 50 years ago, whereas Farey found that farmers from adjoining counties would bring their carts for 40 or more miles to collect Derbyshire lime.

The result was the construction of hundreds of limekilns in the region: these were situated either where the lime was quarried or along canals and later railways, where lime was burnt at wharves and sidings for distribution by cart. At Ticknall in Derbyshire, documentary evidence exists for limekilns as early as the 15th century: by the mid-19th century there were at least 40 kilns, the produce from which was taken away for sale by means of a horse-drawn tramway to the Ashby Canal. Most of these kilns were of the intermittent type, with a cone-shaped pot which was filled with alternate layers of limestone and slack, fired and allowed to burn for several days before being raked out through one or two draw-holes. By the middle of the 19th century, running kilns were in use, which were charged at the top and raked out at the bottom in a continuous process. Banks of kilns were constructed at canal wharves, like those alongside the Ashby Canal at Moira in Leicestershire, and by railways: some of the latter were massive structures, like those by Millers Dale station on the Midland Railway in Derbyshire. Twenty large kilns were constructed in 1840 at Ambergate by George Stephenson, who saw the potential of rail transport for taking lime to other parts of England: these remained in use until

1965 and were demolished the following year. However, limekilns are some of the most common surviving structures from the industrial past and, together with the associated quarries and transport systems, make interesting landscapes for closer study. Derbyshire continues to provide much of the country's lime from massive quarries near Wirksworth and Buxton, whose scale dwarfs that of the water-filled and overgrown quarries of the mid-19th-century industry.

There are two minor products from the limestone belt of the East Midlands which had more than local importance. The first was a hard form of dark grey limestone known as 'black marble', which was quarried at Ashford in Derbyshire from medieval times. By the 18th century water-powered saws were being used both in Ashford itself and in Derby to cut the hard limestone, one of the machines being illustrated in Rees' *Cyclopaedia* of 1819-20. Similar equipment was used to fashion Blue John, a colourful fluorspar often found in association with lead in Derbyshire and used for ornamental vases, candlesticks and so on. More recently, fluorspar has been extracted from the lead rakes for use in the steel industry, destroying in the process much of the lead mining landscape of Derbyshire.

Millstone grit is a familiar sight in much of Derbyshire, where drystone walls are used to mark field boundaries. Its very name indicates its commercial significance and Peak stones were widely used for the grinding of animal feeds, the finer-grained French burrs being preferred for white flour. Grindstones, particularly for the Sheffield steel industry, were another important product. The areas below the Derbyshire 'edges' at Froggatt, Curbar and Hathersage are littered with millstones in various stages of completion. Particularly impressive is the graveyard of small millstones alongside the Bole Hill Quarry Railway above Grindleford: the railway was built in the first decade of the 20th century to convey stone for the dams of the Derwent Reservoirs, but presumably also carried millstones down to Grindleford station.

The Permian and Triassic sandstones which make up much of Nottinghamshire and Leicestershire have been used as building stone, particularly for churches, but do not weather well and are best seen in internal situations, like the famous 'leaves' of Southwell Minster. Where sandstone and limestone are in contact near Mansfield, quarries have been established to provide moulding sand for the iron industry. The Keuper marls contain gypsum, which has been extensively worked in the Trent Valley from Gotham to Newark. This was burnt for plaster of Paris, but also to make plaster for the upstairs floors in houses: gypsum was burnt with clay and then laid on a layer of reeds across the joists to make a hard and durable floor, well able to withstand the vibration of hosiery frames and lace machines. Alabaster is a crystalline form of gypsum which was very popular for church monuments as well as ornamental stonework in mansions like Kedleston, where the columns in the great hall are made from red-veined alabaster quarried at Red Hill, near the junction of the Trent and the Soar. Finally, extensive gravel deposits in the Trent Valley have been worked to provide sand and aggregates for the construction industry: water-filled, abandoned quarries provide wetland habitats for wildlife as well as leisure facilities for boating and ski-ing enthusiasts.

3

MANUFACTURING REGIONS

1: The Bassetlaw Region of Nottinghamshire

This region in the far north of Nottinghamshire represents about one quarter of the area of the county but still remains largely rural in character and very much under-populated by comparison with the Erewash valley and Nottingham's environs. This relative stagnation has been due in some part to a comparative lack of viable mineral resources, at least until the exploitation of the concealed coalfield, and also to poor communications until the railway network was established.

Most of Bassetlaw is relatively flat, with the area bordering the Rivers Idle and Trent being barely above sea level; known as the Carrs, this is subject to flooding and has to be drained artificially by pumping to create valuable agricultural land. Elsewhere the Keuper marls have been suitable for grain, in particular for growing barley, and Worksop and Retford developed as malting centres and also as market towns to service the outlying villages. Malting in Worksop and Retford gradually declined, the trade moving to Newark, but has now ceased. The rich soils and sheltered valleys were also suitable for growing hops, particularly around Tuxford and further south. However, changes in taste led eventually to its decline with the adoption of less harsh-flavoured hops from southern England. Some parts of the region were late being enclosed and a unique survival of the open field system of agriculture is preserved by statute at Laxton, just south of the region.

The two largest towns in Bassetlaw are Worksop and Retford (East and West combined). During the 19th century Retford stagnated compared with Worksop but, even in Worksop, population growth lagged behind the county rate until the 1870s when rapid expansion took place, coinciding with the opening of the concealed coalfield.

Industrial development, with the exception of abortive attempts to establish textile manufacture, was initially devoted to self-sufficiency including the processing of agricultural products for the immediate local market and the servicing of the needs of agriculture for implements and supplies. Attempts to introduce textile manufacture began in the last two decades of the 18th century. One of the most significant was the Revolution Mill erected at Retford in 1788 by the brother of Edmund Cartwright, the inventor of the power loom. Designed to spin worsted, it was powered by a 30hp Boulton and Watt rotative engine but the enterprise was not a financial success and had closed ten years later. There are no remains of this mill nor of two other textile mills erected at Worksop which were also unsuccessful and later converted to saw and flour mills. The only remains of these attempts to follow the 1780s trend for spinning mills are at Langwith and Cuckney near the southern boundary of the region.

The construction of the Chesterfield Canal passing through both major towns had little influence on their industrial expansion. Not until rail connections were made did new industries like rubber manufacture and engineering become established, the latter sustained by the demand for coal mining machinery.

The turnpike road system provided reasonable north-south road communications but access to the east was limited by the River Trent. A bridge was built at Gainsborough in 1791 but the next bridge up-river was at Newark until the construction of the Dunham toll bridge in 1832. The Trent itself had been navigable from the Humber up to Burton-on-Trent by the early 18th century and the River Idle along the northern boundary of Bassetlaw was navigable from Bawtry to the Trent at Stockwith from the 1760s. This was the main outlet for Derbyshire lead and Sheffield iron products which were brought by packhorse to the inland port. The Idle navigation was replaced by the only canal in the region, the Chesterfield Canal. This was promoted by Derbyshire lead interests, the Cavendish iron and coal masters at Staveley and other land owners wishing to exploit their coal reserves. The canal was surveyed by James Brindley in 1769, who commenced its construction, but it was completed for opening in 1777 by Hugh Henshall. It was 46 miles in length from Chesterfield to West Stockwith on the Trent, with 65 locks. The canal was narrow as far as Retford and then broad to the Trent; the major engineering feature was a 2,850-yard tunnel at Norwood, west of Worksop, which collapsed in 1908 due to mining subsidence and caused the closure of the canal west of Worksop. The canal company was purchased by the railway interests but continued to operate goods-carrying services until 1892.

The main line railway system began with the opening of the Sheffield to Grimsby line for the Manchester Sheffield and Lincolnshire Railway through Worksop and Retford to bridge the Trent at Gainsborough in 1849; a branch to the south east from Clarborough to Lincoln bridged the river at Torksey. The Great Northern line from King's Cross to York via Doncaster was completed through Bassetlaw by 1852, to be followed by the link from Gainsborough to Doncaster in 1867 and the Mansfield to Worksop railway in 1875. The system was completed with the opening of the line from Chesterfield to Lincoln in 1897, which crossed the Trent at Fledborough. Of the east-west railways, only the Gainsborough line remains open to passenger traffic; the two other lines across the Trent are maintained for servicing the large electricity generating stations on the banks of the river at High Marnham and Cottam with coal supplies from the concealed coalfield.

Extractive industries include dolomitic limestone, once supplying the Sheffield Bessemer and open-hearth steel plants as well as use for refractory brick manufacture. Other brickworks were established beside the Chesterfield Canal and those at Walkeringham provided the last commercial traffic along the waterway in 1955. Gypsum was quarried on higher ground east of Retford.

The first coal mine to be opened on the concealed coalfield in Bassetlaw was at Shireoaks, west of Worksop, which was sunk for the Duke of Newcastle in 1854 on land acquired by him in the 1840s. The productive seams were located at considerable depths, 346, 381 and 428 yards below surface. Two more mines were opened near Worksop in 1859 and 1873 which brought sharp increases in the town's population; by 1911, 30 per cent of the resident males in the town worked on the coalfield and by the 1930s the three mines gave employment to 4,000 people. Each of the mines was well placed with rail connections. The easternmost sinking in Bassetlaw was at Bevercotes which began production in 1960.

46. The working windmill at North Leverton.

GAZETTEER
(OS Maps 112,120 and 121)

Agriculture-based Industries

Bolham Watermill (SK 705826) on the River Idle north of Retford, on an old water power site, was formerly used for paper making and later for tanning and leather manufacture. The early 19th-century mill building lies at the foot of a cut-away sandstone cliff.

Carlton-in-Lindrick Watermill (SK 588838) just off the A60 north of Worksop on a tributary of the River Ryton. This is stone-built with wheel and machinery *in situ*; the chimney stack, now reduced in height, indicates that a steam engine has also been employed.

Laneham Maltings (SK 816772). One three-storey range fronts the River Trent bank with three two-storey ranges behind, all of red brick and now used as farm buildings.

North Leverton Windmill (SK 775820) is the only commercially working mill in the East Midlands. This four patent sail tower mill with three pairs of stones began life as a subscription mill in 1813 and worked as such until 1956; visits may be arranged (Tel. Gainsborough 880573).

Oldcotes Watermill (SK 596884) is a derelict two- and three-storey stone-built mill with pantile roof. Part of it dates from 1792 but the waterwheel *in situ*, dated 1875 and installed by Thorntons of Worksop, drove three pairs of stones.

Ranskill Maltings (SK 662877) lie on Station Road beside the GNR, with a double kiln at the roadside but the malting floors have been removed. On the west side of the level crossing are the former Globe spade and fork works, now used for engineering.

East Retford Maltings (SK 707808), situated on Thrumpton Lane, is a large complex with four kilns beside the Sheffield to Grimsby Railway, now used for rubber manufacture.

West Retford Maltings (SK 698803) are late 19th century with five storeys. They are situated off Ollerton Road beside the link line between the Great Northern and Great Central Railways and now used for dairying.

Monks Mill, Scrooby (SK 651910) is a former watermill on the River Ryton, built of red brick and dating from the 17th century. The derelict mill was restored as a residence in the 1950s; it has an interesting flight of steps at the rear utilising old millstones.

Tuxford Windmill (SK 761694). Only the four-storey tower survives, complete with curb.

Worksop Steam Mill (SK 588793) beside the Chesterfield Canal, known as Albion Mill, is dated 1906 and has five storeys with Dutch gables.

47. The converted watermill at Scrooby.

48. The Albion steam flour mill at Worksop, beside the Chesterfield Canal.

49. The lock at the junction of the Chesterfield Canal with the River Trent at West Stockwith.

50. The ornamental bridge over the Chesterfield Canal at Wiseton.

51. The Chesterfield Canal warehouse at Worksop, showing the bridge hole for loading boats.

Worksop Brewery (SK 590793) on Kilton Road, beside the Chesterfield Canal, has an arched gateway. Nearby workers' cottages have been converted to small workshops. On the opposite side of the road are a group of stone buildings associated with the canal wharf.

Extractive Industry

Shireoaks Colliery Housing (SK 553810) built by the Duke of Newcastle in 1864 to house workers at his newly opened colliery on the concealed coalfield.

Walkeringham Brickworks (SK 753926). On either side of the Chesterfield Canal are remains of kilns and drying sheds.

Transport

Drakeholes Tunnel (SK 706905) is one of the earliest broad canal tunnels and, unusually, is situated on an acute bend on the Chesterfield Canal but is only 154 yards long.

Fledborough Viaduct (SK 813714) carried the 1897 Great Central line from Chesterfield to Lincoln across the Trent and its flood plain. It consists of a blue brick approach viaduct and a four span girder bridge.

Gainsborough Bridge (SK 814891) has three arches and was erected to replace a ferry across the Trent in 1791 by a Turnpike Trust. Although widened in 1964, one of the original toll houses remains.

Littleborough Toll House (SK 814831) was built beside the turnpike from Retford through Littleborough to a ferry crossing of the Trent.

West Stockwith (SK 787947) is the eastern terminus of the Chesterfield Canal with an entrance lock and basin beside the Trent. Some early buildings survive of this once prosperous inland port with boat yards, rope works, warehouses and maltings.

Torksey Bridge (SK 835792) is a lattice girder bridge erected by Fairbairn in 1850 over the Trent for the Sheffield to Lincoln railway. About half a mile downstream is the entrance lock to the Fossdyke, a Roman canal, built around A. D. 120 to connect the Trent to the Witham at Lincoln and hence to Boston and the North Sea.

52. The former cotton spinning mill at Cuckney, with its large mill pond.

53. The pumping stations at Misterton Soss for draining the carrs.

54. The Kilton lock on the Chesterfield Canal at Worksop, with the derelict sewage pumping station in the background.

Wiseton Bridge (SK 715903) is an elegant accommodation bridge over the Chesterfield Canal with stone heads on the keystones and ornamental iron railings instead of a parapet wall.

Worksop Canal Aqueduct (SK 598790) near Kilton, built in stone but refaced with brick, carries the Chesterfield Canal over the River Ryton.

Worksop Canal Warehouse (SK 586792) is situated in an enclosed yard with a Georgian gatehouse and is still occupied by BWB. The classic three-storey brick building has a low wide segmented arch bridging the main canal line.

Worksop Railway Station (SK 586797), built in 1850 of local Steetley stone, has a range of low Jacobean-style single and two-storey buildings.

Manufacturing Industry: Textiles

Cuckney Mill (SK 560710) is located below its storage pond and is now used as the village school. It was built for worsted spinning and later used for cotton spinning by Hollins of Pleasley. There are workers' houses and an apprentice house nearby.

Langwith Mill (SK 548703) is also located on the River Poulter but is derelict. The mill was built in 1786 for cotton spinning, water power being supplemented by a steam engine, and was later converted to a corn mill.

Public Utilities

Misterton Soss Pumping Stations (SK779951). The derelict pumping stations, dated 1828 and 1839, were built on either side of the Mother Drain beside the River Idle. Both formerly housed beam engines driving scoop wheels to drain the Everton, Gringley and Misterton Carrs. One engine was retained as a standby when the other was replaced in the 1890s by a horizontal engine driving a Gwynne centrifugal pump. The latter operated until 1941 when replaced by a Diesel-powered installation at Gringley Carr.

Retford Water Pumping Station (SK 706827) is a two-bay symmetrical building, dated 1880, and built of yellow and red brick.

Worksop Sewage Pumping Station (SK 597790) on the High Holt Road near the canal aqueduct was erected in 1881. Built in decorative style of red brick, it has a tall square chimney on an ashlar pedestal. It is now redundant and derelict but contains the remains of beam engine entablatures and vertical electric pumps.

2: The Upper Trent Valley and Rural East Nottinghamshire

The 'smug and silver Trent', of which Hotspur spoke in Shakespeare's *Henry IV*, runs through its broad flat lowland vale forming a natural barrier between the northern counties of the East Midlands. The 170-mile long river carries the natural drainage from most of Derbyshire, Staffordshire, Leicestershire and Nottinghamshire to its outlet in the Humber. The extremes in flow, coupled with low gradients — only a 76 feet fall in as many miles from Trent Lock to Stockwith — make the valley highly susceptible to flooding and consequently almost completely unsuitable for driving waterwheels. There were therefore few weirs but the presence of shallows and tortuous bends made the river extremely hazardous for navigation.

However, the river served a large and important region and some improvements were carried out enabling vessels to reach Nottingham by 1600. Following further improvements, it was possible to reach Burton from 1699 onwards, but the line to Burton above King's Mills lock at Castle Donington was abandoned around 1780. Improvements in the lower reaches of the river included the deepening of the channel through Newark and the building of two barge locks in 1772, which brought considerable prosperity to the town. Five years later, the Trent became part of the Grand Cross scheme to link it with the Mersey, Severn and Thames. The Trent and Mersey canal was opened to Wilden Ferry in 1777 and the scheme was completed by the opening of the link to the Thames at Oxford in 1790. Gainsborough was the transhipment point for goods entering the Trent in sea-going vessels, which were transferred to barges of up to 35 tons in weight to travel the 71 miles from Gainsborough to Shardlow. Here, goods were stored in warehouses awaiting loading on to narrow boats for the journey along the canal.

Traffic along the river increased considerably following the opening of the canals along the Erewash valley and over 320,000 tons of coal were shipped down to the Trent in 1809. New cuts were made at Sawley in 1793, at Cranfleet in 1797 and at Holme below Nottingham in 1800. The 1796 cut at Beeston, which linked to the Nottingham Canal at Lenton, bypassed hazardous shallows on the river above Trent Bridge. By that date some 140 broad beam barges were being man-hauled or sailed along the river and Nottingham became an important port since all traffic passed its river wharves. A steam packet service was introduced to Gainsborough in 1817. Railway competition took its inevitable toll on river traffic and eventually the Trent Navigation Company countered this with more improvements beginning in 1896. After 1906 depths were increased to five feet below Holme with a minimum channel width of 60 feet which entailed the building of the new Town Lock at Newark. Further improvements continued sporadically until the 1960s.

The river terraces have valuable reserves of sand and gravel as well as workable deposits of gypsum in the Keuper marl which are one of the major sources in Britain. Otherwise industries along the valley were mainly agriculture-based until textile manufactures became important in the towns of the upper valley. Of the towns along the Trent in 1801, only Newark with a population of 6,730 and second to Nottingham in the county, together with Castle Donington (population 1,959) were of any size. Malting and brewing in Newark is discussed in Chapter 5 Section 2 and basket making and hosiery knitting were carried out in Castle Donington. Both places stagnated relative to their respective counties over the next century, Newark falling to tenth position by 1901. It was manufacturing industry, not river traffic, which was responsible for the emergence of new centres at Long Eaton, Draycott, Sandiacre, Beeston and Stapleford — all looking towards Nottingham for their growth. They all offered good communications, cheap building land and unfettered labour relations to the Nottingham machine lace manufacturers.

The Gazetteer which follows includes sites within a three to four mile distance of the river; sites in the lower valley are included in Section 1 of this chapter on Bassetlaw and those in Nottingham itself are included in Section 1 of Chapter Five.

GAZETTEER
(OS sheet 129)

Agriculture-based Industries

Shipstones No 4 Maltings, Dovecote Lane, Beeston (SK 532361) were built beside the Midland Railway in the 1880s for the Beeston Brewery and have been operated by Shipstones since 1922. They illustrate the contrast between the older floor and modern silo malting processes.

55. Waterwheels at King's Mills on the River Trent at Castle Donington.

56. The Clock Warehouse on the Trent and Mersey Canal at Shardlow.

57. A converted maltings at Southwell.

58. Caudwell's corn mill on the River Greet at Southwell.

Kings Mills, Castle Donington (SK 417274) is a Domesday site on a separate channel off the river Trent and its weir was a hazard to navigation. The site has been used for corn grinding, fulling, paper-making and button making over the years but the last use was for gypsum grinding in plaster manufacture. There were two mill buildings at right angles, one with two undershot iron wheels and separate tail race and the other with a single low breast wheel. The mills were severely damaged by fire in 1927 and demolished but the impressive water wheels remain. The mill house, now a hotel, and a row of renovated workers' houses can also be seen.

Fiskerton Mill (SK 742517) is still a working mill and was formerly powered by the River Greet. The four-storey seven-bay building was rebuilt after a fire in 1851 and possibly used for cotton spinning in the 1790s.

Fiskerton Wharf (SK 737510), at a former ferry crossing of the Trent, has a group of brick buildings which include a floor maltings with double kiln and hipped pantile roof.

Hoveringham Mill (SK 685466) was a working cornmill until the early 1960s, one of seven water power sites on the Trent tributary known as the Dover Beck. The oldest section dates to 1778.

Lowdham Mill (SK 660476) has now been converted to residential use but was once one of the largest corn mills on the Dover Beck and still possesses its wheel.

Cavendish Brewery, Shardlow (SK 448299). On the south bank of the river are the extensive remains of a large brewing and malting complex, including kilns complete with cowls.

Maltings, Burgage Green, Southwell (SK 705543) were built in 1825 and subsequently used for cheese manufacture. They have now been converted into housing; the two-storey block has a kiln at the rear.

Caudwell's Mill, Station Road, Southwell (SK 706544). This large flour mill astride the River Greet has four- and five-storey blocks, one of them dated 1867, marking its rebuild after a fire. A further fire occurred in 1893 when the other blocks were built, together with the water tower for a sprinkler system. Milling ceased in 1969.

Transport

Beeston Railway Station (SK 533362) remains substantially unaltered. A pair of gabled pavilions with openwork bargeboards and finials are linked by a single storey section. The gables are dated 1847 and bear the company monogram.

Trent Lock (SK 490312) is the entrance to the Erewash Canal from the river and was once the scene of great activity with coal shipments. There are remains of a toll house, warehouse and boat building yard with a dry dock which once served as a weighing lock. Canal horses were taken by boat across the Trent into the mouth of the Soar Navigation below Red Hill. Boat traffic for Nottingham and further east passed into the Cranfleet Cut just downstream which was opened in 1797 to bypass Trent shallows.

Railway Depot, Long Eaton (SK 488321) complete with canal basin, was built in 1840 as a coke store for the Midland Railway, supplies being brought down the Erewash Canal. Once coal was introduced for firing locomotives, the building became a tarpaulin and sack factory and store for the railway goods traffic.

Red Hill Railway Tunnels (SK 496308). The earlier west tunnel was opened in 1840 and the east freight line tunnel in 1875. Both have elaborate north portals with castellated parapets flanked by octagonal turrets and are listed Grade II. The original Butterley bowstring girder bridge over the Trent has been replaced.

Derby Canal Junction, Sandiacre (SK 4832358). The Derby Canal is in water from its junction with the Erewash Canal only as far as the first stone bridge. The lock cottage with toll booth is used by a canal preservation group.

Harrington Bridge, Sawley (SK 471311). The Nottingham to Birmingham road was turnpiked in 1758-9 with a ferry across the Trent which was not bridged until 1790 and then freed from tolls in 1882. The three main elliptical sandstone arches were replaced in 1906 with steel girders but traces remain of the twin toll houses, demolished in the 1930s, at the northern end.

Shardlow Inland Port developed as a transhipment point between Wilden Ferry, the real head of the Trent Navigation, and the Trent and Mersey Canal. The ferry was replaced in 1759 by the Cavendish Bridge which was

59. The station house at Southwell, typical of T. C. Hine's designs for the Midland Railway in Nottinghamshire.

60. The Gothic Anglo-Scotian lace mill at Beeston.

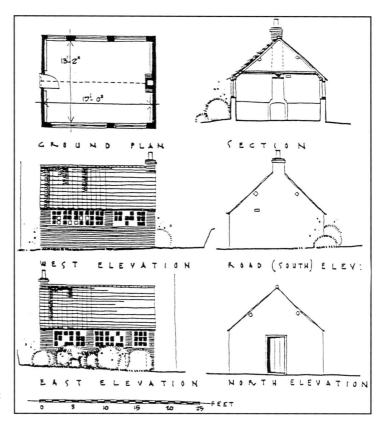

61. The framework knitter's workshop at Caythorpe (drawn by John Severn).

destroyed by floods in 1947; a plaque from it is displayed by the A6 road at SK 446299. Numerous warehouses were built in the last quarter of the 18th century, many with semi-circular headed cast iron windows, and industries such as rope-making, corn milling, brewing and malting developed. Most of these canal-side buildings survive within the Conservation Area; of particular interest is the Clock Warehouse, straddling a canal arm, which is now a pub and restaurant (SK 442303).

Station House, Southwell (SK 707543), a typical Midland building with barge boarding, was built in 1847 for the former line to Mansfield; this has now been lifted and the bed forms the Southwell Trail.

Swarkestone Bridge (SK 370279), with its causeway, is three quarters of a mile long and parts date from the 13th and 14th centuries, some 17 old arches remaining. The actual river bridge, in classical style with five arches, spans 414 feet and is 18th century. Just upstream from the bridge, on the north bank, is an old lock chamber at the entrance into the Derby Canal which linked to the Trent and Mersey Canal just to the north. On the opposite bank can be seen some of the many sand and gravel workings of the Trent valley, many now fulfilling leisure uses.

Thurgarton Station (SK 698485) of 1846, is in the Neo-Tudor style of the buildings on the Midland Railway's Nottingham to Lincoln Line. The characteristic scalloped bargeboards and diamond patterned lattice iron window frames remain, although the Grade II listed building is now in residential use.

Toton Sidings (SK 487350). An extensive marshalling yard was developed from the 1860s just to the north of Long Eaton alongside the Midland Railway's Erewash Valley line. Its main purpose was to handle coal traffic.

Manufacturing Industries: Textiles

Anglo Scotian Mills, Wollaton Road, Beeston (SK 527372) is one of the most ambitious tenement lace factories and dates from 1892; its Gothic style facade has five bays each side of a two bay central section flanked by narrow turrets with crenellated tops. The symmetrically placed windows have pointed arches and the pattern of recessed crosses in the brickwork, highlighted with white brick, is repeated in the pediment of the three-storey mill to the rear.

139-143 Derby Road, Bramcote (SK 504378) are three framework knitters' houses, built c.1830, some with the typical long windows in the upper storey.

Castle Donington has a tradition of domestic industry which included framework knitting, embroidery of twist net lace and later basket making utilising osiers from the Soar and Trent valleys. There is some evidence of top shops on *Bondgate* (SK 446275) and many examples of garden workshops. On *Station Road* (SK 448278) is Donington Mill, a two-storey red brick building with cast iron windows and a small engine house to the rear. This was built in 1877 for silk throwing by a Beeston firm, thus continuing the village's tradition of working to Nottingham masters.

Caythorpe Framework Knitter's workshop (SK 687457). A single storey garden workshop with large windows on the longer sides, where framework knitting continued into the 20th century. The shop accommodated at least six frames. Nearby, behind a farmhouse (SK690455), is a two-storey workshop in a poorer state of repair.

Victoria Mill, Draycott (SK 446333) is the second largest of the region's tenement lace factories; the brick built 600-ft. block is four storeys high. It was begun in 1888 by the speculator E. T. Hooley and completed by Jardine, a Nottingham lace machine manufacturer whose name is on the tower with copper dome which bears the date 1906. The rear elevation to Town End Road has four staircase turrets but the engine houses have been demolished; two Hick Hargreaves engines formerly drove rope races incorporated in the main block. Nearby in *Market Street* (442332) is an earlier mill complex with dates of 1850 and 1860 to be seen. Here most of the buildings are single storey including one with barrel arched roof and cast iron columns; they feature blind arcading and round headed windows.

62. Harrington's tenement lace factory at Long Eaton, one of the largest in the area.

63. Victoria Mill at Draycott, a tenement lace factory in which 'room and power' for machines could be rented.

64. Bridge Mills lace factory, beside the Erewash Canal at Long Eaton.

LONG EATON grew rapidly in the 1850s, the population rising from just over 900 in 1851 to over 13,000 by 1901. Growth in the early part of this period was due to railways with marshalling yards and wagon building and repair shops being established. In the later years, tenement lace factories were built, many of them on sites bordering the Erewash Canal. The surviving factories illustrate very well the change from multi-storey to single storey works. The town specialised in curtain net making on large Leavers machines, each weighing 20 tons and occupying a floor space of 40 by 8 feet. Net production continues in the town but many of the mills are still in multiple occupation and others changed to upholstery and furniture manufacture. The townscape along the canal and Leopold Street is reminiscent of the Colne valley in West Yorkshire.

Bennett and Bridge Street (SK 488340). The lower ends of these streets are lined with semi-detached houses with gardens, built in the 1900s, which housed lace factory workers in better conditions than those in the crowded slums of Nottingham.

Bennett Street and Canal Street (c.SK 485345). Several single storey lace factories, all dating from the first decade of the 20th century, serve to illustrate the boom in the industry. Many of them are now occupied by upholstery manufacturers.

Bridge Mills, Derby Road (SK 488340) is one of the last tenement lace factories to be built; the three-storey brick factory was commenced in 1902. The engine house survives with a tall circular brick chimney which has a large bulbous cast iron cap. Coal supplies came via the adjoining canal to fuel the former 170hp steam engine, which drove by line shafting to each floor. The machines in the later single storey workshops had individual electric motors.

High Street Mills (SK 493336). The oldest section, dated 1857, has six bays and the adjoining seven-bay section, also three storeys, was added in the 1870s. Its increased size reflects the change to larger machines.

Harrington Mills, Leopold Street (SK 488337) is a 550 feet long tenement lace factory, named after its builder and erected between 1885 and 1887. The front of the building faces the cemetery and the rear, with four staircase turrets, the street. At one time it had 26 separate tenants.

West End Mill, Leopold Street (SK 488338) is 350 feet long and was built in 1882 beside the canal. By 1886 there were 24 lace manufacturers renting space in the four-storey block. The adjoining Whiteley's Factory was built for Henry Whiteley, a lace manufacturer, and is in two three-storey sections. The first was built in 1883 with a 1903 extension to the south and an engine house is sandwiched between. The factory backs on to the canal.

Mills, Milner Road (SK 489346). Alexandra, Edward and Victoria Mills on the opposite side of the canal to Leopold Street contrast sharply with the tall tenement factories. They are single storey, built between 1905 and 1909, to house heavy lace machines powered by electric motors. At the north end of the street is the electricity generating station built by the UDC in 1903 for which coal supplies arrived by canal. Some of the lace factories had already switched to electric power by the installation of individual steam-driven generating plants.

Austin's Factory, New Street (SK 492337) has five storeys with two staircase turrets and tall circular chimney; it was built in 1884 as a tenement lace factory and now makes elastic braids.

Maythorne Mill (SK 697556) is an early 19th-century self-contained industrial community based upon a former silk mill powered by the River Greet. Two multi-storey mills, built end to end, have been converted into flats and opposite is a row of three-storey workers' houses. The owner's house and farm buildings remain.

Springfield Mill, Bridge Street, Sandiacre (SK 480366), backs on to the Erewash Canal. The 400-feet long block has four storeys and the central pedimented block contains the rope race and bears the date 1888. Ornamental tie bar ends have the initials 'T H Ltd' and the adjacent office block carries the name 'T Hooley Ltd', the company which built the factory. At the rear are four semi-circular staircase turrets and an engine house with elaborate chimney stack.

Nottingham Road, Stapleford (SK 495375). On the south side of the road, there are two blocks of three-storey framework knitters' cottages with long top-floor workshop windows.

65. Springfield Mill, a tenement lace factory beside the Erewash Canal at Sandiacre.

66. Maythorne silk mill on the River Greet near Southwell, the centre of a working community.

Manufacturing Industries: Engineering

Former Humber Works, Humber Road, Beeston (SK 536369) are an early purpose-built engineering works, built originally for cycle manufacture in 1885. They were abandoned in 1908 when car manufacturing was transferred to Coventry, after which the works were used for lace net manufacture. The decorative roundels reflect the early Humber trade mark.

Manufacturing Industries: Chemicals

Boots Factory, Beeston (SK 543367). Development on this 156-acre site was begun in 1929 by the Boots Pure Drug Company, established in 1883 in Nottingham to supply a chain of stores. The first building was a soap factory, but two important reinforced concrete buildings were added in 1933 and 1938, designed by Sir Owen Williams to house the wet and dry goods sections. The former has a 550-feet long canopy on the south face to cover the loading dock and is listed.

3: The Wye and Derwent Valleys

The River Derwent and its major tributary, the River Wye, pass through some of Derbyshire's most attractive scenery but have also supported a considerable variety of industry. It was to these valleys that lead mining companies drove their soughs to un-water mines to the west. Cromford Sough was begun in 1673 to drain the mines of the Wirksworth area, while Magpie Sough was built as late as 1873. Some of these soughs still discharge millions of gallons of water a day into the rivers. The veins of galena and other minerals may be seen in the limestone show caves around Matlock, and an extensive lead mining landscape survives on the plateau to the west. Many of the early rakes have been destroyed in the search for secondary minerals, particularly barytes. The limestone itself has been extensively exploited for burning, ironmaking and more recently for roadstone, but the huge modern quarries tend to destroy the traces of earlier working. Remnants of the extensive millstone industry can be found in the northern part of this region.

The Derwent, described by Defoe as 'a frightful creature when the hills load her current with water', was a source of power rather than a means of navigation, although the lower reaches were improved to Derby by 1720. Corn and fulling mills made use of its power from the Middle Ages onwards and the water resources of the valley were utilised for the first powered textile mills in Britain. The pioneering use of the Derwent for silk throwing by Lombe is described in Chapter Five. Arkwright fought shy of the river for the first of his water-powered cotton spinning mills at Cromford in 1771 by using the sough and then the Bonsall Brook, but later mills made use of the Derwent itself. The distance of the region from centres of population made it difficult to obtain labour and so complete communities were established at Cromford, Belper, Milford and Darley Abbey. Only Milford has been substantially altered, although several early mills at Belper were demolished in the 1960s. Isolated mills like Litton and Cressbrook made use of pauper apprentice labour, often from London.

Good transport routes along the Derwent valley were not easily achieved. Turnpike roads did not extend along its length until the early 19th century and many important routes, like the Salt Ways from Cheshire, crossed it with considerable difficulty, at first using fords, and later pack horse bridges at, for example, Cromford and Hathersage. Arkwright promoted the Cromford Canal along the Derwent valley in 1773 which brought coal northwards and linked Cromford to the national waterway network. The canal was engineered by William Jessop who became one of the founders of the Butterley Company. Attempts to extend the canal to the north west failed and not until the Cromford and High Peak Railway was constructed in 1831 was any direct communication established with the Manchester area. George Stephenson's North Midland Railway from Derby to Leeds, opened in 1840, clung to the river as far as Ambergate, piercing the Chevin Hill at Milford rather than following the valley floor where it would have disrupted the water supplies to the mills. From Ambergate, the Manchester, Buxton, Matlock and Midland Junction Railway had followed the Derwent as far as Rowsley by 1849. As the Midland Railway, the line was extended to Manchester in 1867 along the Wye valley, creating a pattern of viaducts and tunnels which, although now disused, survive as a tribute to the persistence of Victorian engineers.

GAZETTEER
(OS sheets 110, 119 and 128)

Agriculture-based Industries

Victoria Mill, Buxton Road, Bakewell (SK 216687). This former corn mill, built of gritstone, has three storeys and occupies a Domesday site on the River Wye. It once belonged to the Duke of Rutland and the 16-feet diameter 14-feet wide water wheel with rim drive remains.

Crossroads Farm, Blackbrook (SK 337479) is a substantial stone-built farmstead built by the Strutts in 1830 to supply fresh foodstuffs for their mill hands in nearby Belper.

67. Caudwell's flour mill, whose turbines are powered by the River Wye at Rowsley.

Corn Mill, Chatsworth Park (SK 259688) on the Derwent was built in the late 18th century for the Duke of Devonshire. The three-storey stone building is now just a shell but fragments of the wheel remain. The village of *Edensor* (SK 250699) was moved to this site between 1838 and 1842 by the Duke so that it was not visible from Chatsworth; the village was laid out by Joseph Paxton.

Corn Mill, Cromford (SK 293569), powered by the Bonsall Brook, was built by Arkwright to provide flour for the inhabitants of his expanding town. The complex includes a drying kiln and is undergoing restoration by the Arkwright Society as a working museum and information centre.

Elvaston Castle Museum (SK 408330) is based in the estate buildings of Elvaston Castle and the displays depict the working of a close-knit self sufficient community of craftsmen, tradesmen, labourers and their families at the beginning of the 20th century.

Caudwell's Mill, Rowsley (SK 256658) on the River Wye was operated by the same family for over a century until 1978, since which time operations have continued by a Charitable Trust. The present gritstone building dates from 1874 and originally there were two waterwheels driving a total of 11 pairs of stones. These were replaced by roller mills and the wheels by turbines which still power a complete roller milling plant. (For opening hours tel. Matlock 734374.)

Extractive Industries

Hillcarr Sough Tail (SK 258637). The sough was begun in 1766 to drain the mines of Alport Moor, but the important Guy Vein was not reached until 1787. The sough and its many branches were 140 feet below the water table but by 1800 all the attainable ore deposits had been exhausted. Steam engines were rejected on grounds of cost and so water pressure engines were installed below ground to pump to sough level. By 1848 there were eight such engines in use on the Alport lead field.

Peak District Mining Museum, Matlock Bath (SK 294581) is housed in the former spa pavilion and contains displays on the local lead mining industry. Exhibits include the water pressure engine rescued from a 400-feet deep shaft near Winster. The Museum is open daily (tel. 0629 583834). Access is possible to *Temple Mine* nearby where old lead and fluorspar workings are displayed.

Meerbrook Sough Tail (SK 326554). The tail arch bears the initials 'FH' (Francis Hurt) and the date '1772', indicating its commencement to un-water the Wirksworth lead mines. When completed the total length with its branches was about five miles and its level, some 100 feet below the 17th-century Cromford sough, caused disputes with Arkwright at Cromford whose water resources were thereby diminished. Since 1902 water from the sough has been used for mains supply.

Good Luck Mine, Via Gellia, near Middleton (SK 269565) is situated just off the A5012 road. Although privately owned, the underground workings are occasionally opened to the public (enquiries tel. 0629 583834). The mine was largely worked out by 1840 and visitors can experience something of the life of the 'old man' without concessions to floodlights and concrete paths.

Lime Kilns, Millers Dale (SK 139732). At the eastern end of the rail viaducts and further west beyond the former station are two sets of massive lime kilns formerly serviced by rail. The four derelict eastern kilns were built in 1878 and worked until 1930 whilst the two western ones were built into the rock face in 1880 and substantial concrete buttresses were added in the 1920s. These kilns worked until 1944 and have been restored and interpreted by the Derbyshire County Museums Service. The quarries which these kilns served have now been abandoned but limestone quarrying continues on a large scale at *Tunstead* in Great Rocks Dale (SK 100730), opened in 1929, with rotary kilns used for lime and cement manufacture.

Millstone Edge (SK248800). To the north of the A625, there are many unfinished millstones in the small quarries on the western side of the Edge. Immediately south of the road is a small quarry containing part-finished mushroom type and flat monolith millstones. A footpath to the south follows the track of a railway built to carry stone for the construction of the dams in the Upper Derwent valley. The path is lined with hundreds of abandoned small millstones or grindstones quarried in the nearby Bole Hill Quarries.

Magpie Mine, Sheldon (SK 173682). Lead mining on this site continued for over 300 years, but most of the present remains date from the second half of the 19th century. John Taylor, the Cornish engineer, became manager in 1839 and brought with him Cornish men and methods. A large 70-inch engine house survives, built in 1868, together with other surface remains from operations which continued until 1966. The site is a scheduled Ancient Monument in the care of the Peak District Mines Historical Society and is opened to the public at weekends (enquiries tel. 0629 583834).

Mill Close Mine, near Wensley (SK 258618). This once prosperous lead mine was operated by the London Lead Company in the 18th century. It became the richest lead mine in the country and over 300 years some 450,000 tons of lead and zinc concentrates were produced. At Watts Shaft there are remains of an 1859 Cornish pumping engine house but eventually the workings were drowned by water and operations ceased in 1940. The lead smelter nearby continues in use.

Moot Hall, Chapel Lane, Wirksworth (SK 287542) is a reminder of the town's former importance as a lead mining centre. The present hall was built in 1814 and housed the Barmote Court for the King's Field until 1988. The stone panels on the front showing lead miners' tools were retained from an earlier building of 1773; the standard ore measuring dish, made in 1512 and presented by Henry VIII, is kept here.

National Stone Centre, Ravenstor Road, Wirksworth (SK 286552) is located among disused limestone quarries. Displays interpret the quarrying industry and highlight its regional differences. The use of stone and its products is also promoted through the National Stone Trade Centre (tel. 0629 824833).

Transport

Belper Railway Cutting (SK 348478) was excavated in 1840 by George Stephenson to avoid tunnelling beneath the established settlement. The railway passes through the stone-walled narrow cutting which involved building ten overbridges in a mile to accommodate the existing streets.

68. The Wigwell aqueduct, built by William Jessop, carrying the Cromford Canal over the River Derwent.

69. The attractive station at Cromford, still in use for the Ambergate to Matlock section of the former Midland Railway's line from Derby to Manchester.

70. The portal of the Chevin tunnel, near Milford, *above left*, was built in 1840 for the Midland Railway line to Leeds.

71. The two viaducts at Millers Dale, *above right*, were built to carry the Midland Railway from Derby to Manchester over the River Wye.

72. The former cotton spinning mill at Bamford on the River Derwent retains its horizontal steam engine.

73. The Leawood pumping
station with a working
steam engine for lifting
water from the River
Derwent into the Cromford
Canal.

Bull Bridge Wharf (SK 359524) on the Cromford Canal was the terminus of a tramway from the Hilts Quarry near Crich which was worked by the Butterley Company until about 1929. Lime kilns, now derelict, were built about 1800 and used coal brought in by canal whilst limestone was also shipped out; eventually a rail connection was made to the Midland

National Tramway Museum, Crich (SK 345549) is sited in a former limestone quarry which was developed by George Stephenson from 1840. Stone was taken by a 2.5-mile waggon way, incorporating inclines, to kilns and wharves at Ambergate beside the Cromford Canal. The Museum, opened in 1962, has a large collection of working tramcars, reconstructed buildings and a streetscape; it is open daily, except Fridays, from May to September and at weekends and bank holidays at other times (tel. 077 385 2565). There is an open air display on lead dressing part way along the working tramroute.

Cromford Canal. The canal, promoted by Richard Arkwright, opened in 1793 to the Erewash Canal at Langley Mill. The *Wharf* terminal basin (SK 300570) retains an original stone-built warehouse and further south is the *High Peak Wharf* (SK 313560) of the Cromford and High Peak Railway, an interchange between canal and railway at the foot of the Sheep Pasture incline. The former railway workshops house a small information centre and the catch pit for runaway wagons may still be seen nearby. Further along the towpath is a transit shed and the *Leawood Pumping Station* (SK 316557). This retains its original Watt single-acting beam engine, built at the Milton Ironworks at Elsecar in 1849, which pumped water from the Derwent into the Canal. The engine is still regularly steamed. Just to the south is the stone-built three-arch *Wigwell Aqueduct* (SK 316556) which carries the canal over the river. At the south end of the aqueduct is a short canal branch to Lea where a lead smelter and textile mills were located.

Cromford Station (SK 303574) lies near the mouth of a tunnel on the Derby to Manchester railway opened by the Midland in 1849. Built c.1860 the diminutive station buildings and adjacent house are in French chateau style. A lattice iron overbridge is also retained.

Middleton Top Engine House (SK 276552) was erected in 1829 to house a winding engine for the 708-yard long double track Middleton incline (1 in 8.25) on the Cromford and High Peak Railway. The Butterley Company engine is still *in situ* and has been restored to operation; it consists of two rotative beam engines driving a common crankshaft to haul a continuous wire rope on to which two loaded or five empty waggons were attached at a time. Traffic ceased in 1963 but the railway with its incline and locomotive worked sections now forms the High Peak Trail linking Cromford and Buxton.

74. The Middleton Top winding engine house for the incline on the Cromford and High Peak Railway. The Butterley engine is preserved.

Chevin Tunnel, Milford (SK 347456). The north portal of this 836-yard tunnel on the North Midland line is built of rusticated stone with ring arches in the Norman manner. The south portal has a roll cornice. A gritstone sighting tower, nearly 50 feet high, still remains on the Chevin Hill; it was built by George Stephenson to accommodate a rotating alignment telescope to check the tunnel line.

Millers Dale Viaducts (SK 139732) carry the trackbed of the Midland line to Manchester across the River Wye just to the east of the former station, with five platforms, near the junction to the Buxton branch. The arched iron viaduct was built in 1863 and the later steel one in 1903. The track bed now forms part of the Monsal Trail.

Monsal Head Viaduct (SK 183716) across the Wye has five stone arches and is 300 feet long; it was denounced by John Ruskin for spoiling the landscape beauty of the dale.

Rowsley Station (SK 258660) was designed by Sir Joseph Paxton and acted as the terminus of the Ambergate line to Buxton from 1849 until 1867 when the line was extended westwards along the Wye valley. The gable ends of the roof are pedimented and the curved roof brackets match the round headed windows.

Manufacturing Industries: Textiles

Bamford Mill (SK 205834) is a stone-built complex, the oldest part dating from 1791 when the original cotton doubling mill was destroyed by fire. The mill was once powered by a breast wheel supplemented by a beam engine: both were replaced, the former by turbines and the latter by a tandem compound horizontal mill engine by Musgrave of Bolton in 1907. The weir and leat may still be seen at the back of the mill. Now occupied by Carbolite Furnaces Ltd, who occasionally operate the steam engine.

BELPER was a large village dependent on agriculture and nail making until Jedediah Strutt realised the potential of the River Derwent for cotton spinning. The Strutt family erected their first mill there in 1776 and built seven more over the next 40 years. Unfortunately not all have survived demolition but the *North Mill* (SK 346481), erected in 1804 to replace an earlier mill destroyed by fire, does survive as the second oldest fire-proof mill. The five-storey plus attic brick-built mill has a cast iron frame with brick arched vaulted floors. The housing for the 23ft-diameter breastshot wheel can still be seen in the projecting wing. The mill is presently undergoing conversion to residential use. The bridge over the road which gave access to the now-demolished Round and West Mills was constructed around 1795 and incorporates gun ports in the walls which were intended to be used in the

75. Brettle's hosiery factory at Belper, the centre of an extensive domestic industry.

event of hostile attack. The round weir behind the mill, rebuilt in 1796 and subsequently heightened, once provided a head of water for at least three wheels.

The adjacent square seven-storey *East Mill* in Accrington brick was erected in 1912, dominating the North Mill. Originally steam driven, the adjoining engine and boiler house remain but the chimney has recently been cut down. Fortunately much more survives of the early housing and community buildings erected by the Strutts. North of the mill on *Wyver Lane* (SK 346484) is a terrace of workers' houses; the lane led to a farm belonging to the Strutts. South of the mills off Bridge Street is *Long Row* (SK 348479) with its original stone paving and terraces of three-storey houses lining either side. North Row, of gritstone, was built 1792-3 whilst South Row is later and brick built. The three parallel streets to the south are named after Jedediah Strutt's three sons, William, George and Joseph, and several blocks of four houses, known as 'clusters', two facing one way and two the other, may be found. These houses have generous gardens and were intended for foremen. In *Joseph Street*, a small nail maker's workshop still exists; although in decline by the 1840s, nail making still gave employment to over 600 people in the town. In *Field Row* to the east is the Unitarian Chapel, built in 1788 by Jedediah Strutt; he is buried there.

Brettle's Factory, Chapel Street (SK 346473) is a classical stone three-storey building with 19 bays flanked at each end by three-bay pedimented wings. It was built in 1834-5 by master hosiers as a distribution centre for yarn for domestic framework knitters and as a warehouse for finished goods. In 1829 this firm, established in 1802, were renting 400 frames for silk hose and gloves and a further 2,500 frames making cotton hose.

The Dale, Bonsall (SK 279584). Until the opening of the cotton mills at Cromford, Bonsall was mainly a lead mining village but by 1844 there were 143 stocking frames in use in the village, probably working to Brettles at Belper or Smedleys at Lea Bridge. A typical stone building survives on the left side, dated 1737, and has an upper floor workshop with long window reached by external stone steps. Near the village cross to the east is a brick and stone workshop of later date which is known to have housed six knitting frames.

Calver Mill (SK 247745) is an austere seven-storey former cotton mill with a central pediment and staircase turrets to the rear. It was built 1803/4 to replace an earlier mill of 1778 erected under licence from Arkwright on a former corn milling site. The company was financed by Leicester bankers and hosiers and continued to supply thread to Leicester until spinning ceased in 1923. The wheelhouse once contained two 22ft-diameter waterwheels side-by-side, each developing 80hp.

Cressbrook Mill (SK 173727) lies in an attractive setting at the confluence of the Cressbrook and the River Wye. The first mill on the site was erected by Arkwright in 1779 and was powered from the brook but the present four-

76. The 'clusters' at Belper, two pairs of back-to-back houses built by the Strutts for their foremen.

storey pedimented Palladian structure, topped by a cupola, was powered by the Wye; it was erected in 1815 by William Newton. Single storey north light weaving sheds were added during this century and the twin water wheels were each replaced by a turbine which remain to the west of the main mill. The site is proposed for conversion to hotel and residential use. Some 200 to 300 pauper apprentices were housed in the long row to the north with its Gothic-style end overlooking the mill leat.

Crich (SK 350543). In the main street are some three-storey stone-built houses, one with an upper floor framework knitters' workshop having long windows.

CROMFORD is a lead mining village transformed in the 1770s by Richard Arkwright who used the Bonsall Brook and the Cromford sough to power his water frames for cotton spinning. Of his first mill (SK 297569), only the lower storeys survived a fire but the iron aqueduct remains, dated 1821. It replaced the original wooden launder which took water to a large overshot wheel. Further buildings, also using water power, were added nearby late in the 18th century. The whole complex is in the care of the Arkwright Society and restoration is continuing. The site is open to the public.

Masson Mill (SK 294573) was also built by Arkwright. It was begun in 1783 to utilise the power of the River Derwent and illustrates the trend towards more ornate architectural style with its central pediment, Venetian windows and cupola. The large brick chimney indicates the subsequent addition of a steam engine.

The village itself was expanded by the Arkwrights, who built and lived in *Willesley Castle* (SK 297572). They provided less ostentatious accommodation for their workforce in *North Street* (SK 294568) where the two three-storey stone terraces, built 1771/6, had upper floor through workshops lit by long windows. Some have been restored by the Landmark Trust. The school and schoolhouse at the end were built in 1832. A market was held from 1790 to 1880 in the *Market Place* (SK 295569) and the elegant *Greyhound Inn* was built in 1778. There are two watermills in the village, the corn mill already mentioned above and the former paint grinding mill at the head of the pond. This building still has an external overshot iron wheel supplied by overhead iron pipes.

DARLEY ABBEY is a third well preserved integrated cotton spinning community on the Derwent. The *Boars Head Mills* (SK 354386) on the east bank were begun in 1783 by the Evans family who had interests in lead mines at Bonsall, iron slitting and copper rolling mills in Derby, as well as banking. The earliest surviving mill dates from 1789/1792 and is a five-storey brick block with segmental headed windows. Later buildings of similar style

77. Houses in North Street at Cromford, originally built with a through attic loomshop for Richard Arkwright's employees.

78. The weir and sluices which controlled the River Derwent for the Strutt cotton mills at Milford.

also remain. Accommodation for workers was built on the west bank, with access by a toll bridge. Here rows of three-storey cottages were built, separated by small squares; by 1830 there were nearly 200 dwellings for the 500-strong workforce. The *Village* (SK 354385) with its houses and school is now a Conservation Area.

Litton Mill (SK 161730) is a former cotton spinning mill on a site first used in 1782. The present gritstone mill buildings date from the late 19th century and the turbine installation, powered by pipeline from the River Wye, can be seen at the west end. Such isolated sites made extensive use of pauper apprentices and the tale of the sufferings of Robert Blincoe at Litton, published in 1828, is undoubtedly a highly coloured version of the treatment they received.

Lumsdale Valley (SK 312613 to 313600). This Conservation Area includes the remains of at least four textile mills and a bleach works which were powered by the Bentley Brook. The mills have since been used for grinding bone, minerals for paint manufacture and for corn; the succession of water courses and ponds may be followed down the valley.

MILFORD (SK 351452) is another integrated village community bearing the imprint of development by the Strutt family who built the first cotton spinning mill here in 1780. Unfortunately this, and a later cruciform warehouse of 1792/3 which had timber beams fire-proofed by cladding with sheets of tinplate, have been demolished. Columns and a roof arch from the dye house of 1832 have been rebuilt and a works bell dated 1781 displayed by the river bridge. There are, however, considerable remains of the water channels and weirs to harness the river. North of the road are sluices and controls dated 1857 and 1858 at the end of the mill leat. South of the road the tail race can be controlled by three further sluices, two of which can be traced to existing wheel pits and the third to a small turbine powered electricity generating station dated 1936.

There are more remains of houses and community buildings erected by the Strutts. On the west bank of the river are houses, chapels and a school close to the bridge and further north are *Bank Buildings* (SK347454), a row of workers' cottages. Several terraces of houses remain on the east bank at *Hopping Hill* (SK 350455) and some of them retain large windows indicating domestic framework knitting activity. Stone for the various mills came from a quarry nearby (SK 352453). South along the A6 is *Moscow Farm* (SK 346444), built in 1812 by the Strutts to provide meat, milk and vegetables for their workers.

WIRKSWORTH has already been mentioned as a lead mining centre but water power brought cotton spinning into the town, the manorial corn mill, *Speedwell Mill* (SK 283529), being converted in 1790. This gritstone mill of three and four storeys has been subsequently enlarged. Nearby, *Haarlem Mill* (SK 284526) may be seen, which was leased by Arkwright and opened in 1780. The small original building is brick-built on stone footings and behind it is a brick building, erected in two phases in 1832 and 1885. These two mills are powered by the Ecclesbourne Brook. To the east a tributary stream powered two more mills: *Gorsey Bank* (SK 291531) and *Willowbath* (SK 288533). The former was built on the site of a saw mill about 1881 as Providence Mill, with associated cottages, and the latter was begun in 1816. Both were used for tape manufacture and Wirksworth became renowned as the centre for the production of Government red tape.

The *Wirksworth Heritage Centre, Crown Yard* (SK 286540) is housed in a former silk and velvet mill which has been restored with various grants: there are displays on local industry and the development of the town which was the subject of a Civic Trust regeneration project in 1979.

Public Utilities

Upper Derwent Valley Reservoirs, near Bamford form a striking series of reservoirs and dams erected to supply Nottingham, Leicester and Derby by pipeline. The first two masonry dams, the Howden (SK 170924) and the Derwent (SK 173897), completed in 1912 and 1916 respectively, were built of stone from Grindleford brought to site by a special railway. The third dam, the Ladybower (SK 198855), was completed in 1945 bringing the storage capacity to 10,400 million gallons.

79. Haarlem Mill, an early Arkwright-type mill at Wirksworth.

Little Eaton Waterworks (SK 364406) were erected in 1848 to pump water for Derby from the Derwent by means of a system of perforated brickwork laid in the gravel bed. The beam engines were removed from the Gothic-style brick pumphouse in 1948.

Miscellaneous

Peckwash Mill, near Little Eaton (SK 354423) was a former paper mill on the Derwent which has been derelict for some years. It was an ancient corn mill site which changed to paper making in the 17th century and this continued until 1906. Since that time the three-storey late 18th-century stone building, with adjacent north light sheds, had various uses until around 1960. Wheelpits are visible showing the positions of five wheels and steam-driven turbines were added in 1894 at which time the brick chimney stack was added.

4: The Grand Union Canal and the Soar Valley

Unlike the Derwent Valley, this section is concerned with the transport systems and industries which developed along and around a navigable river and its canal connections to the south. The Roman Watling Street, now the A5, descends from the Northamptonshire uplands into the Nene valley and then passes through the watershed between the Nene and Severn river systems. The important transport corridor of Watford Gap was later utilised by canal, railway and most recently motorway. North of the Gap, higher ground was tunnelled through by the canal at

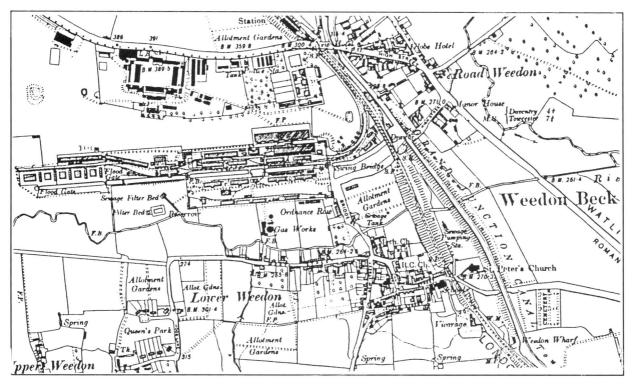

80. The Weedon Military Depot served by the Grand Union Canal and later by railway, from the 6" Ordnance Survey map (Sheet 43.SE).

81. The locks on the Grand Union Canal at Stoke Bruerne in winter.

82. A detail of the elegant iron work of the Horsley Company on a towpath bridge at Braunston.

83. A lift bridge at Rothersthorpe on the link from the River Nene at Northampton to the main Grand Union Canal at Gayton.

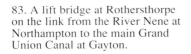

84. Towpath bridges at the junction of the re-aligned Oxford Canal with the Grand Union Canal at Braunston.

85. One of the massive ventilation shafts for the Kilsby tunnel on the London to Birmingham railway.

Crick and the railway at Kilsby. Once in Leicestershire, the canal leaves its summit at Foxton Locks and begins a slow descent into the Soar valley. North of Leicester, this now navigable river runs between the Pre-Cambrian rocks of Charnwood Forest to the west and the Jurassic ridge to the east. This is another important transport corridor, also followed by the earliest Leicestershire turnpike road, the Market Harborough to Loughborough turnpike of 1726, now the A6. The river and road were later joined by the Midland Counties Railway of 1840 and the Great Central Railway of 1899. The river joins the Trent near Red Hill opposite Trent Lock which provides access to the Erewash Canal.

The present Grand Union Canal was formed as late as 1929 by the amalgamation of several linked waterways. The earliest element of the system in the East Midlands was the Soar Navigation from the Trent to Loughborough, opened in 1778. This proved so profitable that it was extended to Leicester in 1794 with an unsuccessful branch to the west Leicestershire coalfield across Charnwood Forest. The Wreake Navigation from the Soar to Melton Mowbray opened in 1797 with a canal extension to Oakham in 1803. Meanwhile routes to London were being developed south from Northamptonshire, first the narrow Oxford Canal opened in 1790 and then the more direct broad Grand Junction Canal opened from the Thames at Brentford in 1800 to join the Oxford Canal at Braunston, albeit with a tramway over the uncompleted Blisworth tunnel. As London's demand for coal increased, ways were sought of transporting Erewash valley supplies south beyond Leicester to link up with the Grand Junction system. The projected link from Leicester to the Nene at Northampton was frustrated by lack of funds and was only completed as far as Debdale in 1797. Not until 1814 was a link finally established through the Watford Gap between the Soar Navigation and the Grand Junction Canal at Norton Junction. Due to continuing financial stringency, this link was built as a narrow canal and its multiple locks at Foxton and Watford remain a bottleneck in the Grand Union system. A year later, the Nene at Northampton was connected with the main system by a five-mile branch to Gayton with narrow locks.

The river navigations are themselves of considerable interest. Both the Soar and Wreake have a shallow profile and consequent tendency to flood, yet have been used as power sources for cornmills. The water rights of the miller had to be protected with locks and weirs when the improvements for navigation were carried out, as may be seen at Cossington and Zouch. The Soar valley is the most industrialised part of this waterway system, with granite, limestone, sand and gravel all being quarried along its banks. The valley also became one of the major centres of the hosiery industry which extended to villages south of Leicester such as Wigston and Fleckney. Comparable development is not found further south. The canal in Northamptonshire runs through a largely rural landscape lacking in settlements, and even the arrival of the London and Birmingham Railway in 1838 through the same transport corridor did not stimulate any industrial growth. Only the M1 has brought any such development with its vast distribution depots at road interchanges.

The contrast between the environment of the southern and northern sections of this waterway route will be appreciated by visiting the sites listed in the following Gazetteer.

GAZETTEER
(OS sheets 129, 140, 141 and 152)

The entries in this section are not arranged thematically but in a South to North sequence. They include sites of interest which can be visited within reasonable distance from a canal boat along the Grand Union system.

Wolverton Aqueduct (SP 801418). The Canal enters Northamptonshire from this cast iron aqueduct built which spans the River Ouse. In order to get the canal open, nine locks were constructed up and down the valley sides while a brick aqueduct was being built. This collapsed in 1808 and was replaced three years later by the present structure. In the interim the original locks were brought back into use, of which one remains at the Cosgrove end. At *Cosgrove* (SP 793427) an elegant gothic bridge of 1800 spans the canal.

Stoke Bruerne The Grand Junction Canal was opened here from the River Thames at Brentford in 1800, climbing via seven *Locks* (SP 750489 to 744499) to the level through Blisworth tunnel; this connection to the north was not opened until 1805. By the top lock of the flight is a canal settlement which includes a former steam corn mill now used as a *Waterways Museum*. The broad locks were duplicated in 1835 in order to speed up traffic and combat expected competition from the London and Birmingham Railway. In the original top lock a boat weighing machine dating from 1834 is displayed; this was removed from the Glamorganshire Canal at Cardiff and carries a horse-drawn narrow boat.

Blisworth Canal Tunnel (SK 739503 to 7295299) is almost 1.75 miles (2.81km) long. Its construction began in 1793 but was abandoned in 1796 and work did not recommence until 1802. When finally opened in 1805 the temporary plateway from the bottom lock of the Stoke Bruerne flight over Blisworth hill, which had been in use since 1800, was abandoned. At Blisworth wharf a warehouse, dated 1879, remains.

Gayton Junction (SP 720550). The plateway removed from Blisworth tunnel served for ten years as a link from here for the five-mile descent to the River Nene at Northampton until the canal arm was completed in 1815. There are 17 narrow locks in all, 12 in the *Rothersthorpe flight*, a lock-keeper's cottage and three timber lift bridges between SP 723560 and 727571. It provides a link from the Fenland waterway system to the main canal network.

Weedon Ordnance Depot (SP 629595) is a relic of the Napoleonic Wars when construction of an arsenal and barracks, together with special buildings to accommodate George III and his family, was begun in 1803 on a 125-acre site. Gas works and sewage disposal works were also erected. The Depot was served by an arm of the Grand

Junction Canal and later by a connection to the London and Birmingham Railway. The barracks and royal pavilions have been demolished but a remarkable series of buildings remain within a rectangular walled compound. These include a main entrance with water gate over the canal arm, complete with portcullis and clock tower. The canal arm continues westward flanked by a series of eight multi-storey brick-built depots designed to take 800,000 stands of small arms. The canal then passes through a second water gate into the powder storage area. Here a series of double skinned powder magazines are separated by dummy buildings which are earth-filled to minimise any blast damage from accidental explosions. The whole complex has been vacated by the Government and re-use proposals have so far not been carried into effect.

Whilton Locks (SP 619643 to 617649). A flight of locks, with side ponds now disused, ascends to Long Buckby Wharf.

LONG BUCKBY. The wharf at SP 613654 was once part of a busy canal settlement and a few of the buildings remain. Within sight from the canal are the Watling Street (A5), the London and Birmingham Railway and the M1 Motorway, all following a transport corridor northwards through the Watford Gap. The village lies about 1.5 miles to the north-west of the wharf and is still a shoe making centre; the industry was established here in the 1830s, working to Daventry manufacturers. In the village centre at SP 629676 are some two-storey workshops packed in behind stone cottages; nearby are other single and two-storey hand workshops. The first phase of mechanised production is epitomised by the Castle Factory in *King Street* (SP 627676), a three-storey building constructed in two phases between 1885 and 1890, one with three bays and the other with six bays plus entrance; a wall crane remains *in situ*. At South Place on *Station Road* (SP 625672) is a nine-bay pedimented single storey factory, reflecting the change towards heavier machinery. This was erected in 1903 together with a row of 20 houses.

Norton Junction (SP 602657). Here the old Grand Junction line turns westwards and the former Leicester and Northampton Union Canal continues northwards. Along the Grand Junction the 2,042 yard (1.86km) *Braunston Tunnel* (SP 576651) is reached; opened in 1796, this has a tight 'S' bend in it due to a surveying error. *Braunston Wharf* (SP 545659) is reached via six locks. Braunston was on the line of the original Oxford Canal, opened in 1774; then the Grand Junction was opened in 1805 and it became an important junction. Between 1829 and 1834 the sinuous line of the Oxford Canal was re-routed and a new connection located at SP 533660; here the 'Y' junction has elegant Horseley Ironworks bridges for the towpath. Nearer the wharf the original Oxford junction has a further footbridge and the red brick toll office remains. Adjacent to the bottom lock is a covered dry dock and the former engine house where water was pumped back up to a small reservoir located near the top lock.

Watford Locks (SP 593687) lie between the A5 and the M1, on the link from the Grand Junction to the Leicester and Northampton Union Canal at Foxton which opened in 1814. The locks are narrow and there are seven in all, including a staircase of four, climbing to reach the 22-mile long summit level. There are tunnels at *Crick* (SP 592707) and *Husbands Bosworth* (SP 632845).

Kilsby Railway Tunnel (SP 578697 to 565714) was completed in 1838 by Robert Stephenson for the London and Birmingham Railway. Nearly 1.4 miles long, the tunnel was then a pioneering venture for steam trains. It was built to large dimensions, 28 feet high and 25 feet wide, for fear of suffocating the passengers. The size of the bore can be appreciated at the portals. There are several ventilation shafts, including two of 60-feet diameter, which can be seen from the the A5 road, together with the spoil heaps from the tunnel construction.

The Welford Arm (SP 627826) begins here. The 1.5-mile branch has a single lock before the terminus wharf at Welford. The branch serves as a feeder from Naseby, Sulby and Welford reservoirs.

Claybrooke Mill (SP 499891). This site on the Soar was used from the 13th century until 1953. The three-storey brick mill then went out of use but recently the internal pitchback wheel and the mill machinery have been restored and the mill is once again operating commercially using water power.

Stemborough Mill (SP 532911) on a Soar tributary was first mentioned in the 13th century, although the present buildings date from the early 19th century. Milling ceased in 1944 and the mill has now been restored to residential use. However, much of the machinery remains including a 15.5ft-diameter overshot iron wheel, dated 1901, made

86. The working watermill on a source stream of the River Soar near Claybrooke Magna.

87. The two staircases of five narrow locks on the Grand Junction Canal at Foxton.

88. The steam corn mill on St Mary's Road in Market Harborough.

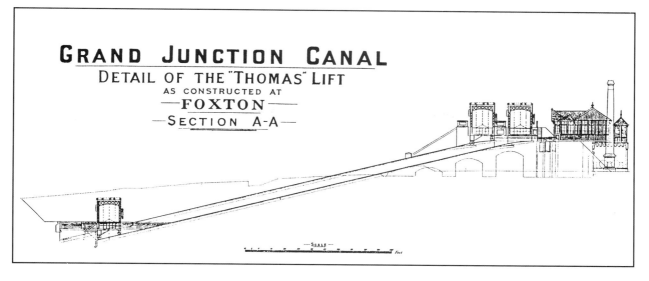

GRAND JUNCTION CANAL
DETAIL OF THE "THOMAS" LIFT
AS CONSTRUCTED AT
—FOXTON—
—SECTION A-A—

—SCALE—

89. A section drawing for the Thomas boat lift constructed at Foxton for the Grand Junction Canal.

90. Symington's elaborately fenestrated corset factory in Market Harborough.

by William Cartwright of Loughborough. Unusually, there are two wallowers on horizontal shafts which mesh with the pit wheel: these drive two pairs of stones through bevel gears. One of the shafts is extended and carries a belt pulley for driving the grain feeders and sack hoist system; these have been removed in the subsequent conversion.

Foxton Locks (SP 690892 to 692898) begin the descent towards the Soar valley and the Trent. There are two staircases of five narrow locks descending 75 feet which are separated by a passing pound. These locks and those at Watford formed a narrow bottleneck between two broad canals and eventually the carrying firm of Fellows, Morton and Clayton pressed for improvements. In 1900 a boat lift was constructed, working on the inclined plane principle: both caissons could accommodate two narrow boats and counterbalanced one another, friction being overcome by a steam engine. The *inclined plane* worked only until 1911 when it was abandoned. The Foxton Inclined Plane Trust has cleared the incline remains and provided interpretative material. A replica of the original boiler house has been constructed which contains a small museum and the long term aim is to restore the incline to working order. A nucleus of the original canalside buildings also survives.

MARKET HARBOROUGH may be reached via the 5.75-miles long level canal branch from the foot of Foxton locks to a *Terminus Basin* at SP 727879. Several timber merchants were once located here but the area is due for residential and marina development, including the early warehouse buildings. The *Station* (SP 741873) in Queen Anne style was built in 1883, replacing the previous station erected for the Rugby to Stamford line in 1850; subsequent lines were laid to Leicester and Kettering in 1857, to Northampton in 1859 and to Melton Mowbray in 1879. Only the second, the main line to London, survives.

Market Harborough was the market centre for south east Leicestershire, serving the Welland valley which was a good cattle rearing area. As a result, a tannery, woollen manufacture, grain warehouses and maltings were established. There are grain warehouses in *Fairfield Street* (SP 731872) and near the railway in *Great Bowden Road* (SP 740873). On *St Mary's Road* (SP 739872) there is a former steam cornmill which was erected in the 1860s. The main block is three storey and is built of brick with decorated cornice and round headed windows. Also on the south side of *St Mary's Road* at the corner of Kettering Road is a further corn warehouse and nearby, at Number 84, a former woollen merchant's warehouse. The steam mill on *Northampton Road* (SP 736868) was erected by Symingtons for grinding pea flour and coffee. It is dated 1881 and has three storeys and decorated gables. The former *Symington's Corset Factory, Adam and Eve Street* (SP 734873) has been re-used to house Council Offices and Library and Museum. The business was established in 1848 in a former carpet factory and used American sewing machines. Victorian fashion ensured the rapid expansion of the industry and extensive four- and six-storey blocks with elaborate windows were erected, some of which have since been demolished.

Kibworth Harcourt Windmill (SP 689944), the only surviving post mill in Leicestershire, stands some 30 feet high and has a brick round house. The mill, possibly dating from 1711, was in use until 1912 and has been restored. There are four sails and two pairs of stones.

FLECKNEY was an important framework knitting centre in the early 19th century, with 126 frames in 1844. On *Kilby Road* (SP 649937) an early powered hosiery factory can be seen; this three-storey block was built in three phases of four, six and four bays with adjacent dyeing sheds. This business was established by Robert Walker in 1859 and became part of Wolsey. A later single storey hosiery and knitwear factory can be seen on the *Saddington Road* (SP 651931) which was built in 1886 as the Victoria Mill of R Rowley & Co, another prominent East Midlands manufacturer. The factory has few windows on the street frontage. The firm also built houses nearby in Gladstone Street.

WIGSTON MAGNA was the subject of W. G. Hoskins' The *Midland Peasant*. As early as 1801 half the population were engaged in trade and industry and by 1845 there were over 500 stocking frames at work. There are few remains of the domestic phase, but small hand-powered hosiery workshops may be seen off *Moat Street* (SP 605986), *Spa Lane* (SP 608988) and *Mowsley End* (SP 609989), the latter having later single storey north light workshops behind. Other later hosiery factories may be found at *Newtown Lane* (SP 610985) and *Paddock Street* (SP 608989).

The most important relic of the hand-powered phase of the hosiery industry is at *42/44 Bushloe End* (SP 603987) where the Wigston Framework Knitting Museum has been established in former glove and stocking workshops. The master hosier's house, complete with mending windows, is listed Grade II and a detached 19th-century two-storey workshop at the rear contains most of its original machines and ancillary equipment. The Museum is open to the public (enquiries tel 0533 883396).

Wigston was also a railway junction where lines to Leicester, London, Rugby and Birmingham met. Engine sheds were once located here and some of the 300 railway staff lived in houses erected by the Midland on the north side of *Station Road* (SP 595986).

SOUTH WIGSTON. Adjacent to the canal is *Crow Mill* (SP 590977) which was once powered by the River Sence (the Soar tributary); the canal proprietors bought the mill, along with an associated windmill in 1818. A steam engine was installed to supplement the internal wheel but milling seems to have ceased by 1900 and the buildings have been converted to residential use. The village itself lies to the north and may be approached along *Canal Street* (SP 590983) which runs parallel to the former line of the Midland line to Rugby. The works which line the east side of this street included an iron foundry, biscuit factory, and shoe and hosiery factories, many built of bricks made at the Wigston Railway Junction works. The factories themselves and at least 600 identical terraced houses were erected by Orson Wright, a speculative builder, who was also a hosiery and boot manufacturer. W. G. Hoskins wrote: 'The sight of South Wigston on a wet and foggy Sunday afternoon in November is an experience one is glad to have had. It reaches the rock bottom of English provincial life and there is something profoundly moving about it'.

Pack Horse Bridge, Aylestone (SK 566009). This and its causeway was built to accommodate the growing coal trade between the north west of the county and Leicester – its distance from the town indicates the problems of flooding in the river valley to the north.

St Mary's Mills, Leicester (SK 577025) lie on an island between the Soar and the Biam. In the 15th century the corn mill belonged to the College of St Mary in Leicester, then passing to the Westcotes estate. In 1867 the mill was converted by William and Arthur Bates first for the manufacture of rubber thread for elastic sided boots and later for making cycle tyres. Various buildings were added before 1909 when the use of water power ceased and a 250hp gas engine supplied power; by 1917 there were over 1,100 employess. The business was acquired by Dunlop in 1925 and the manufacture of Lactron thread and tyres continued. This has now ceased and the parallel ranges of buildings are occupied by various tenants.

Former Town Gas Works, Aylestone Road (SK 582024). Begun in 1878, these were the second gas works to be built in Leicester beside the navigation with a direct connection to the Midland line to Burton. Most of the original buildings have been demolished but the former offices house the John Doran Gas Museum, open to the public, and some stylish workers' houses remain along the road frontage.

Electricity Generating Station (SK 582028). This is now a stand-by gas turbine station and was the City's third facility; development on this site, served by canal and railway, began in 1920.

The LEICESTER STRAIGHT (SK 581030 to SK 582043) is nearly a mile long and was constructed as part of the flood prevention scheme, begun in the 1870s, which largely used the line of the leats and tail races of three former water mills. The Old River Soar on the original line still flows to the west of the new cut. There were four new bridges erected as part of the scheme. *Walnut Street* (SK 581034) and *Mill Lane* (SK 581038), two bridges of identical design, were erected by Gimson & Co of Leicester and are dated 1890; the roadway is supported by steel arches with ornamental cast iron parapets. *The Newarke* (SK 581040) bridge has stone parapets with turrets and was opened in 1898 whilst the first West Bridge (SK 581043) reverts to cast iron parapets and was built by Butler of Leeds in 1890. On the towpath just to the north of *West Bridge* the initials 'U.N.' mark the 1886 boundary between the Leicester Navigation and the Union Canal. The Old River Soar rejoins the new line slightly further along (SK 580045): adjacent was the site of the first terminus station of the Leicester and Swannington Railway which opened in 1832.

The flood prevention scheme allowed large tracts of land to be made available for building, and sites were immediately taken up for industrial development. On the west bank, the Bede Meadows were utilised for the *Great*

91. A former worsted spinning mill beside the River Soar at West Bridge in Leicester.

92. The Stephenson lift bridge which once carried the Leicester and Swannington Railway over the Leicester Navigation at Soar Lane in Leicester, now located at Snibston Discovery Park.

Central Railway goods yards (SK 580036) where the former electric and hydraulic power generating station remains adjacent to Mill Lane bridge; the goods warehouse and office block also survive. On the east bank, between Walnut Street and The Newarke bridges, a refuse destructor plant was built (now replaced by student accommodation) and ornamental gardens were created below the Castle incorporating the site of the former water mill. Several early 20th-century factories line the Eastern Boulevard and The Newarke, reflecting the prosperity of Leicester's shoe and hosiery industry. By *Walnut Street* (SK 582034) is the former Liberty Shoe factory, a steel framed four-storey building complete with statue which was erected in 1919. Further north along *Eastern Boulevard* is an 11-bay three-storey plus basement former shoe factory of 1900 and at the corner of *Mill Lane* (SK 582037) the elaborate four-storey factory erected in several phases from 1899 to 1925 for Russells, hosiery manufacturers, successors to a business established elsewhere in the town in 1815. The south side of *The Newarke* (SK 582040) is also occupied by factories of similar age. Nearest the canal, the former Adelaide Works of Wildts, hosiery machine manufacturers, were begun in 1905. Adjacent is Baker's hosiery factory, begun in 1912 and still in original occupation. At the corner of *Gateway Street* (SK 583040) are the four-storey Portland Shoe works begun in 1904 with later extensions along Goswell Street.

West Bridge Mill (SK 581042) is a fine five-storey worsted spinning mill erected c.1848 and until recently manufacturing hosiery. The chimney and engine house have been demolished and an imaginative glass panelled modern extension added on the river side. The viaduct of the former Great Central Railway now finishes near the north end of a lattice girder bridge; it formerly extended across the West Bridge linking to the station. The island viaduct site of the station still remains, now a trading estate, but the street level buildings on *Great Central Street* (SK 581047), with their extensive terracotta decoration, are still extant.

Friar's Mill, Bath Lane (SK 580046) has a belfry tower with the Ibex trade mark of Donisthorpe's, the old-established wool and worsted thread spinners. The listed buildings, the finest of Leicester's textile mills, include the central pedimented four-storey block of the early 19th century with an engine house at either end. Later additions have recently been demolished and the original buildings sympathetically restored.

Soar Lane Bridge (SK 580048) is dated 1876 and was constructed by Richards the local ironfounders to improve access to the goods yards of the Leicester and Swannington Railway on the west bank of the river. Immediately adjacent are traces of a wooden lift bridge which was designed by Stephenson to carry the railway into the goods yard on the east bank of the canal where a goods shed remains. The bridge has been removed and will be re-erected at the Snibston Heritage Museum at Coalville.

Leicester Mills. Several water mills on the Soar have disappeared, many of them during the flood prevention scheme. Between the West Bridge and the canal cut to Belgrave are two large weirs, Evans' and Hitchcock's, both named after millers. The latter operated *North Mill* (SK 580052), the water rights for which were bought by the Corporation in 1876 for £8,060. The inlet leat, once much wider to provide boat moorings, and the tail race may still be seen. The mill had a horizontal steam engine installed in 1888 and its foreshortened chimney stack can now be seen behind the four-storey building. The mill ground corn until 1905, since which date it has been used by dyers and finishers and hosiery manufacturers.

From *North Lock* (SK 581052) *St Leonard's Mill, Northgate Street* (SK 581053) may be reached. This fine-four storey pedimented block was erected in 1867 for wool spinning and later changed to hosiery manufacture. Continuing to North Bridge, various dye works can be seen along the river bank, which once used river water but are now reliant on deep well and mains supplies. The canal cut passes Abbey Park, opened in 1882, on the left bank and several textile works, with dyeing sheds along *Friday Street* (SK 585053). Nearby in *St John Street* is St Margaret's Works (SK 587052), belonging to the Corah knitwear group. An early three-storey plus basement building dating from 1865, with prominent central entrance fronting north-light sheds, is now hidden by extensive later additions. In *Watling Street* (SK 587052) is the former engineering works of Goodwin Barsby which surround an earlier building with decorated round headed windows. In *Canning Place* (SK 586052) are Leeson's hosiery works, the earliest section of which is dated 1877.

Belgrave Wharf (SK 590057). Near Limekiln Lock is a former canal basin which once served lime kilns on the north bank, the existing canal warehouse and the original town gas works on the south bank. The warehouse has been converted for use by the Charles Keene College and a new access bridge erected to the main site which

93. The St Margaret's Works, pictured above, is a large hosiery factory belonging to Corahs in Leicester.

94. Worsted spinning and hosiery factories beside the Leicester Navigation on Abbey Park Road.

95. The former tannery at Frog Island near the North Mill in Leicester.

utilises the former generating hall of the *Lero Power Station*. This opened in 1904 to supply DC power for the tramway system and became redundant in 1949.

Textile Factories, Abbey Park Road (SK591058). This range of buildings has been erected over 60 years, with the earliest section along the canal bank being the steam-powered Abbey Mills of 1884 for the worsted spinners, Fielding and Johnson. The later buildings fronting the street date from 1887 to 1923 and were erected for R. Walker & Co. hosiery manufacturers, later becoming Wolsey Ltd.

Abbey Meadow Mills (SK 589064) lie between the Canal and the river near Belgrave Lock. The complex, established in 1902, includes dyeing sheds with characteristic louvred roofs as well as extensive north light sheds. The complex also incorporates a former rope works by the river bank and is still occupied by Wolsey (Courtauld group).

Museum of Technology, Corporation Road (SK 589066) is housed in a former sewage pumping station built in 1891 which retains its four Woolf compound beam engines built by Gimsons of Leicester. These engines and others in the Museum are regularly steamed. (Open weekdays 10 to 5.30, Sundays 2 to 5.30.) After Belgrave Lock the waterway resumes a sinuous course to Birstall lock, passing on the east bank the *Belgrave Pumping Station* which was erected in 1902 for sewage pumping. The building with round headed windows once contained three vertical compound condensing engines with single action pumps, supplied by three Lancashire boilers.

Cossington Mill (SK 596129) is a Domesday mill site on the Soar and was used for fulling cloth, paper-making and corn grinding until 1928. The external undershot wheel has now been removed and the water courses filled in. The timber-framed mill standing beside a lock on the Soar navigation is now a restaurant.

SILEBY, half a mile east of Sileby Lock (SK593147), is another of the Soar Valley's industrialised villages. The church is a good example of construction using the hard Mountsorrel granite with limestone and gritstone quoins. The most striking buildings are the brewery and maltings in *High Street* (SK601157), which date from the 1860s. The village was a hosiery and boot and shoe centre, and there are examples of workshops and early 20th-century factories.

Mountsorrel Quarry (SK577148). The hill at Mountsorrel, by the Soar, was extensively quarried for granite for setts and road stone but the plant now processes stone from *Buddon Wood* quarry nearby (SK 562152). Although much of the stone is now carried by road, the original transport connections are of interest. By the river

96. The distinctive outline of the former brewery and maltings at Sileby.

97. The Lower Mill on the River Soar at Cotes, near Loughborough.

(SK 579153) remains of wagon tipplers for loading canal boats can be seen whilst the adjacent elegant red brick bridge, dated 1860, carried a rail link to the Midland Railway at Barrow on Soar. The bridge is still in use, now carrying a conveyor to the concrete works and rail loading point at Barrow. There was a second rail link to the Great Central to the west and a cutting and overbridge can be seen at SK572147.

QUORN contains many houses of local granite; those in Station Road date from around 1800 and are also roofed with local Swithland slate. It was once a busy knitting centre and *Bridge Mills* (SK562165) were built by the Wright family for elastic web manufacture. The attractive four-storey brick building has round headed cast iron windows, large roof ventilators and a tall chimney with ornamental top; later north light sheds adjoin.

Lower Mill, Cotes (SK 554206) continued to use water power until 1973 for grinding animal feeds. It too has been converted to a public house and restaurant. Nearby a 15th-century bridge and causeway carries the Nottingham road over the flood plain of the River Soar.

Loughborough Canal Basin (SK 533200) was the terminus of the original Soar Navigation opened from the Trent in 1778. All the original wharf buildings which lined both banks have been demolished, but the towpath can be followed to the Chain Bridge where the later Leicester Navigation branches off. No traces remain of the Nanpantan tramway, part of the Charnwood Forest Canal system, which terminated here. The former electricity generating station remains in *Bridge Street* (SK 535199), whilst the town gas works were on the opposite side of the Derby Road, both well sited for canal borne coal supplies, but some distance from any rail link. Other sites in Loughborough are included in Chapter Five: Section 5.

Zouch Mill (SK 508234). Zouch has been a bridging point on the Soar since the Middle Ages and the watermill lies between the river and a canal cut. The gaunt brick building has been used for both corn and gypsum grinding but is now converted for residential purposes.

HATHERN is to the south from Zouch. Another former framework knitting village working to Loughborough, workshops survive at *The Green* and *Green Hill Rise* (SK 503223). To the east of Zouch along the A6006 by the railway are the *Hathern Station Brick and Terracotta Company Works* (SK 515242) which were established in 1878. Terracotta and faience tiles are still made here which are a distinctive feature of cinemas and other public buildings of the 1920s and '30s.

Soar Lane, Sutton Bonington (SK 503256). This village had 110 stocking frames in 1844. A good example of a domestic frameshop survives which is dated 1661. The house is timber-framed with brick infill and has long windows on both ground and first floors, the latter clearly being a later insertion.

KEGWORTH. The village was an important hosiery centre but little evidence survives except for the two-storey workshop behind the Britannia Inn on the A6 (SK 488265). This has windows on all sides on both floor levels and an external staircase. One of the last hand operated workshops to be built in the East Midlands, frames were used here as late as the 1950s.

5: The Nene Valley of Northamptonshire

The fertile valley of the River Nene is primarily an agricultural area with pastoral farming providing the raw materials of wool and leather for the early worsted and boot and shoe industries of the county. The river is 115 miles long, falling 300 feet in 17 miles from the source to Northampton and a further 160 feet over the 49 miles to Peterborough. Nearly every village along the Nene and its tributaries possessed its own water mill for grinding corn or, more rarely, for fulling cloth. At many mill sites the river divides into several channels, thereby providing natural by-passes. There are surviving buildings at over 30 of these sites, many of which were rebuilt as large mills in the mid-19th century, indicating the continuing dependence of the region on water power. These often straddle a major arm of the river and, because of insecure foundations, the walls are strapped by numerous tie bars.

Until the Middle Ages the river was bridged only at Oundle, Thrapston, Wellingborough and Northampton. These places later developed as trading centres with river wharves. The Nene was improved and made navigable to Oundle by 1730, to Thrapston by 1737 and to Northampton by 1761. This provided a 92-mile waterway connection to the Wash and therefore to the coast-wise coal trade, bringing much needed fuel to the county. Navigation was made possible by means of both staunches and pound locks; in 1852 there were 11 staunches, 34 locks and 33 watermills between Northampton and Peterborough. Some of the locks between Wellingborough and Northampton were donated by local gentry striving for political positions. The River Commissioners commemorated these gifts by the erection of inscribed stones at the locks, two of which still survive at Abington and Clifford Hill.

The river navigation was later connected to the main canal system by means of the Northampton Arm of the Grand Junction Canal which was opened from Gayton to Northampton in 1815. By the early 20th century, due to silting at both the outfall and in the upper valley, the river was only navigable with great difficulty and in 1930 the Nene Catchment Board was formed and new improvements began. Between 1937 and 1944, the vertical gate staunches were replaced by locks and pound locks reconstructed. The modern locks are characterised by their mitred top gates and single vertical guillotine bottom gates which are normally left raised to allow flood waters to pass easily. Two locks at Rush Mills and Ditchford have curved bottom gates which swing in an arc whilst Abington lock has mitred bottom gates. The river regularly carried goods until 1969 when grain supplies to Whitworth's mill at Wellingborough ceased to be brought from London by canal to Northampton and then by river.

A railway was opened in 1845 from Blisworth, on the London and Birmingham Railway, to Peterborough. This ran beside the Northampton Canal arm and then along the Nene valley to Peterborough. The tracks have all been lifted except for the section from Wansford to Peterborough which is now worked by the Nene Valley Railway. The valley was crossed at Wellingborough by the Midland Railway's Leicester to Hitchin line, opened in 1857, and later at Northampton in 1881/2 by the Roade to Rugby link of the London and Birmingham Railway. The construction of the Midland Railway led to the discovery of vast ironstone reserves and subsequently provided transport for both the ore and iron foundry products. Blast furnaces were erected locally but a large proportion of the ore, often calcined on site, was taken to Derbyshire, South Wales and the West Midlands. Several of the ironstone quarries have now been converted into Country Parks.

The river valley remains a rich source for gravel extraction and flooded pits at Billing, Ringstead, Titchmarsh and Barnwell are also now used for leisure purposes. Bullrushes were cultivated and used for the manufacture of horse collars and rush mats, particularly in Islip. Towns and villages like Wellingborough, Earls Barton, Raunds and Irthlingborough also developed as tanning and boot and shoe manufacturing centres. Earls Barton illustrates the transition from back garden workshops to multi-storey factories, while in Irthlingborough it is possible to observe the evolution of shoe factory design.

GAZETTEER
(OS sheets 141, 142, 152 and 153)

Agriculture-based Industries

Ashton Mill (TL 051875) is a Domesday mill site which was later used for fulling and then for corn grinding until 1900 when it was converted by the first Lord Rothschild to provide piped water and DC electricity supply to his mansion, model village and farm. Two turbines and a Crossley hot bulb engine were installed, the latter subsequently replaced by two Blackstone diesel engines; clutches were fitted to allow either source to power Crompton dynamos and piston pumps which lifted 4,000 gallons of water daily to reservoirs in the village. Adjacent is the *Fish and Bygones Museum* which has displays concerning fishing and river management as well as rural industries. The site is open on weekend afternoons in the summer.

Barnwell Mill (TL 038870) is stone-built with a wooden lucam and part of the building is dated 1746. The mill has been converted to a restaurant. It is a good example of a mill associated with a river navigation with a typical lock beside it with mitred top gates and guillotine lower gate. Nearby is a 37-acre country park which was established in 1971 in gravel workings dug between 1957 and 1968.

Billing Mill (SP 814611) was recorded as a fulling mill in 1274 and belonged to St James' Abbey until 1538. The present building dates from the 19th century and contains an iron wheel together with two of the original three pairs of stones. It has since 1968 been maintained as a museum with displays on mills of the county. A horse engine removed from a farm at Eversholt in Bedfordshire is also preserved here. (For opening times tel. 0604 408181.)

Heygate's Mill, Bugbrooke (SP 679586). The tall profile of the modern buildings is easily visible from the M1 but closer inspection reveals the earlier three-storey stone-built watermill and its adjoining mill house which is dated 'ABM 1866'. The mill straddles the River Nene and had an internal wheel, later a turbine. The modern mill still produces flour.

Cogenhoe Mill (SP 832613) is a three-storey brick mill built across the River Nene, with lock alongside. The adjacent stone house, once thatched but now tiled, has a datestone 'EW 1725'. The mill is at the centre of a caravan site.

98. The interior of the former corn mill at Ashton near Oundle, showing the conversion for water pumping and electricity generation for the nearby estate village.

99. The watermill at Barnwell with the adjacent guillotine lock on the Nene Navigation.

Cotterstock Mill (TL 047904) has been reduced in size for road widening, but the remaining stone building has been restored as offices; the wheelpit of the former low-breast wheel is visible. A private river wharf was built here in 1729 by Lord Cardigan of Deene Park.

Hardwater Mill, Great Doddington (SP 876637) with mill house attached, is a two-storey stone building straddling one channel of the Nene. The Navigation channel and lock is on the north side of the mill.

Harlestone Mill (SP 708647) lies on a Nene tributary. The derelict brick and stone building retains its machinery. Nearby the *Model Farm* (SP 702646) belonging to the Althorp estate is an impressive complex of ironstone buildings with four square towers and a Palladian pedimented portico.

Islip Mill (SP 992792) is a stone building with a brick upper storey and wooden lucam. This had two wheels, one breastshot and one undershot; one remains *in situ* and the other was removed on conversion to electricity in 1954. The mill worked until 1970 but is now used as a residence.

High Street, Islip (SP 987791). Two families, the Lovedays and Knights, were involved in using bulrushes for making horse collars, matting, baskets and seats. The industry continued into the 1950s and Knights' three-storey rush factory has now become a club.

Kislingbury Mill (SP 694595) is brick-built with the adjoining mill house of stone; the tail race is visible but the leat infilled. The mill is now used for fireplace manufacture.

OUNDLE has many remains of its once extensive brewing and malting industry. Several examples in East, South and North Roads have been modified to other uses. A substantial brick maltings with lucam at TL 044888 has

100. The empty shell of Warmington mill on the Nene.

101. Victoria steam corn mill, served by road, water and railway in Wellingborough.

102. The Neneside Ironworks of Smith and Grace in Thrapston.

been converted to housing and there is a stone one at TL 044885. *Anchor Brewery* on South Road (TL 038879) was established in 1864 and the three-storey brick buildings remain.

Titchmarsh Mill (TL 015809), on a Domesday site, is a low stone and brick building beside a river lock. The mill worked until the 1950s and since 1967 has been the HQ of the Upper Nene Sailing Club. The millstones were in line and driven by a long layshaft; an external drive pulley remains on the downstream side.

Upton Mill (SP 721592) is a gaunt three-storey ironstone mill and adjoining house straddling the main river channel. It was rebuilt in 1815 and the mill is now disused.

Wadenhoe Mill (TL 013833) is an attractive three-storey stone building with prominent tie plates, rebuilt in 1838 and now converted into a residence.

Warmington Mill (TL 074916) with its own wharf is now semi-derelict. The large four-storey stone building has segmental headed cast iron windows with yellow brick lintels. The mill was built in two phases in the 1830s and 1890s and two wheel pits remain which held low breastshot wheels. Unusually in the Nene valley, the parallel river lock is a third of a mile away.

Victoria Mill, Wellingborough (SP902665). The four-storey brick steam corn mill is dated 1886. It was built by J. B. Whitworth beside the Nene and waterborne deliveries continued until 1969. It also has road and rail access. The plant was electrified in 1958 and the buildings are still occupied by Whitworths.

Great Addington or Woodford Mill (SP 973752), also known as Willy Watt mill, has two storeys and is stone-built with ornamental ironstone banding. Two low breastshot wheels are still *in situ*, one internal and one external. Primarily a corn mill, it was at one time used for paper making. Alongside are a lock with guillotine gate and also a flood control gate.

Yarwell Mill (TL074973), close to a typical lock with guillotine gate, is dated 1839. Some windows in the stone mill have been infilled and a modern extension mars the rear of the building.

Extractive Industries

Hunsbury Hill (SP 738584) is now a Country Park created among old ironstone workings. There is evidence for early iron working in the Iron Age hill fort which was itself damaged by the ironstone extraction in the 1870s. The stone was processed at two blast furnaces erected near to the Northampton Canal Arm but quarrying ceased in 1921 and the furnaces closed. The park is now the home of the Northamptonshire Ironstone Railway Trust with a collection of working steam and diesel locomotives which is operated on Sundays.

Irchester Countryside Park (SP 910660) was formerly an ironstone quarry operated by the South Durham Iron Company until 1969. Although planted with trees, the hill and dale formation of the backfill after ironstone working may still be discerned. Around the perimeter are exposed quarry faces and the remains of calcining clamps at SP 908659. There are traces of early narrow gauge and later standard gauge mineral railways. The Irchester Narrow Gauge Railway Trust is based here.

Smith and Grace Ironfoundry, Thrapston (SP 995783) This business was established in 1857 for manufacturing farm implements but later concentrated on foundry work and the making of pulley blocks, as is reflected in the inscription 'Smith and Grace Screw Boss Pulley Co Ltd' on the 1898 office block. An earlier two-storey workshop with cast iron windows adjoins.

Transport

Medieval Bridge, Irthlingborough (SP 957706), now by-passed, dates from the 14th century. It has ten pointed arches with five refuges on the downstream side.

OUNDLE's importance as a market town increased after river traffic was possible after 1730. Near to the *North Bridge* (TL 045888) is a disused arm of the navigation with now-converted warehouses remaining. The former *Railway Station* (TL 046981) in neo-Tudor style was erected in 1845 and has been converted to residential use; a nearby inn was built in similar style.

Thrapston Bridge (SP 991786) is a long medieval crossing of the Nene but has been widened to accommodate modern traffic.

Manufacturing Industries: Boots and Shoes

EARLS BARTON changed from an agricultural village of c.700 people in 1801 to a small town of 2,900 in 1901, indicating its transformation into an important boot and shoe manufacturing centre with 16 factories at that time. Here may be seen the backyard or garden 'shops' where outworkers carried out the closing and finishing operations. Garden workshops may be found behind houses in *Broad Street* (SP 854636) and in *Sunnyside* (SP 848636) is a terrace of cottages built as a speculative development between 1886 and 1900 with workshops at the street side. Also on *Broad Street* (SP 853636) is a manufacturer's house with two-storey workshops attached.

Factories may be seen in *Harcourt Square* (SP 853636) and in *Station Road* (SP 852633) where Barker's original factory remains. In *Park Street* (SP 850637) is a former leather works, dated 1879, and further along a terrace of cottages c.1860 with back garden workshops. On the *Doddington Road* (SP 858636) is another large factory erected by White's in 1893.

IRTHLINGBOROUGH also developed during the 19th century, its population growing fivefold to 4,300 by 1901. Employment was provided both by ironworking and also by boot and shoe manufacture. There are few signs of the domestic outwork system remaining. On *Victoria Street* (SP 942703) is the Tower Factory with its chateau-style tower attached to the three-storey 12-bay building with prominent 'S' tie bars; some smaller two-storey workshops survive below the works. Further along *Victoria Street* are the three-storey Atlanta Works (SP 942704). Another works at the corner of *Queen Street*, now a leather warehouse, has an elaborate gateway.

103. Purpose-built domestic boot and shoe workshops in Earls Barton.

On *Scarborough Street* (SP 945706) are the Excelsior Boot and Shoe Works which were built in four phases from 1893. They are a good example of the transition from the three-storey block to the single storey buildings at the rear which were necessary to accommodate larger and heavier machinery. Near the *Church* (SP 958707) are the Express Works, dated 1937, with an imposing stone frontage to a steel framed building.

RAUNDS developed into an important boot and shoe manufacturing centre specialising in boots for the Services; wars in the late Victorian period did much to stimulate the trade. Most of its factories and terraced housing are built of locally made red and yellow brick from the Manor works. The factories provided outwork for garden workshops into the 20th century and a group of these can still be seen in the terrace off *Gladstone Street* (TL 000727). The small single storey workshops are separated from the back yards of the houses by a common access passage. The extensive three-storey plus basement factory, formerly Adams Brothers, fronts both *Gladstone Street* and *Spencer Street* and has loading doors on both streets. There is a datestone of 1904 and separate entrances labelled 'Office' and 'Workmen'. On *Midland Road* (TL002733) is a three-storey factory in two adjoining blocks with a datestone inscribed 'CEN 1896', referring to C. E. Nicholls. There is a wall crane serving three loading doors in the gable end and the factory is now operated by Coggins, like Adams a firm established at the end of the 19th century. The *Wellington Works* (SP 993722) are marked by an entrance archway, adorned with a boot motif, between two pairs of semi-detached houses. Formerly a shoe factory, the present tannery was established during the first World War. Adjacent is a three-storey factory with wall crane and identified by a roundel engraved 'John Horrell & Son, Boot and Shoe Manufacturers and Contractors, 1889', the latter referring to their position as government suppliers.

Ringstead (SP 990752). On the main street is a three-storey yellow brick boot and shoe factory with cast iron windows, dated 1895. It is inscribed in a small roundel 'Ringstead Britannia Cooperative Society Ltd, Solid and Reliable' with a boot motif.

RUSHDEN. Like its immediate neighbour Higham Ferrers, boot and shoe making was superimposed on a small town. In Rushden this resulted in very rapid growth in the late 19th century, the population trebling between 1871 and 1891. A branch railway, now closed, from the Midland main line was built to serve the town's industries in

104. A classic boot and shoe factory on Rectory Road in Rushden, with loading doors and wall-mounted crane.

105. An elaborate boot and shoe factory on Cromwell Road in Rushden.

106. This single storey boot and shoe factory on Allen Road in Rushden is typical of the last decade of the 19th century.

107. The elaborate polychromatic brick water storage tower at Finedon.

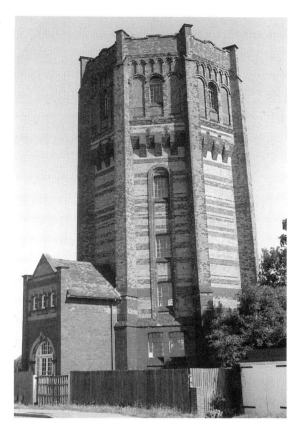

1893/4. The integrity of the industrial development of the town has been lost because of demolition and new road schemes, but the variety of buildings connected with the leather trades of Rushden may be seen by following a short trail on the east side of the A6 trunk road. Starting at the north end of *Rectory Road* (SP 957671), on the west side a terrace of six cottages have back garden workshops with their blank back walls facing the street. On the opposite side of the road is a further terrace, *Beaconsfield Place*, also with garden workshops. Further along *East Grove* is a small three-storey factory in domestic style with centre loading bay. Returning to *Rectory Road*, at the corner of Victoria Road is a plain two-bay three-storey brick factory with a surviving wall mounted crane serving a row of loading doors. Further south, at the corner of *Albert Road* (SP 958670), are two factory blocks, each with two-storey offices fronting single storey north light workshops. Some more back yard workshops are visible on the west side of the road.

Further south at the corner of *Portland Road* is Highgrove, a refurbished three-storey 20th-century shoe factory which has been converted to housing; extensive workshops at the rear have been demolished for new houses. On *Portland Road* (SP 959669) two single storey factories face each other, the one on the north side having an elaborate entrance vestibule with decorative leaded lights illustrating the markets supplied. Opposite the end of Portland Road is *Allen Road*, with a pedimented single storey factory, dated 1895, which has large cast iron segmental-headed windows. At the corner of *Cromwell Road* and *Upper Queen Street* (SP 962671) is an elaborately fenestrated four-storey factory with corner tower, the home of 'Grenson' shoes. Adjacent on *Cromwell Road* is a small factory manufacturing boxes, an essential element in the shoe trade.

WELLINGBOROUGH, at the confluence of the River Ise with the Nene, witnessed the transformation of its industrial activity from home-based pillow lace and shoe making in the early 19th century to factory-based boot and shoe manufacture, iron making and engineering later in the century. The town's population trebled between 1851 and 1901. Iron making was commenced in the town in 1852, utilising local ores, but the works were off the route of the Leicester to Hitchin railway constructed in 1857. This exposed further ore deposits and new furnaces were erected near the railway in 1867. These were shut down in 1925 and demolished, but the site remains in use as an ironfoundry (SP 907677). A large coal distribution depot employing 400 people in 1900 was established on the railway.

The shoe industry came to specialise in upper manufacture only, rather than complete shoes. Clicking and closing of uppers was carried out in factories and the uppers sent elsewhere for lasting and finishing. The basket-work system did not therefore operate to the same extent as in other shoe towns and this may help to explain why there were fewer garden workshops here. Some survive behind a terrace of 20 houses on *Colwell Road* (SP 903678), separated from the rear gardens by an alley. The town centre has been largely rebuilt but several shoe factories do remain, largely of 1890s date.

North of the centre in *Herriotts Lane* (SP 891681) is a 3½-storey brick factory with a central pediment, inscribed the 'Wellingborough Boot and Shoe Company'. Between *Alma Street* and *Chequers Lane* (SP 894681) are several small workshops in very plain style. On *Great Park Street* (SP 892681) are two three-storey factories of *c*.1900. In *Mill Road* (SP 896681), at the corner of *Strode Road*, a three-storey plus basement factory whose corner block is dated 1898 has later extensions. On the other side of the church, at the corner of *Thomas Street*, is a similar factory with central loading doors, dated 1890. On *Stanley Road* (SP 897683), at the corner of Grant Road, is an impressive red brick factory with yellow string course and cast iron windows. On the corner of *Cannon Street* (SP 895683), unusually for Wellingborough, an integrated shoe factory has north light sheds to the rear. A large clothing factory dominates *Victoria Road* (SP 895678), whose two similar blocks are dated 1916 and 1928. This was established by Ideal Clothiers, who had branch factories in several adjacent villages; the firm closed in 1980.

Public Utilities

Water Tower, Finedon (SP 926717). An elaborate Victorian polychromatic brick structure with a castellated top which was erected in 1904/5 to supply the village.

4

Extractive Regions

1: East Derbyshire and Nottinghamshire Coalfield

The landscape of the coalfield consists of rolling hills in the west, with the higher ground only 200m above sea level, becoming flatter in the east. In the north the gradients on the rivers Leen, Maun, Meden and Poulter were sufficient to power first corn mills and later cotton spinning mills from the late 18th century. The Coal Measures outcrop along a line running north-south from Chesterfield to Belper which then swings south east to Stanton. To the east, they are overlain by younger Permian rocks, Magnesian limestones, Bunter sandstones, mudstones and alluvium across to the Trent valley bordering Lincolnshire. The sandstones are highly porous and, since they rest on an impervious marl, form a reservoir or aquifer of vast capacity which provides around 70 per cent of Nottinghamshire's water. The outcropping coals have been worked at least since the 13th century for local use as part of a dual economy with farming. As mining technology improved and demand increased, the mining industry moved eastwards to exploit deeper seams.

Drainage of the shallow mines was achieved by soughs or simple mechanical means. The first sough was constructed at Wollaton in 1552 and another begun by Sir John Molyneux in 1703 from Blackwell to Teversal was five miles long when completed by the Duke of Devonshire in 1774. A system of soughs was constructed during the early 18th century by John Fletcher and family; these included the Loscoe, Langley and Owlgrove soughs draining into the River Erewash. After the introduction of steam engines for pumping in Derbyshire lead mines, they soon arrived in the coalfield. One of the first was at the Middleton's colliery at Trowell Field in 1733 and by 1777 there were seven atmospheric pumping engines at work on the Derbyshire coalfield, some of them made in the county by Francis Thompson of Ashover. But the market was limited to the local region within reach of packhorse or waggon. An early attempt to improve transport was made in 1604 by Huntingdon Beaumont with the construction of a wooden waggonway from bell pits at Strelley down to Wollaton Lane for carriage to the Nottingham market. It was canal transport which first really provided the means for expansion of the market for coal, first with the opening of the Chesterfield Canal to the Trent at West Stockwith in 1777, then with the Erewash Canal from Langley Mill down to the Trent in 1779. These links served wharves along the Trent itself and then further south via the Soar Navigation to Loughborough. The Erewash line was extended northwards by the Cromford Canal to Cromford with a branch to Pinxton. The canal network was completed with three more links, the Nottingham Canal from Langley Mill down the east bank of the Erewash direct to Nottingham, the Derby Canal from the Trent and Mersey Canal to Derby and Little Eaton and the Nutbrook Canal from the Shipley mines, all opened in 1796.

Following this expansion of the canal network, coal mining activity in the Erewash valley grew considerably and many of the entrepreneurs were the land owners themselves, for example the Morewoods of Alfreton, the Drury Lowes of Denby, the Miller Mundys of Shipley and the largest of all, the Dukes of Newcastle. Many of these mines were managed for them by mineral agents such as the Boots of Huthwaite, who also acted as mining consultants over a period of 120 years. In addition, other entrepreneurs from yeomen stock took leases on mineral rights and managed their mines themselves, for example North, Barber, Fletcher, Walker and Outram whose businesses grew to very large companies. Improved steam pumping enabled deeper sinkings to be made on the edge of and in the concealed coalfield. One of the first of the deep shafts was begun in 1841 at Cinderhill, later Babbington Colliery, north of Nottingham, where two 7ft-diameter shafts were sunk to a depth of 203m. Thomas North, the lease holder, established a brick works there and built a new village, as well as an extensive internal railway system. Further north, the first deep sinking in the Leen valley was at Hucknall in 1851 whilst at the Shireoaks pit near Worksop the top seam was found at 316m below surface. Even today new shafts are being opened at Asfordby in the Vale of Belvoir, just over the border in Leicestershire, where the shaft depths are over 500 metres with recoverable seams between 400 and 700m below surface.

Much of the later expansion was made possible by railways linking the coalfield to a national network and an almost insatiable market which the region was well able to sustain. The first significant line was the horse-drawn tramway between Pinxton and Mansfield opened in 1819. Thirteen years later, the concern of the Erewash valley coal producers over the loss of their Leicester markets through the opening of the Leicester and Swannington Railway in 1832 led them to promote a steam-hauled railway from Pinxton to Leicester. The original scheme was abandoned, but their efforts led to the building of the Midland Counties Railway opened between Derby and Nottingham in 1839 and southwards to Leicester and Rugby in 1840. A line up the Erewash was not in fact completed until 1847. The second railway, the North Midland, was constructed from Derby to Leeds in 1840. George Stephenson, already an established coal owner in Leicestershire, was also engineer for this line. Several coal seams were discovered whilst driving the Clay Cross tunnel and he established what later became the Clay Cross Company to exploit these reserves. He also built coke ovens supplying fuel for railway locomotives but his main output of coal went out by rail to the London market.

The rail network expanded rapidly, with a second line up the Erewash valley and further lines up the Leen valley. East-west links were provided by the Sheffield to Lincoln line opened in 1849 and the Derby to Nottingham line opened in 1878. Any new shaft sinkings were all immediately provided with main line rail access. D. H. Lawrence in *Lady Chatterley's Lover* captures the scene with his description of Uthwaite [Chesterfield]:

down in the valley, with all the steel threads of the railways to Sheffield drawn through it, and the coal-mines and the steel-works sending up smoke and glare from long tubes, and the pathetic little corkscrew spire of the church, that is going to tumble down, still pricking the fumes.

The excellent house coal carried by rail to London soon began to make inroads into the traditional sea-borne coal from the North East and by the 1880s had exceeded the shipping tonnage. The prosperity of the coalfield was further enhanced by the location at greater depths of the Top Hard seam of good coking and steam coal, first in the Leen Valley in 1876 but followed by mines in the Mansfield district in the 1890s.

108. The principal railways of Nottinghamshire, showing opening dates.

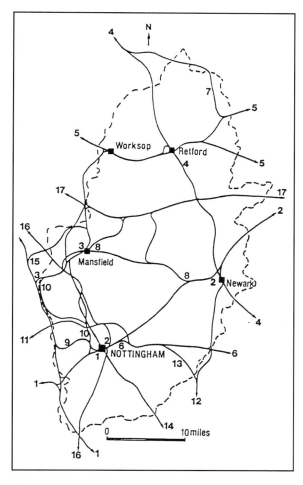

1. 1839-40 Nottingham to Derby and Leicester, via Trent Junction
2. 1846   Nottingham to Lincoln, via Rolleston and Newark
3. 1849   Pye Bridge (Erewash Valley line) to Mansfield
4. 1849-52 York, Doncaster to London (King's Cross), via Retford, Newark, Grantham and Peterborough
5. 1849   Sheffield to Gainsborough, with spur to Lincoln, via Worksop and Retford
6. 1850   Nottingham to Grantham, via Bingham and Bottesford
7. 1867   Doncaster to Gainsborough
8. 1871   Mansfield to Rolleston Junction via Southwell
9. 1875   Nottingham to Trowell Junction
10. 1875-6   Radford to Awsworth, via Kimberley, with branch to Pinxton along the Erewash Valley
11. 1878   Nottingham to Derby, via Kimberley
12. 1878   Newark to Melton Mowbray, via Bottesford and Harby
13. 1879   Bingham to Harby
14. 1880   Nottingham to Kettering, via Melton Mowbray and Manton
15. 1886   Westhouses Junction to Mansfield Woodhouse
16. 1893-9   Sheffield to London (Marylebone), via Beighton, Nottingham, Loughborough and Leicester
17. 1897   Chesterfield to Lincoln via Duckmanton and Langwith Junctions
18. 1901   Pye Bridge to Duckmanton Junction

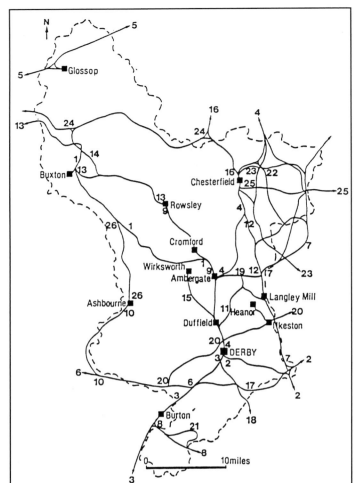

109. The principal railways of Derbyshire, showing opening dates.

1.	1830	Cromford and High Peak Railway, from the Cromford canal to the Peak Forest Canal at Whaley Bridge, via Parsley Hay
2.	1839-40	Derby to Nottingham and Leicester, via Trent Junction
3.	1839	Derby to Birmingham, via Willington and Burton
4.	1840	Derby to Leeds, via Duffield, Ambergate, Clay Cross and Chesterfield
5.	1842-7	Manchester to Sheffield, via Woodhead Tunnel
6.	1848	Willington to Stoke-on-Trent, via Eggington and Uttoxeter
7.	1847-9	Trent Junction to Mansfield along the Erewash Valley, via Langley Mill, Pye Bridge and Pinxton
8.	1849	Burton to Leicester, via Ashby
9.	1849	Ambergate to Rowsley, via Cromford
10.	1852	Uttoxeter to Ashbourne
11.	1856	Little Eaton to Ripley
12.	1862	Pye Bridge to Clay Cross
13.	1863	Rowsley to Manchester and Buxton, along the Wye Valley
14.	1867	Great Rocks Dale to New Mills
15.	1867	Duffield to Wirksworth
16.	1870	Chesterfield to Sheffield
17.	1873	Willington to Trent Junction
18.	1874	Derby to Ashby, via Melbourne
19.	1875	Ambergate to Pye Bridge
20.	1878-80	Derby to Nottingham and Eggington Junction
21.	1884	Swadlincote Loop
22.	1890	Staveley to Pleasley
23.	1893	Beighton to Nottingham
24.	1894	New Mills to Dore (Sheffield), via Cowburn and Totley Tunnels
25.	1897	Chesterfield to Lincoln
26.	1899	Ashbourne to Parsley Hay Junction

Once coke smelting had been perfected, local coal was converted for use in blast furnaces to replace charcoal for the production of iron. There were profuse deposits of ironstone in Derbyshire at Codnor Park, Morley Park, Somercotes, Chesterfield and Staveley which had been smelted in a dozen charcoal furnaces. By 1800 these had been replaced by a similar number of coke furnaces which had increased to 15 by 1827. By 1847 there were 30 furnaces, 20 of which were in blast producing a yearly output of 95,000 tons of pig iron. The exploitation of coal, clay and ironstone from the same locality gave rise to the establishment of several businesses which became very large combines. The Butterley Company, originally Benjamin Outram and Company, by 1829 had blast furnaces, foundry and steam engine works at Butterley and similar works at Codnor as well as three collieries and limestone quarries; these activities employed 1,500 men. By 1870 the company operated 15 collieries and their workforce had expanded to 8,000, most of them accommodated in new purpose-built housing at Ironville. In the Chesterfield area, the Staveley Coal and Iron Company originated in the 1780s and continues to trade in association with the Stanton company. The Sheepbridge Coal and Iron Company was a later formation in 1864; by 1871 it was operating four collieries which had resulted in the doubling of the population of Whittington in a decade.

The coal from north east Derbyshire was particularly suitable for coking and in the late 19th century over 1,000 beehive coke ovens were operating, most of them concentrated in a small area between Dronfield and Chesterfield. But the end of the 19th century was a period of considerable change. Many of the older pits on both the exposed and concealed coalfields were either worked out or uneconomic to operate and many closures took place in the Erewash valley and the Dronfield and Unstone district. In addition many of the ironworks became uncompetitive and switched to coal production only and into coke and chemical by-products such as tar, sulphate of ammonia, sulphuric acid and benzol. This industry continues to supply metallurgical and smokeless fuel requirements.The opening of large fully mechanised mines in the concealed coalfield, particularly in the Dukeries area of Nottinghamshire, involved the construction of new accommodation and facilities for the miners and families. The labour force came from other coalfields out of the region and also from the closed mines further west. These new mines employed on average 600 men each and the new company settlements, such as Blidworth, Bolsover, Clipstone, Creswell, Edwinstowe, Forest Town, Rainworth and Ollerton reflect in their planning and construction the changing fortunes and aspirations of their builders and the need to attract key personnel. At New Ollerton, developed in the 1920s by the Butterley Company, a factory was erected by them for rent and it was occupied by a hosiery manufacturer, so providing employment for 600 women and girls. The present day output of coal feeds not only the by-product industry but also the electricity generating stations along the Trent valley which now provide the sole use for some of the extensive railway network.

As with many coal mining landscapes, there are few early remains to be seen. Many sites have been completely cleared and spoil heaps reshaped and planted whilst others have been re-used as industrial estates. Sometimes, as at Bestwood in the Leen valley, a solitary winding engine has been preserved without any of its associated coal screens, albeit with the company housing built for the employees in the 1870s. The significant remains of the industrial heritage are mainly of service and secondary industries in the older market towns and the new or expanded village settlements. Many of the former have found new prosperity based upon their long established framework knitting, hosiery and lace manufactures which provided an alternative to coal mining as a by-employment of farming. When these industries were mechanised, employment was provided for women in towns such as Bulwell, Heanor, Hucknall, Ilkeston and Kirkby in Ashfield which continue to prosper long after the coal mines have closed.

GAZETTEER
(OS sheets 119 and 120)

Agriculture-based Industries

Chesterfield, Lords Mill Street (SK 385707). The former Hipper Corn Mills, large steam powered corn mills formerly beside the Great Central Railway, which was opened in 1897. The railway has been used for the Inner Relief Road, and the terminus station and goods yard site redeveloped as a shopping centre. Only the *Hotel Portland*, opened in 1898 to serve railway users, survives.

Dale Abbey Post Mill (SK 438398) is also known as the Cat and Fiddle mill. It was built before 1788 with a stone roundhouse added below the wooden body in 1844. The only post mill remaining in Derbyshire, it is being restored.

Heage Tower Mill (SK 368508) is a stone-built tower mill having six sails and ogee cap which has been partly restored by Derbyshire County Council.

Kimberley Brewery (SK 497450), situated in Hardy Street, is a large tower brewery and maltings complex, formed by the merger of two breweries in this fast growing mining village. The site was served by the Midland Railway, which like the later Great Northern line through Kimberley is closed. Adjacent to the main complex are another maltings and cottages and further north west along *Hardy Street* at SK 495453 is 'Maltsters Terrace', six decorative brick houses.

Langwith Maltings (SK 526696) are dated 1876 and were built beside the Mansfield to Worksop railway. There are brick-built floor maltings and kilns and the decorative features of the brickwork are repeated in the nearby terraces of workers' houses.

Mansfield, Cattle Market, Nottingham Road (SK 539606) was built in 1877 to the design of the Nottingham architect Watson Fothergill. The former market tavern is an ornate polychrome brick structure with a round tower.

Mansfield, Midworth Street Maltings (SK 540609) date in part from the 18th century. They are stone-built with two floors with additional bays and kilns to the rear, now converted to a restaurant complex.

Mansfield, Mustard Mill (SK 543613) lies in Rock Valley and ground mustard using water power from the River Maun. The building survives as offices within the modern factory complex of Metal Box who took over the business created for the making of tins for packaging the mustard.

Extractive Industries: Coal and Ironworking

New Annesley Village (SK 513535) is just off the A611 road and was built to house miners for the new colliery sunk in 1865. There are 160 cottages in ten rows of eight on either side of an open area.

Bestwood Coal and Ironworks (SK 553477) is a planned settlement begun in 1874 by the Bestwood Coal and Iron Company who once operated four blast furnaces here until iron making ceased in the 1920s; their coal mining activities continued, here and elsewhere. The planned village survives with dark brick houses bearing the company crest. Close by at SK 557475 is the preserved vertical twin cylinder *steam winder* which was probably built at Worsley Mesnes Ironworks in 1873. The engine house now stands in isolation complete with pit head gear in the care of the Leen Valley Country Park.

110. The restored windmill at Heage.

111. Hardys and Hansons
Kimberley Brewery and Maltings
See Frontispiece.

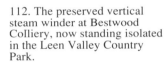112. The preserved vertical
steam winder at Bestwood
Colliery, now standing isolated
in the Leen Valley Country
Park.

113. Housing erected by the
Bestwood Coal and Iron
Company for their workers in
1876, bearing the company's
crest.

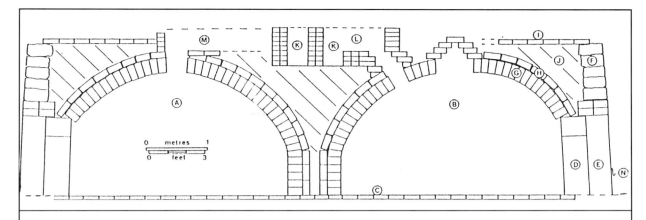

Summerley Coke Ovens - typical cross section

Key:

A Typical oven with centre hole only (based on 9-East)
B Typical oven with centre hole and back flue (based on 9-West)
C Brick floor
D Firebrick inner arch
E Red brick inner arch
F Freestone retaining wall
G Firebrick inner lining
H Red brick outer lining
I Red brick top floor
J Rubble fill
K Longitudinal flue to chimney
L Transverse flue
M Diagonal flue
N Iron hook

114. The beehive coke ovens at Summerley drawn by the Industrial Archaeological Section of Derbyshire Archaeological Society.

115. The remnants of an early coke-fired blast furnace at the Butterley Company works near Ripley.

Blidworth Village (SK 595565) is one of the later planned settlements on the concealed coalfield, built for the new mine opened in 1926.

New Bolsover (SK 465703) lies below the early 17th-century Bolsover Castle and is the first and best of the mining villages built by the Bolsover Colliery Company which leased 7,000 acres to work for coal from the Duke of Portland in 1890. There are 194 houses arranged in double rows around three sides of a square and semi-detached overseers' houses on the access road. Although providing a better standard of housing for the miners, they were criticised by D. H. Lawrence as 'set down like a game of dominoes, with spaces and gardens, a queer game of dominoes that some weird masters were playing on the surprised earth'. He resented their rawness in the landscape and preferred the 'intimacy and smallness of colliers' dwellings over a hundred years old'. By 1930 the Bolsover company was operating six mines and had built nearly 3,000 houses, some 44,000 people being dependent upon it for a livelihood.

Butterley Ironworks, Ripley (SK 401516) was the creation of the company founded by, among others, William Jessop and Benjamin Outram in 1790. The site is still enclosed by its forbidding stone walls and gatehouse. The headroom of the machine shops has been increased by superimposing modern metal cladding on older stone foundations. Heavy engineering still continues here and recent demolitions have revealed remains of a blast furnace of 1838 which still incorporates a 1791 date-stone from the earliest furnace. The Cromford Canal passed under the site through the Butterley tunnel and boats could be loaded via a shaft within the works. The company also built a road and tramways to link to their other works at Codnor Park to the east and they were among the first to provide model housing for their workforce (see Golden Valley and Ironville below).

New Clipstone (SK 587631) is west of the old village. The mine began sinking in 1914 but did not produce coal until 1922. There are two shafts of 21-feet diameter down to 1,920 feet, sunk by the Bolsover Colliery Company who built the spacious new village.

Creswell Village is another creation of the Bolsover company for Creswell colliery which began production in 1894. There are two contrasting settlements, the earlier one at SK 522740 being planned round an elliptical open space, with short rows of houses ranged around it with subtle changes in style. The second at SK 525742, east of the railway, is in rectilinear form with tightly packed houses of inferior quality built in terraces round a recreation ground.

Eastwood (SK 465470). A colliery village noted as the birthplace of both the Midland Counties Railway at the *Sun Inn* and of D. H. Lawrence, a miner's son, at *8a Victoria Street*. There is a museum in his birthplace and other displays in the Library in *Wellington Place*, where trails may be obtained of the town with its restored miners' housing, once dominated by the Barber Walker Company.

Eckington, Seldom Seen Engine House (SK 422800) on a coal mine near to the Yorkshire border, is a large red brick structure, with remains of boilers and coke ovens in the vicinity.

Golden Valley (SK 427513). Along the Cromford canal is a terrace of 20 restored Butterley Company houses built of stone between 1797 and 1813.

Ironville (SK 436517) was also built by the Butterley Company between 1834 and the 1860s with rows of houses, church, Mechanics' Institute and school. Many houses have been demolished but three rows remain in Casson Street, Queen Street and Market Place dating from the second phase of building between 1858 and 1863. Many of the later houses are constructed of random slag blocks with red brick quoins. The isolated stone bridge (SK 434516) beside the canal reservoir crosses the dried-up arm of the branch to Pinxton.

Mansfield, Forest Town (SK 563620) is another Bolsover company village constructed for their new Crown Farm colliery opened in 1905. The housing density contrasts sharply with New Bolsover; here there are 324 houses laid out in nine rows of 18 on either side of a central access road.

Morley Park Ironworks (SK 380492) possess two blast furnaces now in the care of the Derbyshire Archaeological Society. They are stone-built, cold blast coke-fired furnaces, the first built by Francis Hurt in 1780 and modified in 1818, and the second in 1825. They ceased to work in 1875 and were preserved by the Stanton Ironworks Company.

Newstead Colliery Village (SK 520530) with its unpretentious red brick terraces was built by the Sheepbridge Coal and Iron Company for their new mine opened in 1875.

Pleasley Colliery (SK 498644) was begun by the Stanton Ironworks Company in 1871 and used steam winders until closure in 1985. Two stone-built engine houses with head gears remain, one engine house being dated 1873. Nearby at *Pleasley Hill* (SK 509637) beside the A617 road are long rows of monotonous brick terraced houses which were built for miners and their families.

Rainworth Village (SK 586587) is another colliery village constructed for the Bolsover company's Rufford Colliery in the 1910s. 114 houses are laid out in stepped blocks of 2,4,6 and 7 along four avenues between the A617 road and the railway.

Ramshaw Coke Ovens, near Unstone (SK 375770) were used to carbonise coal from the Ramshaw colliery into coke for the Sheffield steel industry; the beehive kilns, in four ranges, appear to have been used only for about 20 years until the Unstone collieries closed by 1895. Some more modern beehive kilns survive nearby at *Summerley Colliery* (SK 368778).

Ridgeway (SK 402807) had industries more akin to Sheffield. There were once scythe and sickle works here, and along the *Moss Beck Brook* to the south east (SK 402804) are remains of several dams which operated grinding hulls and forges.

Shirebrook Village (SK 525669) is a late 19th-century development of red brick miners' houses in short terraces with a variety of styles.

116. Company housing at Barrow Hill erected for the Staveley iron works in the 1850s.

117. The pottery kiln at West Hallam, now preserved as part of a craft centre.

The Staveley Coal and Iron Company built several settlements near their works north east of Chesterfield. One, *Poolsbrook* (SK 443735), has been almost completely cleared but there are substantial remains at *Arkwright Town* (SK 429703) with its plain terraced houses and the far more imaginative settlement at *Barrow Hill* (SK 417755), dating from the 1850s, which probably reflects company prosperity or its closer proximity to their main works.

Strelley Bell Pits (SK 514418) probably date from the 17th century and may be found either side of the minor road leading to Strelley village.

Warsop Vale (SK 546679) was the village created by the Staveley Coal and Iron Company for their Warsop Main colliery opened in 1890. It has short terraces of brick houses grouped around three sides of a square with the mine on the fourth.

Extractive Industries: Clay

West Hallam Pottery, High Lane West (SK 434420) has a listed bottle kiln which is now incorporated into a craft pottery and garden centre. It was one of two kilns forming part of John Derbyshire's Peak Pottery which opened c.1922 and worked until 1940.

Ilkeston, Oakwell Brickworks (SK 460412) date from the 1870s and were attached to Oakwell Colliery. There is a listed Hoffman kiln without chimney stack and a Scotch kiln nearby. The works, disused since 1966, were once served by a rail connection to the Great Northern Nottingham to Derby line.

Watnall Brickworks (SK507480). Four chimney stacks, prominent features beside the M1 motorway are, along with some houses, the only remains of an extensive colliery brickworks; the Hoffman kilns have been demolished.

Transport

Bennerley Viaduct (SK 470437) now stands in isolation between Awsworth and Ilkeston. One of two wrought iron viaducts remaining, it was erected in 1876/7 to span the Erewash valley by the Great Northern Railway for its new Nottingham to Derby connection. In addition to the river, the viaduct also crosses the Midland Railway and there were additional bridges over the Erewash and Nottingham Canals. The listed structure is 484 yards long with 14 lattice-work piers and three brick piers; the ironwork was supplied by Easton Swingler and Company of Derby.

118. The Bennerley viaduct, a landmark in the Erewash valley, which once carried the Great Northern Railway from Nottingham to Derby.

119 & 120. Little Eaton canal and railway and *below* the coal dock (Derbyshire County Libraries).

Cossall (SK 485418). Here are substantial remains of the Nottingham Canal which contours along the east side of the Erewash valley. There is a short branch eastwards, the Robbinetts Arm, opened in 1796. Extensive remains of feeder tramroads from mines on the edge of the concealed coalfield can be traced.

Little Eaton (SK 363410) lies at the head of the filled in Derby Canal. Here was the interchange between the Gangroad from Denby colliery where loaded containers were lifted from waggons and transferred to barges. The line of the Gangroad may still be traced (SK 363411 to 364221) and the listed clock house, dated 1793, still remains.

Golden Valley (SK 422512). The eastern portal remains of the 3,063-yard Butterley tunnel on the Cromford Canal. There is no towpath and boats took three hours to be legged through; the collapse of the tunnel through subsidence in 1900 caused the isolation of the Cromford end of the canal. Beside the entrance is a cascade which supplied water from Butterley Park reservoir. The canal had been built to take broad craft as far as this tunnel.

Langley Mill Great Northern Canal Basin (SK 454472) was constructed by William Jessop in 1796 at the end-on junction of the Erewash and Nottingham Canals with the Cromford Canal. Only the Erewash Canal now remains in water and nearby are remains of an extensive system of tramroads linking mines to canal wharves.

Mansfield, Kings Mill Viaduct (SK 519598) bears a date-stone 'M & P 1817' and was built for the Mansfield and Pinxton tramroad which linked Mansfield to the Cromford Canal. The stone-built viaduct became disused when the tramroad was re-aligned in 1849 by the Midland Railway and converted to standard gauge for locomotives.

Mansfield, Station (SK 537608). The former stone-built Midland station of 1872 in Italianate style was closed in 1964 and is now used as a bar. Mansfield is probably the largest town in England without a main line passenger station. Further east (SK 539610) is the 350-yard curved *Viaduct* with which the Midland line to Worksop sliced Mansfield in half. There are 15 spans with arches 30 to 40 feet high together with 250 yards of embankment.

Ripley, Midland Railway Centre (SK 402519-415520). An exciting steam centre on a former MR link from Ironville to Ambergate. The museum houses a dedicated collection of locomotives and rolling stock, together with relocated buildings which include Whitwell Station, signal boxes from Ais Gill, Kettering and Kilby, buildings from St Mary's goods yard in Derby and wagon workshops from Nottingham. The centre piece of their Country Park is *Western Pit* (SK 415517), with a small engine house and headgear enclosed in a ventilation tower.

Shipley Wharf (SK 462456) on the Erewash Canal is surrounded by remains of mine transport links. The canal crosses the river by a short aqueduct just to the north and runs parallel to the Nottingham Canal up to Langley Mill. One of the earliest links was a wooden tramroad to the Shipley colliery, opened in 1792 and owned by the Mundy family. This link was subsequently replaced by the Nutbrook Canal in 1796. A tramroad went to Woodside Colliery going under the Midland Erewash line before ascending an incline up the hill to the west. Nearby, also, are traces of the derelict Nottingham Canal with further mine railway connections, derelict lock and swingbridge.

Manufacturing Industry: Textiles

Forge Mill, Bestwood (SK 547471) is on an ancient metal working site on the River Leen. The stone-built mill was built in 1787 by the Robinsons of Papplewick and used for cotton spinning. Following fire damage, the upper storeys were removed and the building was used as a bone mill.

CALVERTON. The birthplace of the East Midlands hosiery industry, it was here that William Lee is reputed to have invented the stocking frame in 1589. Windles Square (SK 621491) consists of two rows of knitters' cottages from the original complex of three; they have been restored by the Nottinghamshire Buildings Preservation Trust. These and other cottages (SK 609493) have ground floor workshops with through lighting. Elsewhere in the village (SK 611492) the next stage in the evolution of the powered hosiery factory can be seen with the grouping of hand frames in small two-storey workshops. A small museum, at SK 615492, may be viewed by appointment (Tel 0602 652886).

CHESTERFIELD. *Wheatbridge Mills* (SK 375709), beside the River Hipper, are part of the extensive works of

Robinson and Sons Ltd. which began the manufacture of pill boxes in 1839. They subsequently spun cotton to make surgical dressings and sanitary goods as well as making packaging. Parts of the buildings are dated 1889, 1907 and 1924. By the gateway is the *Cannon Mill*, on Dock Walk, with its external iron overshot wheel and rim drive. This formed part of the Griffin Foundry which was established in 1775 by John and Ebenezer Smith. There were once three blast furnaces on Furnace Hill to the west and the long mill goyt may also be seen. *Holme Brook Mill* on Chester Street (SK 375712) was also bought by Robinsons for cardboard box manufacture in 1883. Two four-storey blocks have undergone conversion to sheltered and single person's accommodation.

Heanor, High Street (SK 432466). I & R Morley established two large factories here in the 1870s and by 1900 the firm employed 10 per cent of the population of about 10,000, making hosiery and knitwear but also dyeing and finishing. Part of their original works still survive, together with some later factory buildings.

HUCKNALL. There are some remains of the domestic hosiery and knitwear industry which, along with mining, was the mainstay of this town whose population multiplied tenfold during the 19th century. The three-storey brick-built houses on the east side of *Albert Street* (SK 535494) are purpose built for stocking frame knitters and are unusual in having the workshops on the middle floor with the characteristic full width windows in the rear wall. The stone-built houses on the west side have back garden workshops. Similar workshops can be found behind houses in *Cooperative Avenue* (SK 535496) which date from 1901/2. At *68-72 Nottingham Road* (SK 531481) there is a fore-shortened stone terrace of three cottages each with large windows facing north and smaller windows facing south on the middle floor.

ILKESTON. Albion Works, Burr Lane (SK 466418) were built about 1845 and the four-storey works with central pediment and clock are still occupied by Francis Ball and Son, hosiery manufacturers. On *Belper Street* (SK 466413) a three-storey brick factory with segmental headed cast iron windows dates from the mid 19th century. It is still in use for lace manufacture, being occupied by Messrs F. and C. Mason who operate Leavers machines as well as the latest computer controlled Raschel machines. On the other side of the road stands another factory of similar age. There is another pedimented brick factory of four storeys on *Heanor Road* (SK 464427) with ornamental gritstone courses which was erected in 1855; there are adjoining later three-storey blocks. On *Market Street* (SK 466416) the three-storey brick hosiery factory has an ornate central doorway with portico and an off-centre pediment.

Linby, Castle Mill (SK 545510) was one of the water-powered cotton spinning mills erected by the Robinson family of Papplewick. It originally had a wheel at the east end and the ornamental front contrasts with the plain rear wall. The mill was eventually converted to corn milling and then to domestic accommodation.

MANSFIELD. Town Mill, Bridge Street (SK 541610) was originally built as a corn and malt mill in the 1740s. It was converted to cotton spinning in 1795 and, following a fire, two upper storeys were demolished and the building served as a warehouse until conversion to a bar and restaurant. The river still flows beneath it. On the opposite bank is the former steam powered red brick *New Town Mill*, constructed in 1870 for cotton spinning. *Bath Mill* (SK 547617) is a four-storey stone built mill on the River Maun which was constructed in 1792 for cotton spinning, mainly providing thread for the machine lace industry. Since 1880 it has been used for hosiery manufacture. *Hermitage Mill* (SK 524598) has an early stone-built section with later brick additions. This was one of five water-powered cotton spinning mills on the River Maun financed by the Duke of Portland. *Stanton's Mill, Bath Lane* (SK 545615) is the oldest surviving cotton mill in the town, dating from 1785. The older part is the two-storey section which straddles the river and there is a larger three-storey sectio adjoining. *Victoria Street Mill* (SK 536607) was erected in 1833 as a steam powered cotton mill; the 24-bay stone building is now used for the manufacture of electrical components.

PAPPLEWICK was the place chosen by George Robinson to build the first of six cotton spinning mills powered by means of careful conservation of the waters of the River Leen. The first successful application of a rotative steam engine to drive cotton spinning machinery took place in his Middle Mill in 1786, using a Boulton and Watt engine. Unfortunately nothing remains other than the site of this pioneering enterprise but there is evidence of the water storage and leat system at *Moor Pond Wood* (SK 548507) and at *Grange Farm* (SK 549514) are two terraces of workers's cottages.

121. Framework knitters' houses of 1834 at Windles Square in Calverton.

122. Cannon Mill at Chesterfield, formerly part of the Griffin Foundry, powered by the River Hipper.

123. The attractive Albion hosiery factory at Ilkeston.

Pleasley Vale Mills are a large complex site on the River Meden. The first cotton spinning mill was built by William Hollins in 1784 on the site of a disused forge. The firm later experimented with cotton and wool mixtures and used the 'Viyella' trademark. Following fires in the early 19th century, the two original mills were destroyed and rebuilt by 1850. Three mills remain with extensive water storage ponds. The three-storey *Upper Mill* (SK 516649) is on the site of the first mill while the four-storey *Lower Mill* (SK 521650), dated 1847, is on the site of the second mill built in 1798. *Middle Mill*, with much larger windows, was added in 1913. Workers' houses have been demolished but the ornate mill owner's house and gatehouse do, however, convey the atmosphere of the enclosed mill settlement which once employed nearly 1,000 people.

Public Utilities

Bestwood Pumping Station (SK 578483) was the second to be built on the Bunter sandstone by Nottingham Waterworks in 1871-4. It was designed by Thomas Hawksley in Italian-Gothic style and contained two Cornish engines which were scrapped in 1968.

Papplewick Pumping Station (SK 583521) was also built to supply Nottingham and was opened in 1885. Although no longer pumping, the station is complete and in the hands of a Preservation Trust. There are two rotative beam engines built by James Watt and Co which are regularly steamed. The whole is a monument to Victorian municipal engineering and architecture with lavishly ornamented pillars, delicate metalwork and stained glass windows featuring water motifs. The Trust are also erecting a twin cylinder colliery winder built by Robeys of Lincoln in 1922 which has been removed from the nearby Linby Colliery. (For Open Days telephone 0602 632938 or 631409.)

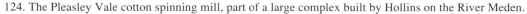

124. The Pleasley Vale cotton spinning mill, part of a large complex built by Hollins on the River Meden.

2: South Derbyshire and Northwest Leicestershire Coalfield

This is a coalfield of minor importance in national terms which has consequently not been extensively developed in recent times and so preserves relics of its past. The Thringstone fault separates the coalfield from an area of Pre-Cambrian rock, Charnwood Forest, whose landscape presents a considerable contrast. The Forest area has also been an important source of building stone and remains a major source of roadstone. Roofing slate has also been extracted from quarries at Swithland and Groby. The high ground of Charnwood, however, proved a major obstacle in transporting coal to the manufacturing centres of Loughborough and Leicester.

Coal was mined in the north and west of the region in the 13th century, and recent open-casting has revealed evidence of medieval workings, including timber-lined shafts. Output was greatly expanded by a partnership between the Willoughbys of Wollaton and the Beaumonts of Coleorton in the early 17th century. The introduction of the Newcomen pumping engine further expanded production, with an engine being installed at Measham as early as 1720. Transport difficulties held up further development of the coalfield and two canals were constructed in the late 18th century, neither of which proved entirely effective. The Charnwood Forest Canal of 1794 was conceived as part of a scheme to extend the Loughborough Navigation to Leicester, thereby enabling Leicestershire coal to compete with Erewash valley coal in the county town. A level canal between Thringstone and Nanpantan was linked by tramways at the west end to the collieries and at the east end to the Loughborough canal basin, which necessitated transhipment of loaded containers. It was never successful and was disused by 1804 following shortage of water aggravated by the bursting of the feeder reservoir dam at Blackbrook.

The second attempt to provide the coalfield with a waterway link was the Ashby Canal, planned as a through route between the Coventry Canal and the River Trent. This was built as a broad level canal as far as Moira, but the company ran out of money and were unable to complete the link to the Trent which would have demanded more complex engineering works. Similar reasons precluded the planned waterway links to the various limestone quarries, which were completed as horse-drawn tramways. The canal was opened c.1804 and took coal southwards to Oxford and London, but not to the Leicestershire manufacturing towns apart from Hinckley. The coalfield did not get an effective transport outlet until the opening of the Leicester and Swannington Railway in 1832-3. The Act allowed for horse haulage but the line, engineered by the Stephensons, was built as a combination of locomotive hauled sections and two inclines, one self-acting at Bagworth and the other wound by a steam engine at Swannington.

Further mine development took place on the concealed coalfield in the south east of the region in the early 19th century when new pits were sunk at Snibston, Heather, Ibstock and Ellistown. The first shaft at Long Lane was sunk in 1822 and was the cause of the hamlet's growth to become the town of Coalville, with a rapid growth in population from 2,887 in 1831 to 20,467 in 1921. Alongside the coal mining activity, brickmaking, railway wagon building, ironfounding and engineering developed as well as female employment in elastic web and hosiery manufacture. This expanding population created a demand for flour which was met by the construction of watermills, especially on the River Sence, where turbines and auxiliary engines were later added to keep pace with rising consumption.

125. The principal railways of Leicestershire (opening dates are shown).

1.	1832	Leicester (West Bridge) to Swannington, via Coalville
2.	1840	Leicester (London Road) to Nottingham and Derby, via Syston, Loughborough and Trent Junction
3.	1840	Leicester (London Road) to Rugby via Wigston
4.	1846-8	Syston Junction to Peterborough, via Melton, Saxby, Oakham, Manton and Stamford
5.	1849	Leicester (London Road) to Burton, via Knighton Junction, Coalville and Ashby, using part of 1832 line
6.	1850	Nottingham to Grantham, via Bottesford
7.	1850	Rugby to Stamford, via Market Harborough, Seaton and Luffenham
8.	1857	Leicester to Bedford and Hitchin, via Wigston, Market Harborough and Kettering
	1868	Bedford to London (St Pancras)
9.	1864	Wigston Junction to Birmingham, via Hinckley and Nuneaton
10.	1873	Nuneaton to Moira, via Shackerstone and Measham
11.	1874	Ashby to Derby, via Melbourne
12.	1879	Market Harborough to Newark, via Marefield, Melton and Bottesford, with branch from Harby to Bingham
13.	1880	Nottingham to Kettering, via Melton, Oakham and Manton
14.	1883	Shackerstone to Loughborough (Derby Road), via Coalville and Shepshed
15	1883	Leicester (Belgrave Road) to Marefield Junction
16.	1894	Seaton Junction to Uppingham
17.	1894	Saxby to Bourne
18.	1899	Nottingham to London (Marylebone), via Loughborough, Leicester (Central) and Rugby

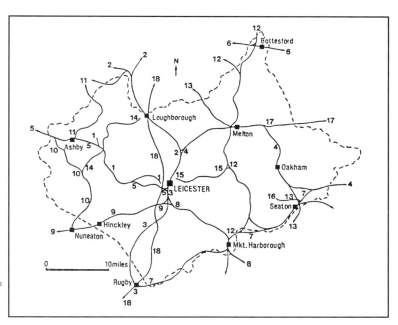

126: The Holywell steam corn mill at Ashby-de-la-Zouch.

127. 'Help Out' mill at Odstone on the River Sence, an important survival of a rural roller mill.

The Leicester and Swannington Railway was bought by the Midland Railway in 1849 and extended to Burton-upon-Trent. This passed through the area of South Derbyshire where fireclay seams were found in the Coal Measures. Established domestic pottery and firebrick industries were able to expand to meet the growing demand from Local Boards of Health for sanitary ware and salt-glazed drainpipes following the Public Health Act of 1848 and further legislation in 1866 and 1875. The earliest works were in the north of the basin where the clay seams were thickest; later expansion took place in the south around Moira where the seams were at greater depth. Rail communication to the clay works was further improved with the construction of a loop line in 1884 through Swadlincote and Woodville. A large urban conurbation evolved comprising Swadlincote, Church Gresley, Woodville and Albert Village. The industry was further sustained by the advent of public electricity supply with its demand for insulators and conduit pipes.

Elsewhere in the region were inliers of Carboniferous limestone, that at Breedon being exploited as early as the 13th century. There were other extensive workings for limestone at Ticknall, Cloud Hill, Barrow Hill and Dimminsdale. The output from these was greatly increased after tramway connections were made to the Ashby Canal and subsequently to the main railway network.

Miners and quarrymen were well paid in comparison with agricultural labourers and secondary employment in textiles was not a major feature of the coalfield. This was not the case in the villages on the edge of the Forest, however, where poor soils brought meagre agricultural returns. Villages within easy reach of a worsted spinning centre, such as Shepshed, became important centres of framework knitting.

GAZETTEER
(OS sheets 128 and 129)

Agriculture-based Industries

Holywell Steam Mill, Ashby de la Zouch (SK 354169) is situated beside the Midland Railway branch from Ashby to Melbourne, as were the former gasworks which are adjacent. The roller mill was built in the 1880s but flour milling had ceased by 1922. The building remains, now in multiple occupation.

Odstone Mill (SK 379078) is a large red brick building with adjoining house and granary. It was powered by the River Sence by means of a long leat and was the last in Leicestershire to mill flour commercially, continuing to use water power until 1970. The lower part of the mill dates from 1811 and the upper storey was added around 1900 when roller mills were installed; the original overshot wheel was not powerful enough to drive the new machinery, supplied by Turners of Ipswich, and a turbine was fitted in 1902. The granary was added in 1912. The mill had a private siding on the Coalville branch of the LNWR and Midland Joint Railway. It is listed Grade II* and remains complete with both stones and roller mills, together with a full set of dressing machinery.

Shepshed Watermill (SK 486207), on the Black Brook, once belonged to the Garendon Estate. The three-storey brick mill retains its pitchback iron wheel, which drove four pairs of stones via spur gear drive from the wheel shaft. The mill was used until 1939.

Shepshed Windmill (SK 462181) has been converted as a residence with an adjoining house which prevents the cap from turning. The tower mill dates from the 1840s and worked until 1935, after which it lay derelict until conversion in 1958/9.

Stretton-en-le-Field Watermill (SK 302123) on the River Mease ceased working in 1938. The mill with its wheelhouse at the north end has been converted to residential use and the mill house has been extended.

Extractive Industries

Bardon Hill Quarry (SK 455131) is located in the highest hill in Leicestershire (278m). Quarrying for granitic roadstone began in 1857 and still continues, much of the output leaving by main line railway. Recently a contemporary terrace of 40 workers' houses with a central reading room has been demolished and replaced by new accommodation nearby.

Breedon Hill Quarry (SK 407233) was worked for dolomitic limestone. The outline of a disused Hoffman-type kiln may be seen, part concealed by waste. The kiln was newly built in 1906. The quarry has always relied upon road transport.

Cliffe Hill Quarry (SK 473108) has been worked for dioritic roadstone since the late 1870s; setts and rail ballast were also produced. Traces may be found of a former two-feet gauge light railway, opened in 1896, connected to a railhead on the Midland line to Burton at SK 443115. The light railway was closed in 1948 but the railhead is still in use.

Cloud Hill Quarry (SK 412215) is now worked out. Limestone was to be sent out by tramway to the Charnwood Forest Canal, but the link was never made. Rail connection was eventually made to the Ashby Canal and the Coleorton Railway.

COALVILLE. Formerly a few houses, known as Long Lane, Coalville grew through the sinking of its first coal shaft in 1824 which was later served by the Leicester and Swannington Railway when it opened in 1833. This was the first of nine pits in Coalville and neighbouring Whitwick. There are few surface remains of them except at *Snibston No 2 Pit* (SK 420144) on Ashby Road which was opened in 1832. This mine closed in the 1980s and is now the site of Snibston Discovery Park, where displays on coalmining and other Leicestershire industries may be seen. The displays include a working steam winding engine and one of the Gimson pumping engines from Hopwas.

128. The blast furnace at Moira early this century, in use as housing.

129. Moira Furnace after restoration in the 1980s.

The brickworks off the *Ashby Road* (SK 418149) are now disused. Two beehive kilns remain of the ten which were constructed in the 1920s and 1930s. These were converted from coal to gas firing in 1970.

Bell Pits, Coleorton survive as earthworks over a wide area of Coleorton Moor (SK 4117), Rough Park (SK 3918) and Birch Coppice (SK 392187). *Coleorton Hall* (SK 391173) was the home of the Beaumont family of coal owners.

Groby Granite and Slate Quarry (SK 527083). The granite outcrop continues to be extensively worked here. Slate was also obtained since the 17th century from the quarry south of the A50 road at SK 522076; this closed in 1908 and the site is now an industrial estate. A single track rail connection to the Leicester and Swannington line near Ratby was made in 1832. Closed in 1967, this can still be traced for much of its length.

Ibstock Brickworks (SK 413108). The manufacture of bricks was begun by the Ibstock Colliery company in the 1830s when suitable brick clays were found near their mine which was sunk in 1825. The brickworks were gradually developed and in 1934 one of the first tunnel kilns in Britain was constructed to the Monnier design.

Moira Furnace (SK 315152) is a brick-built coke fired blast furnace. It has survived because it was unsuccessful and consequently never rebuilt. Restored by the local council, it now forms the centre piece of an excellent museum of ironmaking created by volunteers. The furnace was begun in 1802 for Lord Moira beside the Ashby Canal to process iron ore from clay bands in the Coal Measures. The furnace was completed by 1806 and there were only two blast campaigns, in 1806/7 and 1810/1, after which the furnace was disused and the site was used as a foundry. Cottages were constructed utilising the spaces under the charging bridge. Unfortunately the adjacent blowing engine house, which was also converted to housing, has been demolished but the foundations have been excavated and stabilised. A range of seven lime kilns may be seen along the bank of the infilled canal. At SK 313152 is *Engine House Cottage* which formerly contained a Newcomen engine pumping Furnace Pit. The bricked-up beam aperture may be seen and inside, one of the massive longitudinal floor beams carries a date of 1805.

Oakthorpe Pit (SK 332139). 'Who'd a thought it' colliery engine house stands beside the line of the Ashby Canal. The mine was owned by the Hastings family in the 17th century and leased by Joseph Wilkes of Measham in the late 18th. The brick-built engine house is dated 1859 and was erected during the Moira Colliery ownership.

Shepshed Brickworks, Old Station Close (SK 478185) were opened in 1887, beside the Charnwood Forest Railway which had opened four years earlier. The works are still in operation, using two circular downdraught kilns; clay is brought by conveyor through a tunnel from a pit on the south side of the A512 road.

Dimminsdale, Staunton Harold (SK 376218). Here quarries were worked on a limestone inlier. The Calke Brook passes through the site to the reservoir and six lime kilns may be found on the Derbyshire side of the stream. The flooded area, known as Laundry Pool, conceals both the gallery mining for limestone carried out there and shafts for lead mining; a range of kilns is also now submerged. Traces may be found of the branch connecting the quarry to the main tramroad, which originally linked the Ticknall quarries to the Ashby Canal.

SWADLINCOTE is the largest of a group of communities in the clay-working area at the western end of the coalfield, where extensive fireclay strata are found within the Coal Measures. Many of the sites of sanitary ware and salt-glazed pipe manufacture have been cleared, and some open-casted for coal. However, there are some significant remains near the town centre (SK 298196) of a pottery established in 1821; at *Woodville* (SK 311184) of one established in 1849 specifically to manufacture firebricks and drainpipes. In *Church Gresley* at Pool Road (SK 305187) are the works of T. G. Green where domestic kitchenware is still manufactured. Here numerous bottle kilns can be seen, their bases surrounded by conventional brick-built workshops. A single bottle kiln is all that remains of the Rawdon Pottery at *Woodville* (SK 314192).

Ticknall Limeworks are one of the extractive industries which supported the Harpur-Crewe family at Calke Abbey. The principal remains lie in dense woodland south of the A514 road through Ticknall village, east of the *Tramway Bridge* (SK 356240) which carried the Ashby Canal feeder tramway over the road. Several ranges of kilns have been built on the floor of the quarry and high ground marks out the original limits of the limestone leases. Traces of the extensive network of tramroads may be found, with many stone blocks *in situ*. The lines from the north and south of the village street converge before passing through a 'cut and cover' tunnel (SK 356237)

130. The bridge at Ticknall which carried the Ashby Canal feeder tramroad over the main street.
131. Crushing rollers, driven by a horse engine, at the estate brickworks in Ticknall.

132. The classically-styled railway station in Ashby-de-la-Zouch.

133. Warehouse beside the Ashby Canal at Measham, built of Wilkes' double-sized bricks.

134. Wilkes' brick drying sheds at Measham, now converted to housing.

which passes under the main drive to Calke Abbey. Three ranges of kilns were built in a narrow horseshoe pattern with a tramway system serving to load the kilns at high level and to remove the burnt lime at the kiln base (SK 358238, 359237, and 357241 north of the A514).

To the north of the road were estate brickyards, and remains consisting of a drying shed, Scotch kiln and horse engine-driven crushing rolls may be found at SK 359242.

Transport

Ashby de la Zouch Station (SK 355163) was erected by the Midland in 1849 in a style commensurate with the hotel, baths and large houses which had been erected to accommodate visitors to the spa. This had been financed by Lord Moira to utilise the saline waters found in the Moira coal mines following his successful experiment with baths by the pit head. The more fashionable Ivanhoe Baths in Ashby were completed in 1822 but their popularity had declined by the end of the 19th century. The station is now privately owned. There are traces in the forecourt of the track of the Ashby and Burton Light Railway, a rural electric tramway opened by the railway company in 1906. This connected to Burton-upon-Trent, the trackbed running alongside the present A50 for much of the distance; it was closed in 1927.

Bagworth Incline (SK 446091), part of the Leicester and Swannington railway, was self-acting (1 in 29 gradient) with loaded coal wagons descending towards Leicester. Following its purchase by the Midland Railway, the incline was by-passed in 1848 by a deviation line but has now been affected by mining subsidence. The incline keeper's cottage, two storeys high and bow fronted like a toll house, survived until 1991.

MEASHAM (SK 334121). Two former warehouses, with infilled loading arches over the Ashby Canal, survive on either side of the *High Street*. They are now used for retail purposes but were built c.1802 by Joseph Wilkes for the distribution of canal-borne goods. Their construction is of 'Wilkes' gobs' or 'jumbies' which were double sized bricks. These bricks were made in Wilkes' local brickyard on the *Bosworth Road* and were intended to avoid the payment of the brick tax which was introduced in 1784; any advantage gained was lost when double taxation was imposed on double sized bricks in 1803. The former drying sheds of the brickworks at SK 336121 have been converted to living accommodation. A close inspection of many of the buildings along the main street in Measham will reveal many more of these large bricks and the blind arcading which is a characteristic feature of many of Wilkes' buildings. Clay working still continues to the east of the village at the Red Bank works.

Canal Toll House, near Osgathorpe (SK 427187), is reached from the A512 road. The two-storey house, now derelict, is one of few remaining structures of the Charnwood Forest Canal which was only in use from 1794 to *c.*1802. The house lies at the junction of branches to Thringstone coal mines and Breedon and Barrow Hill limestone quarries, from the termini of which horse tramways were to be laid. The line to Thringstone may be traced, but the other canal arm was never completed.

Shackerstone Station (SK 379066) lies on the former LNWR and Midland Joint Railway from Moira to Nuneaton, just south of the junction to Coalville and Loughborough. The single storey red brick station building with stone window surrounds, bracketed eaves, hipped roof and five-bay platform shelter is especially elaborate as it served nearby Gopsall Hall, once the seat of Earl Howe. The line was opened in 1873 and abandoned in 1964, but the station remains the headquarters of a preserved railway line which extends as far as Market Bosworth.

Snarestone Tunnel (SK 343093), 250 yards long with plain brick portals, was built on the cut-and-cover principle to carry the canal under the village. The present limit of navigation is about half a mile north of the tunnel; the canal line has been progressively abandoned north of this point owing to coal mining subsidence.

Swannington Incline (SK 420157) is now in the care of the Swannington Heritage Trust. The incline, with a gradient of 1 in 17, is about half a mile long and was wound by a small horizontal engine built by the Horseley Iron Works for the Leicester and Swannington Railway in 1833. The engine is preserved at the National Railway Museum in York. The Trust have restored several of the bridges on the incline and have excavated the site of the winder with the aim of restoring working to the incline. Originally loaded coal wagons were drawn up the incline but, in the final years before its closure in 1948, the engine lowered loaded wagons down the slope to supply coal to keep the mine pumping engines working at *Calcutta Pit* (SK 421169), where the engine house still remains.

Manufacturing: Textiles

Pioneer Mills, Belvoir Road, Coalville (SK 424138) were erected in 1878 by a Leicester company for the manufacture of elastic web; the mill was designed to provide female employment in this mining town. The oldest sections are the narrow three-storey block and the north light sheds which adjoin it at the rear. The engine house was located at the rear of the sheds and power was transmitted by line shafting and endless belts. The mill remains in use for shoe manufacture.

MELBOURNE is an interesting small town dominated by a massive Norman church and the Hall. The gardens of the Hall (SK 390250) contain a magnificent wrought iron arbour, the masterpiece of Robert Bakewell of Derby. There is also an estate corn mill powered from the ornamental lake at SK 391249. A charcoal fired blast furnace survived to the south west until it was submerged beneath Staunton Harold Reservoir. This made use of charcoal from local woodland and provided iron for Birmingham ironmasters until the 1770s. It was one of several such furnaces in the area.

The industry of the town looked to Derby and silk warp knitting developed. By 1850, the Castle Mills employed over 1,000 people in the production of figured knitted gloves produced on the jacquard principle. These were demolished in 1990 but the warp knitting mills remain on the west side of *Castle Street* (SK 388253) and there are some remnants of framework knitting shops.

SHEPSHED was an important worsted framework knitting centre at the beginning of the 18th century, dependent on Loughborough for the supply of yarn. A steam powered cotton spinning mill was established by the end of the century but was short-lived. At the time of Felkin's survey in 1844 there were over 1,200 frames in the town, third to Hinckley and Leicester, and more than Loughborough. Almost all the frames were narrow and producing cotton and worsted hose. The village had been on the route of the ill-fated Charnwood Forest Canal, but it was not until the railway was opened in 1883 along part of the former canal route that coal was easily available. This enabled the development of a powered hosiery industry. In spite of extensive clearances it is still

135. A timber-framed house in Forest Street in Shepshed, adapted to house knitting frames.

the best centre in the region to trace the development of the hosiery industry, from the converted houses of the late 17th century to houses with purpose-built integral or garden workshops, workshops for several frames and finally the steam or gas engine-powered factory. Shoe manufacture was introduced into the village, at first into the vacant domestic workshops in the 1870s and then as a factory occupation. Unfortunately many of the small workshops are now sadly neglected.

Looking first at the converted housing, *Forest Street* (SK 483197), beside the school, illustrates the conversion of a thatched timber framed house to accommodate knitting frames, with large windows inserted into the frame and an extension at the north end as a ground floor workshop. The large three-storey house (no 48) was a master hosier's house and has two adjoining workshops at the rear. *9-13 Brook Street* (SK 48052000) is a terrace of three-storey houses with a cart access arch to the rear. The windows have been replaced but the size of those on the upper storey indicate knitting workshops. *4 Hall Croft* (SK47951975) is a well maintained framework knitter's cottage with top floor workshop. *6 Britannia Street* (SK 47901975) is a large three-storey house with top floor workshop with full width windows, facing west.

34 Pick Street (SK 47701975) represents a later phase of the hosiery industry with a two-storey purpose-built workshop in a garden. Nearby on Factory Street is a terrace of four cottages with a central back entry giving an access to a two-storey workshop. These workshops were built to accommodate several hand frames under the control of a master hosier. *26/28 Church Street* (SK48051975) have been renovated. These were knitters' cottages with a two-storey workshop in the garden behind. *23 Moorfield Street* (SK 478195) is a master's house with, in the garden, a large single storey workshop of which both the east and west walls are fully glazed. Behind *11 Kirkhill* (SK 48051950) is a small single storey garden workshop. Nearby are two others, one converted to a garage and the other, of two storeys, with blocked windows. On the north side of *Kirkhill*, behind 11 Freehold Street, is a derelict two-storey back yard workshop. The master hosier's house, known as *The Challottee, 9 Leicester Road* (SK 48201925), has an adjoining three-storey workshop for knitting frames and a terrace of small cottages for his work people. *Springfield Road* (SK476191) has terraced houses dated 1897 and 1902. At the rear of these are two-storey workshops with street access which were built as part of the development.

The factory phase is represented by some early buildings. On *Charnwood Road* (SK 477190) is an elegant two-storey polychrome brick hosiery factory, which still belongs to Whyte and Smith, who were originally established in 1861 as bag hosiers in the village. There are two early blocks, with domestic style windows, and later single storey north light workshops. Queen's Works in *The Lant* (SK 481196) were built for shoe manufacture by a Leicester company, with two-storey blocks to the street and similar blocks and single storey north light sheds extending back to Queen Street. *22 Garendon Road* (SK 480193) was built as a shoe factory. The plain red brick two-storey block was erected in two phases of seven- and eight-bays length. The elegant square engine house chimney still survives. The works are now occupied by Joseph Harriman, an old established Shepshed knitwear firm. On *Sullington Road* (SK 479189) are two factories, now making braids, which were built around 1900, one for hosiery and the other for machine lace manufacture.

Public Utilities

Water Tower, Kilwardby Street, Ashby de la Zouch (SK 353166). This was built when the sewerage system was completed in the 1850s to hold water pumped from the Gilwishaw Brook: a reservoir was later added to augment supplies.

Snarestone Pumping Station (SK 348101) is now a residence. The ornate brick and stone building now stands at the head of the Ashby Canal and formerly received its coal supplies from a wharf at the rear. The station was erected in 1891 and pumped water from an abortive coal mine shaft. Two small beam engines by Bever and Dorling of Dewsbury pumped water 14 miles by pipeline to supply the town of Hinckley.

3: Rural East Northamptonshire and Leicestershire

The area under consideration consists mainly of the former county of Rutland and Northamptonshire east of Kettering, much of it lying astride the Jurassic ridge which extends from Dorset to the Cleveland Hills in Yorkshire. It has long been noted for its pastoral farming: Daniel Defoe in 1724 remarked of Leicestershire that 'the largest sheep and horses in England are found here, and hence it comes to pass too, that they are in consequence a vast magazine of wool for the rest of the nation'. The area concentrated on dairying and cheesemaking, fattening livestock

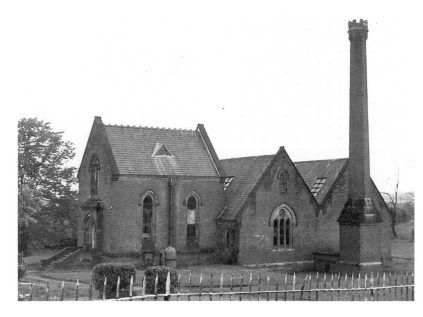

136. This former pumping station beside the Ashby Canal at Snarestone supplied water by pipeline to Hinckley.

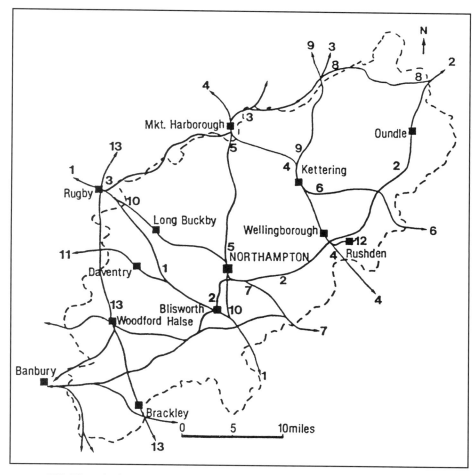

137. The principal railways of Northamptonshire (opening dates are shown).

1.	1838	Birmingham to London (Euston), via Blisworth
2.	1845	Blisworth to Peterborough, via Northampton
3.	1850	Rugby to Stamford, via Market Harborough and Seaton Junction
4.	1857	Leicester to Hitchin (for London King's Cross), via Kettering, Wellingborough and Bedford
	1868	Bedford to London (St Pancras)
5.	1859	Market Harborough to Northampton
6.	1866	Kettering to Huntingdon, via Thrapston
7.	1872	Northampton to Bedford
8.	1879	Seaton Junction to Peterborough
9.	1880	Kettering to Nottingham, via Manton
10.	1881-2	Rugby to Roade, via Northampton
11.	1888	Weedon to Leamington Spa
12.	1894	Wellingborough to Higham Ferrers, via Rushden
13.	1899	Leicester to London (Marylebone), via Woodford Halse

and processing agricultural produce. In the south access was possible to the navigable River Nene, but the Welland was never improved in this region. The north was only opened up with the building of the Wreake Navigation from the River Soar to Melton Mowbray and its extension to Oakham completed in 1803. The economy was transformed with the coming of railways and the re-discovery of iron ore in the mid-19th century, when a vast railway network was established to transport ironstone. Whilst this brought growth to the towns along the Nene and Ise valleys, elsewhere population either stagnated, or even dropped, due to emigration to the manufacturing regions during the second half of the 19th century.

The limestone belt within the Jurassic ridge passes through the former county of Rutland and contains some important freestone quarries which were worked in medieval times. These oolitic limestones are in the Upper Lias deposits and major quarries at Clipsham and Ketton are still operative. This region had extensive ironstone reserves whose extraction was governed by the developing railway system, enabling ore to be transported to Derbyshire, Lincolnshire, Staffordshire and South Wales for blending with other ores for smelting. There were no accessible local coal measures and only now are deep coal reserves being tapped in the area at Asfordby in Leicestershire, at depths of over 500 metres, so return cargoes of coal were essential for local blast furnaces.

Some important boot and shoe manufacturing centres developed in the ironstone belt along the Ise and Nene valleys. Earls Barton, Irthlingborough and Wellingborough have been described in Chapter Three. Kettering will be studied in Chapter Five Section 6. Boot, shoe and hosiery manufacturing, looking to Leicester firms, was established in a small way in Melton Mowbray and Oakham, once coal supplies enabled factories to be built reliant upon steam or town gas for power.

138. The watermill at South Luffenham after conversion to restaurant use.

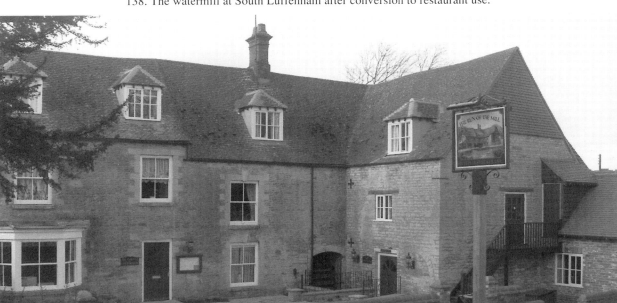

GAZETTEER
(OS sheets 130 and 141)

Agriculture-based Industries

Ketton Mill (SK 981042), on the River Chater, is built of local limestone. The three-storey building in Georgian style had an external wheel and ground corn until 1856; it was later used to pump water for a village supply but is now used as a residence. Nearby at SK 972046 is the shell of a tower mill which was built in 1800.

Langham Brewery (SK 845110) is the home of Ruddle's beer. A brewery was established here in 1858 but the early buildings have been much altered; traces of maltings and the original tower brewery may be discerned.

South Luffenham Mills (SK 945027). This village has an interesting group of mills, all at one time operated by the same miller; the watermill on the River Chater, a tower windmill and, beside the railway, a multi-storey steam mill. The water mill is on a Domesday site and worked until 1948; all the machinery survived until the recent tasteful conversion of the mill and house into a restaurant. Much of the gearing and the stone vats have been retained and the breastshot wheel remains. The tower mill, dated 1832, is now only a shell. It once had three pairs of stones and continued working until after the steam mill was completed. The steam mill opened in 1892, complete with railway siding, and was equipped with machinery made by Robinsons of Rochdale capable of grinding eight sacks per hour. Milling ceased in 1927 since which date the mill has been used for engineering and recently for plastics manufacture.

Morcott Windmill (SK 930001). This tower mill was built in the 1840s and worked three pairs of stones until 1921 when it was partly demolished. In 1968 the tower was rebuilt, a windshaft brought from Lincolnshire and a cap, sails and fantail added. The mill has no other machinery and is maintained as a residence.

Rutland County Museum, Catmos Street, Oakham (SK 863085) is housed in the 18th-century former equestrian exercise hall of the Rutland Fencible Regiment. It contains an excellent collection of farming implements and tools and carts and wagons. (Open Tuesday to Saturday and Bank Holidays 10am to 1pm and 2 to 5pm and Sundays 2 to 5pm.)

Seaton Mill (SP 908977), on the River Welland, has also been converted to living accommodation. The double gabled mill house backs on to the former water mill and in the field in front the brick piers remain of a former post mill which worked until around 1918.

Shacklewell Lodge Farm (SK 965078), beside the A606 near Empingham, is an excellent example of a model farm which was built in the 1870s and is one of very few in the former Rutland county.

Tickencote Mill (SK 989094) is an attractive stone-built mill on the River Gwash. The three-storey mill, with timber lucam, retains an internal breastshot wheel and an external auxiliary drive pulley; the rest of the machinery has been removed and the mill is now in residential use.

Tinwell is a former estate village, belonging to the Marquis of Exeter. On the main street, the A6121 (TF 005064), are several pairs of houses erected by the estate in the mid-19th century. By the church is the village forge, dated 1848, complete with decorative stone horseshoe around the door. The *watermill* (TF 008062), which once had a steam engine to supplement the River Welland, has been converted into an attractive residential complex.

Tolethorpe Mill (TF 022104), on the River Gwash, lies empty with its adjoining mill house. The mill has attractive cast iron windows but seems to have ceased working by 1910.

Whissendine Windmill (SK 823142). The six-storey tower mill, minus sails and built of ironstone, still contains its machinery including four pairs of stones, three overdriven and one underdriven. It was built in the 1830s and worked until 1922 when it became derelict until re-capped in 1962. Elsewhere in the village is a former *Brewery* (SK 830142) now converted to residential use.

Wymondham Windmill (SK 850192) is also built of ironstone and is being restored to working order. The tower mill, with ogee cap, was built *c*.1813. It worked by wind, with six patent sails driving three pairs of stones, until 1922 after which an external oil engine was used to power the machinery.

139. Tickencote watermill on the River Gwash, now used as a residence.

140. Houses in the village of Tinwell constructed for labourers on the Marquis of Exeter's estate.

141. The windmill tower at Whissendine, where the machinery, if not the sails, remains intact.

Extractive Industries

East Carlton Country Park (SP 835895). This 100-acre park surrounds a hall built in 1873 in the style of a French chateau by the Palmer family of biscuit manufacturers. The estate was purchased by Stewarts and Lloyds in 1933 and 59 houses were built in the village for workers at their Corby works. In the Park remains of ironstone outcrops testify to earlier extraction. The estate now belongs to the Corby District Council and an Industrial Heritage Centre in the former Coach House has displays on ironstone quarrying, steel making and tube forming.

Clipsham Quarries (SK 980155 and 988160). Clipsham limestone was renowned in the Middle Ages and was used for Windsor Castle in the 1360s. It is coarser grained than Ketton stone with a larger proportion of broken shells and other unrounded materials, being buff or pale brown in colour. Since the 1870s the freestone was employed for Oxford colleges and more recently for the repair of the Houses of Parliament. The working quarries bridge the Lincolnshire border.

CORBY. Following the opening in 1879 of the Midland line from Kettering to Manton, ironstone extraction began on the outcrop overlooking the Welland valley, mostly operated by the Lloyd family. Until 1895, when Stewarts and Lloyds was formed, all quarrying was done by hand but in that year a 1.5-cubic yard bucket steam excavator was introduced to dig the ironstone. Subsequent developments here included in 1897 the use of belt conveyors to dump the overburden and two years later the introduction of the long boom steam navvy for stripping the overburden. The whole process became fully mechanised and eventually bucket capacities of 30 cubic yards became the norm.

Two blast furnaces were erected at Corby, managed by Andrew Crawford of the Bestwood Coal and Iron Company, and the first iron was made in 1910; a third furnace was added in 1918. Production was originally limited to pig iron but in 1930 a new basic Bessemer steel making and integrated seamless tube production plant

142. The stone mason's workshop at Greetham, decorated with a variety of stone carvings from other buildings.

143. An old photograph of Corby Steelworks (by courtesy of Northamptonshire Record Office).

was added. This was designed to produce 200,000 tons of ingot steel and 130,000 tons of tubes annually. Construction began in 1933 and the number of employees rose from around 700 to 4,000 in 1939. Their accommodation involved the building of over 2,000 houses and a row of 12 shops and flats in Rockingham Road, together with recreational facilities to accommodate a large influx of Scottish workers. A new coke plant to produce low sulphur coke from South Wales coal was necessary for the steel plant. By 1937 a fourth new furnace had been added and the works were geared up for wartime, during which the renowned PLUTO (Pipeline under the Ocean) pipeline was produced in the works. Subsequently, open hearth furnaces were installed and the last Bessemer blow was in 1966, after which basic oxygen steelmaking was introduced. By 1970 local ore supplies were uneconomic to work and eventually the steel making plant closed. Only the tube plant remains with much of the site now within a designated New Town, cleared and turned over to factory units.

Exton. On the Exton Park estate, ironstone extraction did not cease until 1973 and an extensive standard gauge rail network was laid to the rail head near Cottesmore which connected to the main line railway at Ashwell. Old rail tracks and ironstone faces may be seen between SK 911105 and 910127. The giant excavator 'Sundew', electrically powered and with a bucket capacity of 32 tons, last worked here and on closure was 'walked' overland to Corby where it was dismantled. The journey took 56 days at an average speed of one mile in ten hours.

Greetham Stone Mason's Workshop (SK 926145) is an unusual example of a rural craftsman's workshop, the two-storey stone building incorporating many fragments of ecclesiastical buildings.

Ketton Quarry (SK 985055). Ketton limestone is probably the most perfect oolitic freestone with the grains accurately rounded and graded to a uniform size with a minimum of shelly and unrounded matter; it has creamy yellow and pink colour tints. It was used in many Cambridge colleges from the 17th century and also for Burghley House, near Stamford, as well as in the immediate locality. Little freestone is now produced but the limestone is now used for the production of cement and reconstructed stone. The first cement works were erected in 1928.

Pickworth Limekiln (SK 989138) is located within a small quarry which is being transformed into a picnic site. The single kiln, circular in section with a single draw hole, is built of local stone with brick lining; wooden beams are used in the front wall over the draw arch.

Pilton Ironstone Workings (SK 915028). Near the village cross roads are remains of railway cuttings and bridges. To the south a sinuous quarry face is still exposed although considerable infilling with refuse has taken place.

Wakerley Calcining Kilns (SP 947996) have probably never been used. Of the four circular sectioned kilns on brick pedestals, only two were completed; they were built in 1915 beside the Seaton to Peterborough Railway. Ironstone from nearby workings was to be brought in at high level by narrow gauge railway and remains of the embankments can be seen. The local workings closed in 1921 and the kilns were abandoned.

Transport

Rutland Railway Museum, Cottesmore (SK 886136) is located at the former rail-road interchange for the iron ore traffic. Here a Trust preserves a collection of static and working locomotives and rolling stock belonging to the ironstone railways.

Harringworth Viaduct (SP9197) straddles the Welland valley, its three-quarter-mile length supported by 82 arches. It was built by the Midland Railway for their Kettering to Nottingham line in 1877/9. Fifteen million blue bricks were used in its construction but unfortunately later repairs have been carried out using red brick.

Ketton Railway Yard (SK 984041) remains a largely intact village goods yard, albeit now without railway access. The walled yard is still used for coal distribution. One side of the yard is bordered by a stone floor maltings complete with kiln. A nearby large house was formerly the *Midland Hotel* and the retort house of the village gas works has been converted to a garage.

144. The goods and coal yard at Ketton, a rural distribution depot on the former Syston to Peterborough Railway.

145. Market Overton wharf on the derelict Oakham Canal.

146. The huge provender warehouse at Oakham catered for the Midland Railway's numerous wagon horses.

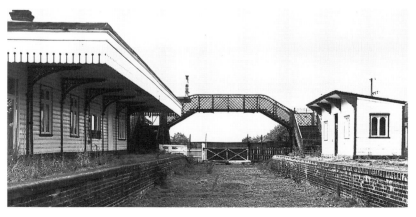

147. Seaton Junction station, still retaining its iron overbridge.

Manton Station (SK 884039) is an elaborate brick structure built, it is said, to placate the people of Uppingham for whom it was originally the nearest rail head. It lies between the diverging Stamford and Kettering lines south of Manton Tunnel with its monumental stone portals.

Market Overton Wharf (SK 881161) was once a private facility erected by the Bennetts beside the Oakham Canal. The attractive stone-built gatehouse leads to a yard enclosed by buildings used to store corn and coal, one of which also functioned as a maltings. Warehouses beside the canal bed have been converted to residential use. The line of the canal, which was closed in 1846, can be traced in the fields nearby on either side of the road.

OAKHAM is the former county town of Rutland and its importance as an agricultural centre was increased with the opening of the Oakham Canal from Melton Mowbray in 1803. This was a continuation of the Wreake Navigation which enabled coal and other supplies to reach the town. The terminus *Canal Warehouse* (SK 862092) has been converted to a theatre by Oakham School and some canal workers' cottages survive nearby. The Canal was sold to the Midland Railway in 1846 and much of its bed used for their line from Melton Mowbray to Stamford which opened two years later. The *Station* (SK 857090) is built of red brick in the Italianate style and to the north is the former *Provender Warehouse* (SK 859099) built by the railway in 1902 to provide feed for their horses. By 1911 this mill supplied feed to 4,100 animals and even by 1947 there were still 2,200 railway horses. The mill was the last of four in the country when it closed in 1954, since which time it has served as a seed store and for other purposes.

Seaton Station (SK 857090) with its remaining iron footbridges was once a busy junction on the line from Rugby to Stamford via Market Harborough which was opened in 1850. In 1879, Seaton became the junction for a more direct line to Peterborough and then in 1894 the 3.75-mile branch line to Uppingham was opened.

Manufacturing Industries: Textiles

Wallis and Linnell's Mill, Brigstock (SP 945856) is an impressive four-storey building of Weldon stone. Its narrow width and extensive fenestration provide maximum interior light. Opened in 1873 as a clothing factory by a Kettering firm, it was converted into offices in 1984 for an architectural practice who won an RICS award for the sympathetic re-use of an industrial building.

Public Utilities

Eye Brook Reservoir (SP 855955) was built in 1936 by Stewarts and Lloyds Ltd. to service their steelworks at Corby. The 300-acre reservoir has a capacity of 1,400 million gallons and the first supplies were drawn off in 1940.

Rutland Water to the east of Oakham was begun in 1971 in the valley of the River Gwash. With an area of 3,100 acres and a capacity of 27,300 million gallons, the reservoir can draw from or deliver to the River Welland at Tinwell and the Nene at Wansford through pumping stations. The former *Normanton Church* (SK 934063), nearly surrounded by water on the south shore, now contains a museum of water supply opened by the Anglian Water Authority in 1985.

5

Townscapes

1: Nottingham and its Satellites

The city of Nottingham is situated in a position of great strategic value with a good defensive position on a Bunter sandstone bluff controlling a crossing point over the River Trent. This was recognised by the Danes at the partition of Mercia in 877, when the town was created one of the Five Boroughs. The pre-Conquest settlement occupied the south east quarter of the medieval walled town which developed on the sandstone plateau, and included St Mary's church. The Market Place lay at the junction of several through routes, the Trent itself first being bridged around 920. The first available map of Nottingham, John Speed's of 1610, probably represents Nottingham as it had been for the previous six hundred years. The town, which then had a population of about 4,000, occupied an area 1.25km west to east and 0.6km north to south and was surrounded by farmland in commonable open fields, except on the west where the Duke of Newcastle had his Castle Park with its hunting reserves. It changed little over the next two hundred years either in plan or extent and Defoe described the town as 'one of the most pleasant and beautiful in England'. Population grew steadily, reaching around 10,000 in 1744 which was largely due to the migration of the framework knitting industry away from London but also to improving communications. Pressure on building space led in the 1740s to the in-filling of narrow burgage plots bordering the north of the Market Place with lean-to houses. By 1801 the population was over 28,000 and 30 years later had doubled to 50,000, all still accommodated with little additional built-up area in the town.

Outward expansion was tightly contained by the survival of common rights on the Clay Field, Sand Field and the Meadows and enclosure was effectively delayed by townsmen who would not relinquish either their grazing rights or the inflated rents they were collecting from the confined building space. The effects on Nottingham were two-fold, first in the town itself and second in the neighbouring parishes. Parts of the town, the infamous 'rookeries' north of the Market Square and Broad and Narrow Marsh, were notorious slums. They were packed with houses and frameshops, many built back-to-back around alleys and courts and even above communal privies. The outcome of this slum creation was epitomised by the Report of the Commissioners for the Inquiry into the State of the Large Towns and Populous Districts in 1845:

> I believe that nowhere else shall we find so large a mass of inhabitants crowded into courts, alleys, and lanes as in Nottingham, and those too, of the worst possible construction. Here they are so clustered upon each other; court within court, yard within yard, and lane within lane, in a manner to defy description..... Some parts of Nottingham [are] so very bad as hardly to be surpassed in misery by anything to be found within the entire range of our manufacturing cities.

Housing density in the Broad Marsh area was 100 to the acre with four or five inhabitants in each. Attempts at building near the Trent were thwarted by flooding problems and the 1847 Improvement Act restricted building on land below the maximum recorded flood level although the Meadows area was developed in the 1860s. Poor living conditions, inadequate drainage and polluted water supplies brought disease and cholera epidemics. Furthermore, poverty among the framework knitters brought labour unrest and Nottingham was the scene of Luddite machine breaking between 1811 and 1814. Thirty years later similar unrest was manifested in Chartism, Nottingham remaining a centre for radical politics.

In the surrounding parishes where earlier enclosure had released land for building, new satellite industrial villages grew. Development either involved expanding existing villages as at Sneinton or building close to old villages as at Radford, Basford and Lenton. Population grew in these villages at a higher rate than in Nottingham itself. Between 1801 and 1901, Radford and Basford grew over three times faster, Lenton seven times and Sneinton ten times, all of them to over 23,000 people while Radford exceeded 35,000 in 1901. Many of the new houses were of three or four storeys with workshops included to accommodate lace making machines. Twist net manufacture which boomed in the 1820s was attracted into the satellite villages by cheap land and labour.

Transport connections into Nottingham were improved with the building of the Nottingham Canal in 1796 which provided links to the Erewash valley coalfield and also down to the Trent, already improved for navigation. The Midland Counties Railway, opened in 1839, provided a route to Derby and a year later to Leicester and further south; further rail development followed in the next decade with eastward links to Grantham and to Newark and Lincoln.

The enclosure of the Nottingham common fields was not accomplished until an Act of 1845, in which the streets and courts of the town were described as 'cribbed, cabin'd and confined' and presented 'a spectacle of the most lamentable description'. New building began to take place but the pace of development accelerated 20 years later when consolidation and re-allocation of holdings took place. During the decade 1851 to 1861 the population increased by over 19,000, of which 11,500 was the result of immigration into the town from the adjoining counties. The expansion of industry and the release of land, coupled with new transport facilities, contributed to a building explosion; houses and factories spread across the former open fields and many of the new roads and terraces reflected former field boundaries. Some of the ground occupied by large mansions and gardens in the old town was freed for commercial development when their owners moved to the private Park Estate, 155 acres of the Duke of Newcastle's land laid out by the Nottingham architect, T. C. Hine, from 1850 onwards.

During the 1870s the expansion of Nottingham began to envelop the satellite villages with serious consequences for water supply and effluent disposal, particularly along the Leen valley. These problems were brought under a single authority by the boundary extension of 1877, whereby the Borough expanded from 808 to 4,425 hectares to include the villages of Basford, Bulwell, Lenton, Radford and Sneinton. The Borough population rose from 87,000 in 1871 to 157,000 with the extension and continued to increase, rising to 240,000 in 1901.

During the 18th century the principal industry in the town was worsted hosiery manufacture using hand frames. The introduction of cotton spinning in the 1780s led to specialisation in cotton and later silk hosiery. Machine-made lace utilised the output of existing spinning concerns and grew rapidly in the 1820s following the expiry of the Heathcoat patent and later modifications to the Leavers machine to produce patterned lace. The twist net boom was based upon hand-powered machines but steam power was introduced into the lace industry in the 1830s, several decades before hosiery. By 1850, Nottingham had 46 warehouses, 110 factories and 500 machines producing lace; over the next five years another 41 warehouses and 76 factories were constructed and, between 1857 and 1858, a further 36 factories were added. At that time over 15,000 lace workers were employed, two thirds of them women. By the middle of the next decade only 90 hand lace machines remained in use compared with over 800 large steam powered machines.

The 'stall' system, that is the provision of machine standing space, heat, light and power for rent, had begun in the 1840s with the adaptation of lace machines to steam power. One of the first of these tenement factories was in Radford, built in 1842 by William Herbert which housed 100 men. The number of lace factories almost doubled between 1870 and 1890. The tenement factories remain a prominent feature of the townscape and have been occupied by a variety of trades besides lace manufacturers and machine holders. These included warpers, winders, Jacquard card punchers, bobbin and carriage makers as well as hosiery manufacturers, printers and cycle makers, the dominance of lace declining in the 1920s. The factories were often built by individual manufacturers both for their own use and for letting off surplus floor space, but capital derived from other sources was also invested in them. For example, the Jardine fortune, made from lace machine manufacture, was invested in a factory at Sandiacre and later in the Colwick Industrial Estate created with the purchase of 340 acres of farmland in 1917.

Bleaching, dyeing and finishing as well as the marketing of lace have always been separated from its manufacture. As the dominance of the town in lace manufacture grew, the marketing branch moved from London and a new warehouse quarter was created in the original town centre around St Mary's church. Most of this survives as a conservation area with tall warehouses dominating the narrow streets.

The hosiery industry underwent a similar transition to factory production in the later decades of the 19th century, which provided an opportunity for female employment as also did clothing manufacture. However, new industries were, by 1900, to reduce the commitment to textiles and to boost male employment with the establishment of the cycle, pharmaceutical and tobacco industries. Cycle manufacture was a logical transition from textile machine making but the wholesale manufacture of pharmaceuticals by Boots and of cigarettes by John Player were established in Nottingham because of its position at the centre of the national market. The retail tobacco trade was widespread but the innovation in 1877 was the pre-packing of specific blends of tobacco and cigarettes. Player's success was manifested in large new factories in Radford, but his caution was such that he let part of his buildings for lace manufacture until his new trade grew sufficiently to require the floor space.

The subsequent development of the extended town was greatly helped by the construction of new wide roads. Gregory, Radford and Castle Boulevards were built in 1883/4, the latter involving the re-alignment and culverting of the River Leen. These acted not only as a ring road around the west, but, like the railways before them, provided attractive locations for industrial development. Railways also helped expansion at the turn of the 19th century with the addition by the Great Northern of a loop line to its 1878 route to Derby through the eastern part of the city. This suburban line through St Ann's Well, Sherwood and Daybrook was welcomed by brick manufacturers at Mapperley and Carlton. The building of the Great Central extension to London through Nottingham in 1898 was itself instrumental in the clearance of a large number of slum dwellings.

The post-1845 phase of development has also left its legacy of sub-standard housing, which although better than the pre-enclosure slums, still lacked basic amenities and were built to high densities intermingled with factory buildings. In areas like St Ann's Well and Broad Marsh complete clearances have taken place, but elsewhere, particularly in the former satellite villages, a more sympathetic policy of partial demolition has been adopted, with benefit to the preservation of the industrial landscape. An example of this may be seen in the Gamble Street Industrial and Commercial Improvement Scheme in New Radford, where selective demolition of some houses and factories and renovation of others has been accompanied by the building of new housing, a school and the provision of parking areas. This policy has restored life to a once run-down area between Forest Road West and Portland Road which was originally developed during the land-famine of the pre-1865 period. Similar schemes have been implemented in New Basford and Sneinton.

Nottingham has been fortunate in its position at the foot of the Bunter sandstone escarpment which forms an excellent source of water. Originally pumped from wells, supplies were increased by pumping from the River Leen but, as these sources themselves became polluted, spring water was obtained from Basford. The Trent Bridge Water Waterworks began the extraction of water from the Trent in 1833, with steam pumps lifting water to town reservoirs. Thomas Hawksley, born in Arnold, had been appointed their engineer in 1830 and he remained as engineer of the new Nottingham Water Works Company formed following the Enclosure Act. New deep wells were sunk in the Bunter sandstone on Derby Road in 1850, at Basford in 1857, Bestwood in 1871, Papplewick in 1884 and further north at Boughton, near Ollerton, in 1901. New supplies were obtained from artesian bore holes in the Trent valley at Burton Joyce in 1908. Since then water from Derbyshire, from the Derwent Valley reservoirs, the Meerbrook Sough and direct from the river at Wilne have augmented local supplies which still account for about three quarters of Nottinghamshire's water. The disposal of effluent, on the other hand, was not helped by the low land surrounding the town and night soil disposal continued into the 1920s, being removed by canal boat to sites along the Grantham Canal and also by rail. The efficient treatment of sewage commenced with the opening of the Stoke Bardolph land irrigation farm in 1880 whilst solid refuse was incinerated at a new destructor opened at the East Croft in 1883. This destructor was an early example of the use of refuse for power generation and district heating and is still in service.

Coal gas manufacture was begun by a private company in 1819 at a works built near to the canal at East Croft and the area of distribution gradually increased to include the satellite villages. By the time the Gas Light and Coke Company was taken over by the Corporation in 1874, there were three plants in operation at East Croft, Radford and Basford. Additionally, the construction of high pressure mains to bring coke oven gas from Pinxton and Stanton provided up to 40 per cent of Nottingham's requirement. Electricity generation, on the other hand, was late to develop with the Corporation-owned station in Talbot Street commencing public supply in 1895; subsequently additional capacity was built at St Ann's Well Road and also attached to the East Croft destructor plant in 1902. The first world war caused postponement of further new building until the erection of the North Wilford station by the Trent, which commenced generation in 1925 and continued until the 1970s. The generating plant has now been demolished.

As far as public transport is concerned, horse tramways were begun by a private company in 1874 connecting to the Midland Station and the routes were extended to Carrington and Hyson Green in 1882. The system was acquired by the Corporation in 1897 and electrification of the system commenced. Subsequently, the electric trams which operated between 1901 and 1936 were replaced by diesel and trolley buses, the latter working until 1966. One long distance electric tramway system was established in 1914, connecting Nottingham to Ripley via the highly populated villages north west of Nottingham. In 1933 trams were replaced by trolley buses and this route eventually closed in 1953.

The gazetteer which follows is arranged thematically and the sites in each category are grouped in quarters NW, NE, SE and SW centred upon Nottingham's Council House.

GAZETTEER
(OS sheet 129)
Agriculture-based Industries

NW *Alpine Street, Old Basford* (SK 550429). The Prince of Wales tower brewery built in 1891, was recently renovated for re-use. On the opposite side of the road is a large floor maltings dated 1899.

NW *Radford Road, New Basford* (SK 556420). A large brewery complex, the Star Brewery was established by James Shipstone in 1852. Various blocks are dated including the 1900 tower. Nearby in *Mosley Street* (556419) and in *Eland Street* (556424) are floor maltings, the latter dated 1931.

NW *490, 576 and 632 Radford Road, New Basford* (SK 556423 - 555428) are three multi-storey brick factories built around 1900 for basket making, wicker furniture and perambulator manufacture. The first, Dyad house, at the corner of Egypt Road, is dated 1901, and has corner pediment features. The second, 576, is a plainer building of earlier date whilst the third, Victoria Works, dated 1896, has three storeys and a single pediment. On the opposite side of Radford Road are the remains of the once extensive gas works.

NE *Mansfield Road, Daybrook* (SK 580450). The Home Brewery was founded in 1880; the present buildings are modern but have decorative stone panels depicting the brewing process.

NE *Sneinton Windmill* (SK 585397). This recently restored five-storey tower mill was built in 1807 for the father of George Green, the mathematician and scientist. It became disused by the end of the 19th century and was burnt out in 1947. It was rebuilt by Thompsons, the Alford millwrights, with two pairs of stones and is now a working City museum with an associated Science Centre.

A short walk up *Windmill Lane* to SK 585400 is rewarded by a panoramic view from the hill top with extensive views of the Trent valley, the East Croft and the Meadows, the Lace Market, St Ann's and Sneinton itself.

SE *Turney's Quay, London Road* (SK 580383) was part of a once extensive leather dressing works, established in 1861 on a site bordering river, canal and road. By 1892 these works were employing 450 people and since closure most of the buildings have been cleared, except for the roadside block built c.1900 which has been converted to residential use.

SW *Leen Gate, Lenton* (SK 551389). This long red brick block, now converted into housing, was formerly part of Bayley's extensive leather dressing works. Adjoining blocks which fronted the now in-filled Nottingham Canal have been demolished.

148. Shipstone's Star Brewery at New Basford, the tower ornamented with terracotta.

149. The windmill at Sneinton which was restored in honour of the mathematician George Green.

150. Turney's extensive leather works at Trent Bridge, Nottingham (from *Nottingham Illustrated*, 1891).

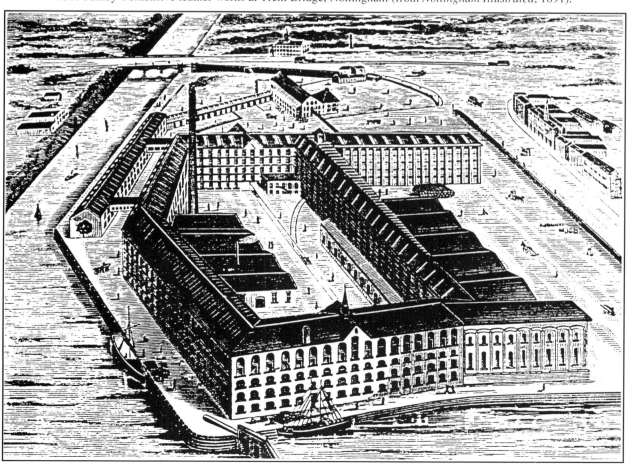

151. The former Bayley's leather works at Lenton, now converted to housing.

152. The Nottingham Patent Brick Company Ltd. works (from *Nottingham and its Industries*, 1925).

THE NOTTINGHAM PATENT BRICK Co.

(Established over Half-a-Century)

LIMITED

Manufacturers of
the Celebrated

Nottingham
Wire-Cut
Common

FACING
BRICKS

Hand-Pressed

Sand-Faced
(red and multi-
coloured)

Multi-Rough
(red and coloured)

A
SPECIALITY

Superior
Wire-Cuts

The Bricks with an
arris like Pressed
Bricks
and

Wire-Cut
Hand-Pressed
Common

for Sewers
Chimneys and
Engineering
Works

THE NOTTINGHAM PATENT BRICK CO., LIMITED

Registered Offices - - 14 GEORGE STREET, NOTTINGHAM

WORKS : Mapperley Hill, Thorneywood, Arnold SIDINGS : Sherwood L. & N.E.R., Thorneywood L. & N.E.R.

Telegraphic Address : " BRICKS NOTTINGHAM."   Telephone : No. **194** NOTTINGHAM

153. Trent Bridge, Nottingham, built by the Borough Engineer, Ogle Tarbotton in 1871.

154. Lady Bay Bridge, now carrying road traffic, was built for the Midland Railway's line to Melton Mowbray and Kettering. The photograph also shows the entrance lock to the Grantham Canal.

155. Wilford Suspension Bridge over the River Trent.

156. Warehouses beside the Nottingham Canal, one of which now houses the Canal Museum.

157. The former London Road Low Level station, designed by T. C. Hine for the Great Northern Railway.

158. The present Nottingham British Rail station in Carrington Street, dating from 1903.

Extractive Industry

NE *Brickworks.* There were once numerous brickworks in NE Nottingham, located on the Keuper Marl at *Arnold, Carlton* and *Mapperley.* The Nottingham Patent Brick Company, established in the 1860s, continues to manufacture at Dorket Head at Arnold (SK 594474). Other former brickworks have been built over (SK 594415) but some claypits remain as recreational areas (SK 598418 and 603412). In the 1850s some 21 million bricks were being produced per annum to build over 150 factories and warehouses and 3,500 houses in the town.

Transport

NE Of the former *Victoria Station* (SK 574403) only the clock tower and the hotel remain. Opened in 1900 and demolished in 1967, it was constructed for the Great Central and Great Northern and large numbers of slum dwellings were cleared before the 13-acre site was excavated. An impression of the magnitude of the earthworks may be seen from the bus station within the complex, and the portal of the northbound Sherwood Rise tunnel, dated 1896, is also visible. The southbound lines also went through a tunnel onto a blue-brick viaduct to *Weekday Cross Junction* (SK 575396) where the GNR line went east to Grantham. Sections of the viaduct still remain as far as Canal Street but the long viaduct south to the Trent has been cleared, as well as the bridge over the Trent itself.

SE *Trent Crossings.* The *Clifton Bridge* (SK 562367), opened in 1958, brought considerable relief for road traffic which had hitherto been channelled over two bridges. The present *Trent Bridge* (SK 581383) was completed in 1871 and its decorative parapet was cast by Handysides of Derby; it replaced an earlier stone bridge, a section of which is preserved in the roundabout in front of County Hall. Upstream is the *Wilford Toll Bridge* (SK 569381) which was opened in 1870 to replace a chain ferry. The original centre sections have been replaced but the brick approach arches and the toll house with tariff board survive; the bridge is now toll-free and only used for pedestrian and cycle traffic. Between the Wilford and Trent bridges is a pedestrian suspension bridge (SK 580377), erected in 1906, which carries water mains and other services across the river. Downstream from Trent Bridge, the three span bowstring *Lady Bay Bridge* (SK 584387) was built in 1878 for the Midland Railway line to Melton Mowbray. This closed in 1967 and the bridge is now used for road traffic.

   Nearby, *Meadow Lane Lock* (SK 581385) gains access to the Nottingham Canal and on the opposite river bank the entrance lock to the Grantham Canal (SK 584386) is now disused. Additional pairs of high gates are fitted at both for flood protection purposes. Considerable boat traffic was drawn across the Trent by rope and windlass between the two canals and eventually the horses crossed by a cast iron bridge erected in 1842 which was removed following flood damage in 1875. The early stone *Meadow Lane* bridge across the Nottingham Canal at SK 580384 is complete with a protective roller against rope wear.

SE *Canal Street* (SK 563393). The Fellows Morton and Clayton warehouses and the adjacent office block, which is dated 1895, are now a *Canal Museum* and public house respectively. The four-storey warehouse spans a short canal arm. Further west along the north bank is another tall warehouse of later date, its floor plan dictated by another basin at the rear which is now infilled. Beyond the Wilford Road bridge with its rosette-panelled balustrades is the *Castle Lock.* On the south bank towpath, between the Wilford and Carrington Street bridges, a hump back bridge spans another canal branch which served the eight-storey Midland Railway Grain Warehouse, now demolished.

SE *Low Level Station, London Road* (SK 580392). This was built by the Great Northern Railway in 1857 and designed by T. C. Hine. The GNR had previously used the Midland station after its line from Grantham opened in 1849. The Low Level station was replaced in 1900 by the nearby *High Level* station on the blue brick viaduct, giving access to Victoria. The old station reverted to use as a parcels depot from 1944 until recently and the buildings have been renovated.

   Further east are two red brick goods warehouses, the nearer two-storey building with lucams and round windows also designed by Hine. The structure is unusual in that the upper floor is suspended from above to give an unimpeded area on the floor below.

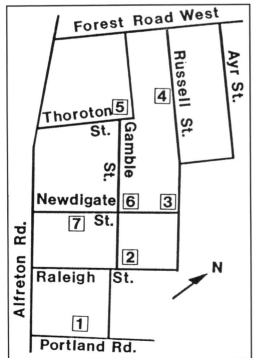

159. Jardine's Factory on Raleigh Street, Radford, *above left* , was used for lace machine manufacture.

160. A tenement lace factory in Russell Street, Radford, *above right*.

161. A sketch map of New Radford.

SE *Midland Station, Carrington Street* (SK 575392). The original Midland Counties Railway station was a terminus on the west side of the street. The first through station on the present site was opened in 1848 with its entrance on Station Street; the present building was completed in 1903. It has an elaborate decorated facade of red terracotta and sandstone with port cochere and wrought iron gates.

Manufacturing Industry: Textiles

NW *RADFORD* (Start at SK 563393 on Alfreton Road)
The following seven sites are all located within the City's Gamble Street Industrial and Commercial Improvement Scheme and are indicated on the map on page 142 . They represent some of the original industrial buildings and are mostly pre-1881 in date. Radford grew in population from 2269 in 1801 to 12,637 by 1851 and to 35,354 by 1901. Sub-standard houses have been replaced and other properties have been renovated. All Saints Church, designed in Gothic style by T. C. Hine in 1864, remains in Raleigh Street, along with its associated parsonage and school buildings; the church was largely financed by William Windley, a Nottingham lace manufacturer.

1 *Portland Road*. The Portland Works were built for a lace machine and bobbin carriage manufacturer, with two three-storey blocks (one with modern fourth floor) with decorative polychromatic brick lintels. To the rear, in Raleigh Street, was the Phoenix Iron and Brass Foundry.

2 *Raleigh Street/Gamble Street Corner*. This building has three storeys and a well-lit attic with stepped end gables, similar to many others in Nottingham. There are loading doors on each floor on the Gamble Street face. This was the Raleigh works of John Jardine and was used for lace machine manufacture.

3 *Russell Street/Newdigate Street Corners*. On the south corner, this four-storey factory plus attic workshop has 10 bays to Russell Street and 17 to Newdigate Street. It has decorated round headed lintels, a corner pediment with clock dated 1872 and continuous attic windows. The chimney stack still remains and in the angle of the L-shaped block are square and round service towers. This was originally Kirk's tenement lace factory and was later occupied by Robinson and Barnsdale, lace manufacturers, who subsequently became tobacco manufacturers. On the opposite north corner is another former lace factory with three storeys and twin gables to Russell Street. Further along Russell Street is another three-storey block and a domestic-style two-storey factory.

4 *Russell Street*. This large five-storey block with attic workshops and staircase turrets either end was known as Russell Street Mill and was originally a lace tenement; it now carries the name 'J B Spray', who were garment manufacturers. It and the adjacent later four-storey factory to the north, built end-on to the road, used a common 50hp engine. The buildings were later occupied by the Raleigh Cycle Company who also used the factory on the opposite side of the street.

5 *Gamble Street*. On either side of the road are former tenement factories. The 13-bay four-storey building on the east side was Albert Factory, a rebuild following a fire in 1891; the three-storey block on the south side changed from lace machine manufacture to cycle making. Opposite the end of *Thoroton Street* is Victoria Factory erected by Adcocks, lace dyers, dressers and machinists, which became a tenement factory.

6 *Newdigate Street*. This utilitarian 16-bay factory with its corner office block was the Provident Works, also a lace tenement factory.

7 *Newdigate Street*. Between Gamble Street and Alfreton Road is a range of buildings of various dates, some pre-1881. The four-storey block in Newdigate Street, the corner building and the three-storey block in Gamble Street with intact chimney stack formed part of Gamble's tenement factory. The four-storey 10-bay gabled block with dormer windows was formerly West's tenement.

NW 238 *Alfreton Road, Radford* (SK 559409). A three-storey house next to the public house with large windows in both front and rear walls of the topshop. Inspection of the back walls of the adjoining properties shows the in-filling of other large windows. These properties would have been occupied by framework knitters or machine lace makers.

NW *Denison Street, Radford* (SK 558405). Clyde Works are one of the largest tenement factories, built in the 1880s by Spowage and Lee to replace earlier buildings. There are two plain six-storey blocks linked at the west end with 22 windows on each floor. The buildings were once surrounded by blocks of terraced and back-to-back housing. In the 1902 Directory some 25 machine holders are listed as tenants and at that time power was derived from a 75 hp steam engine.

NW *Grant and Baldwin Streets, Radford* (SK 560402). This recently renovated three-storey works was originally a tenement owned by Thomas Herbert and Co., lace manufacturers with machine standings let to other lace and hosiery manufacturers.

NW *Ilkeston Road, Radford* (SK 557402). Radford Mills, a red brick four-storey building with yellow terracotta decoration and water tower, were built for William Hollins and Co., wool, cotton and silk spinners, some time after 1913. Along *Norton Street* are single storey louvred roof dyeing sheds of similar construction with adjoining earlier buildings. These were used by Hollins in the 1880s for merino wool, worsted and silk manufacture. The 18-bay block on *Norton Street* has stepped gables with well-lit attics. Another three-storey plus basement building remains on this extensive site fronting *Garden Street* which is dated 1897; adjacent single storey buildings have recently been demolished.

NW *Lonsdale Road, Radford* (SK 552405). In contrast to the multi-storey factories mentioned above, Radford Works, a single storey north light lace factory with five blocks, is post 1900 and illustrates the transition of the industry to the use of large curtain machines. These could be over 50 feet in length, 12 feet high and weigh over 30 tons each.

NW *Radford Boulevard, Radford* (SK 554406). Boulevard Works, 39 bays long, were erected in two stages beside the newly created suburban artery. Several decorative features include a central staircase tower with Dutch gable and at the south end a mansard roof with dormer windows. A parallel block facing *Forster Street*, dated 1896, housed over 20 lace making tenants. These blocks have survived, still used for textiles, whilst the large 1930s works on the opposite side of Hartley Road have succumbed to demolition for supermarket development.

NW *NEW BASFORD* (Start at SK 558422 on North Gate)
The following five sites are located within the City of Nottingham's New Basford Industrial Improvement Area, and are shown on the map on page 145. New Basford, like Radford, expanded rapidly during the last century; the population of the parish rose from 2,124 in 1801 to 10,091 in 1851 and to 27,119 by 1901. This area was, however, predominantly one of factories and considerable demolitions have taken place providing parking and landscape areas around the remaining industrial buildings.

1 *Palm Street, New Basford*. The block dated 1870 with single gable and large Venetian window was originally the warehouse and office block associated with Ward and Cope's lace factories to the rear.

2 *Mount Street, New Basford*. Papyrus works is a long narrow block with 27 bays, mainly three-storey plus attic, with decorated water tower and continuous attic windows. This utilitarian building was erected in several stages before 1881 and has two sets of loading apertures and stepped end gables. It was at one time occupied by T. I. Birkin & Co., lace manufacturers, along with adjoining works in *Palm Street*, now demolished.

3 *Beech Avenue, New Basford*. The Maville factory, a four-storey plain brick building with tall windows, dates from around 1900. Originally a tenement, it is still used for lace manufacture by Guy Birkin.

4 *Gawthorne Street, New Basford*. A terrace of pairs of Gothic-style houses survive, representative of better class housing erected in 1878/9.

5 *High Church Street, New Basford*. On the east side of the road are the Victoria Works, dated 1873, with a cart entrance in the central block; these have been occupied by Swift and Wass, lace machine manufacturers. On the opposite side of the street are two-storey blocks of 15 and 13 bays, bearing a datestone 'HS 1872'. These were built by lace manufacturer Henry Simpson, who had nine tenants. On either corner with *Wycliffe Street* are older buildings, one dated 1853; both were originally Kirkbrides and Clark's tenement lace factories.

162. The Boulevard Works, a decorative tenement factory on the new boulevard in Radford, *above left*.

163. The Papyrus Works, a utilitarian tenement factory on Mount Street in Basford with prominent attic mending windows, *above right*.

164. The former Lambert's bleach works on Talbot Street in central Nottingham, *above*.

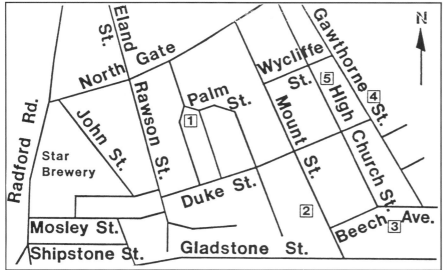

165. A sketch map of New Basford, *left*.

NW *Vernon Road, Old Basford* (SK 553431). One of several dyeworks in the Basford area, the Vernon Road Bleaching and Dyeing Works used water from wells in the Bunter sandstone. Some old wooden fulling stocks are preserved here.

NW *Talbot Street* (SK 568401). Lambert's bleach works were built in 1863 with an imposing frontage to the five-storey building. The clock tower resembles that at Wollaton Hall. Since closure, moves were made to convert to a hotel but this was not successful and attempts to demolish have been rejected following a public enquiry.

NE *Ashley Street, Sneinton* (SK 581401). A range of buildings on the north side, together with adjoining block on *Roden Street* of later date, was originally occupied by lace dressers and finishers.

NE *Handel Street, Sneinton* (SK 582401). On the north side near Alfred Street, and now converted to shops, these three-storey buildings of domestic appearance, together with the buildings to the rear on Ashley Street, originally served as hosiery warehouse and factory belonging to J. & R. Morley.

NE *Robin Hood Street, Sneinton* (SK 580402). The four-storey block at the corner of Roden Street has prominent attic workshops and was constructed for silk throwing. The pedimented corner carries a wind indicator and a stone 'AD 1869 WW', denoting William Windley the lace manufacturer. The adjoining block along *Roden Street* was also Windley's factory and traces of the engine house are visible.

NE *Lincoln Street* (SK 574400). On the corner of George Street there is a small terrace of houses incorporating workshops for the domestic production of lace.

NE *St Luke Street, Sneinton* (SK 581401). At the corner of Longden Street, the three-storey hosiery factory, dated 1866, has round headed windows, decorative eaves and string courses.

NE *Ashforth Street, St Anns* (SK 576409). There has been wholesale demolition in the St Ann's area but a range of single and multi-storey buildings, dating from around 1880, survives at the corner of Peas Hill Road. Originally Carver's tenement factory, they became known as Alfred Street Mills.

NE *Great Freeman Street* (SK 575405). Now linked to a new building fronting Huntingdon Street and being used by Hopewells as a furniture warehouse, this long four-storey block was built for lace dressing and finishing for Harrisons.

NE *Mansfield Road/North Sherwood Street* (c.SK 570410). Many early 19th-century three-storey buildings survive along the west side of Mansfield Road between Shakespeare Street and Forest Road East. From their fronts they appear to be houses converted to shops. However, if the rear walls are inspected from North Sherwood Street, a large number of them have surviving long windows to workshops for framework knitting or lace manufacture, many other windows having been infilled. In addition, on North Sherwood Street there are remains of court dwellings and also a block of back-to-back houses. This assemblage represents pre-enclosure development along the Mansfield Road and is an important early survival.

NE *St Ann's Hill Road, St Ann's* (SK 572411). This imposing brick factory consists of two sections, Oldknows and Clarkes, both pre-1880 lace tenements which dominate the surrounding area from their hill side position. The adjacent four-storey building down *Egerton Street* was W. Clarke's lace dyeing and trimming factory.

NE *Mansfield Road, Daybrook* (SK 580448). One of the many factories which once belonged to J. & R. Morley, originally yeomen farmers from Sneinton who founded a hosiery business about 1790. The building with the clock fronting Mansfield Road dates from the 1860s and the additional block to the north from 1885.

SE *Queens Road* (SK 578391). At the corner of *London Road* are the works built by Cox and Co, lace finishers, and now occupied by Hicking Pentecost, dyers and finishers. The extensive four-storey block along Queens Road was also originally built for lace dressing and finishing. Both works are built by the Tinkers Leen river which flows along the back, now discharging into the canal.

SE *Queens Road* (SK 576391). Meadows Mills, now used by Boots for warehousing, was originally built for cotton doubling and lace manufacture by W. E. and F. Dobson. Attic mending workshops are more or less concealed behind the parapet wall.

166. Carver's tenement factory on Ashforth Street, St Ann's.

167. Houses in Lincoln Street, showing the long windows to workshops for lace or hosiery manufacture.

168. A section of a Goad's Fire Plan, 1889, showing the tightly packed houses and workshops near Mansfield Road.

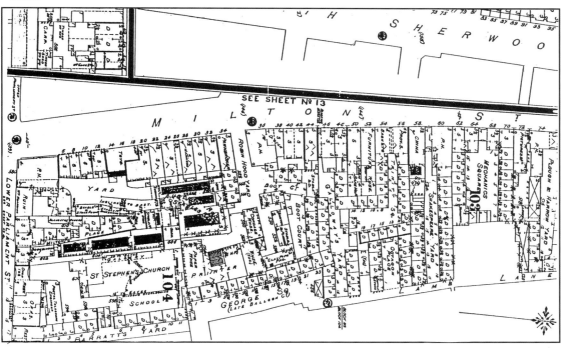

SE *THE LACE MARKET* (Start at SK 575396)

The Lace Market was the commercial rather than the manufacturing centre of the industry, although finishing was carried on in the extensively fenestrated attic workshops of the warehouses. These warehouses were built to impress buyers and their embellishment and quality contrasts sharply with the plain tenement factories where the lace was manufactured. The product was dressed and finished before coming to the warehouse for final inspection, packaging and sale.

The Lace Market, since 1969 a Conservation Area with over fifty Grade II listed buildings, was established in the 1850s around St Mary's church in what was formerly a prestige residential area. Many of the residents had moved to the newly built Park Estate and their large houses were adapted as warehouses, gradually being replaced by new buildings as the wholesale market for lace moved from London to Nottingham. Unfortunately some demolition took place in the 1960s for new road construction but this was halted and the area protected. Most of the cleared areas have now had new houses and car parks erected on them and their style reflects the older buildings of the Lace Market. The following eight sites are located on the map on page 149.

1 *The Lace Hall, High Pavement*. A convenient starting point, the Lace Hall has refreshment facilities, shops and exhibitions including working machinery devoted to the industry. It is housed in the former Unitarian Chapel which was erected in 1876 on the site of a former meeting house. (Tel 0602 484221)

2 *Short Hill*. Some of the original Georgian houses remain here with additional inspection attics added in the roof space when they were converted to lace warehouses.

3 *Kaye's Walk* has a row of six-storey warehouses, largely plain in character.

4 *Broadway*. An interesting example of townscape, the narrow street was laid out by T. C. Hine 1853-5 and has two curves in its short length; it is flanked by tall warehouses of distinctive style constructed on the site of Plumtre House. The warehouse on the south side with its entrance archway was built for T. I. Birkin in 1854. The upper part of the archway is stone but the lower part is cast iron to give protection against damage from carts. The adjacent corner warehouse was Jacoby's, one of several firms of German origin that were established in Nottingham.

5 *Barker Gate*. On the north corner there is a later warehouse designed in 1897 by another prominent local architect, Watson Fothergill. This has an ornate corner feature with tiered oriel windows and a glazed turret separating two pepper pot towers. Further down the hill is Gothic House, another former warehouse, much less ornate, with six storeys, which has been restored from dereliction to office accommodation.

6 *Stoney Street*. This is probably the most impressive of the lace warehouses. Another Hine design, the five-storey E-shaped block was built for Adams and Page in 1855 and incorporated a library, tea room and workers' chapel where services were once held every morning. The rear of the building, in St Mary's Gate, is equally important with loading bays.

7 *Warser Gate*. An interesting tympanum *c*.1860 depicting industrial scenes may be seen at the entrance to the building on the corner of St Mary's Gate. On the north side is another later warehouse of 1890.

8 *St Mary's Gate*. The Bridge Housing Society scheme has been built in keeping with the style of the older lace warehouses with attic workshops; beneath the canopy a series of display panels shows the history of the area.

SW *Castle Boulevard* (SK 570393). Built on land created by the infilling of the Duke's Wharves beside the canal, the four-storey former Viyella building was erected in 1933 fronting an earlier factory of 1919 built by Hollins for garment manufacture. The fully glazed facade has been restored and the rear aspect to the Nottingham Canal rebuilt with viewing terrace.

SW *Stanford Street* (SK 572396). A fine run of lace warehouses, including Pennine House, originally constructed in 1874 and enlarged later in the century. This five-storey warehouse has recently been refurbished for office accommodation.

169. A sketch map of the Nottingham Lace Market.

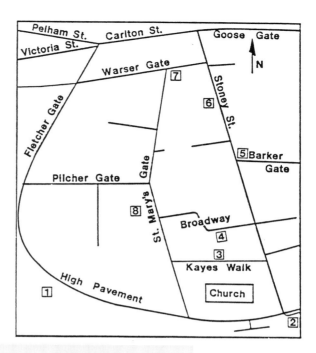

170. The lace dressing and dyeing works of Hicking and Pentecost in London Road.

171. The lace warehouses designed by T. C. Hine on the elegant curve of new street called Broadway.

172. The Thomas Adams building in Stoney Street, designed by T. C. Hine and one of the most elaborate in the Conservation Area.

173. The East Croft Council Depot, reflecting municipal aspirations.
174. The elaborate gateway to Nottingham cattle market.

Manufacturing Industry: Engineering

SE *Crocus Street* (SK 576390). On the south side adjoining Newthorpe Street is a complex of single and two-storey buildings, still used for engineering purposes; they were originally the Arkwright Works of Lee and Hunt machine tool makers, established there by 1875. On the opposite side of the road, the Crown iron foundry and the viaduct of the Great Central have recently been demolished but the 14-bay three-storey building with prominent tie bar plates was in multiple occupation by, among others, needle manufacturers and machine builders, including Moses Mellor and Co.

Public Utilities

SE *East Croft Depot* (SK 580390). The enclosure of the East Croft field in 1845 enabled the Corporation to develop various public services on this site which included a pumping station, refuse destructor, hide and skin market and the night soil sanitary depot. Further south along *Meadow Lane* was the cattle market where many of the original buildings, pens and ornamental gates survive. Off *London Road* there are several examples of Victorian municipal architecture, which include the office block with clock tower and the Nottingham Hide Skin and Fat Co Ltd. building dated 1878 with its distinctive triangular gables. The site is still a municipal depot.

Miscellaneous

NW *Radford Boulevard, Radford* (SK 554407). Several buildings remain of the former Castle tobacco factory of John Player, later part of the Imperial Tobacco Company. The building at the corner of *Beckenham Road* with three gables and semi-circular windows was built in 1892 as a bonded warehouse for tobacco. Further along Beckenham Road are the Castle Cavendish Works, dated 1898, with twin gables and roof vents, also used for tobacco manufacture. On the north side of Beckenham Road demolition has revealed the rear of the original John Player factory which fronts *Player Street*. This was built in anticipation of his requirements and let out as a lace tenement. It had four storeys, 384 feet long by 44 feet wide and provided 176 machine standings, 44 per floor; a 200hp steam engine provided power for this and the demolished Castle Tobacco factory. By 1886 there were 32 different tenants but it was gradually brought into use as required for the tobacco manufacturing business. The 1932 factory on the west side of Radford Boulevard has already been demolished and the deceptively old-looking white weather-boarded block on the east side is actually the former Head Office built in 1967.

NE *Bath Street* (SK 579402). Victoria Dwellings were built in 1876-7 by the Borough to provide housing for their own employees at the markets and the East Croft depots nearby. This is probably the oldest surviving council accommodation block in the country and has been refurbished as apartments, now known as Park View Court.

The facade is enlivened with two gabled sections, complete with twin towers, each above a huge lancet containing balconies.

SW *Castle Boulevard* (SK 569393). The former paper warehouse with towers was designed by Watson Fothergill and built in 1894. The building has been recently renovated for re-use.

2: Newark on Trent

Newark owes its importance as an early settlement to its strategic position as the lowest crossing point of the Trent, a distinction which it held until 1790. It was also the junction of the Fosse Way and a prehistoric trackway known as Sewstern Lane, later utilised as part of the Great North Road. The town developed an extensive coaching trade but most of its traffic was on the river itself. Grain warehouses were established on the banks and by the middle of the 19th century Newark was one of the most active malting centres in the country but no working maltings or breweries now survive. It was later served by two railways, the Midland in 1846 and the Great Northern east coast route from King's Cross in 1852: the two lines crossed on the level. Many of the maltings and breweries had both river wharves and rail connections.

GAZETTEER
(OS sheet 121)
Agriculture-based Industries

Albert Street, Castle Brewery (SK 798536), away from both riverside and railway, was built for James Hole; the stone-built office block in Renaissance style with pediment and central clock tower is dated 1882. The red brick tower brewery to the rear was erected in 1889 and brewing ceased in the early 1980s.

Castle Gate, former Corn Exchange (SK 796539). This was built on the riverside in 1847/8 and its elaborate Italianate features reflect the town's reputation as the granary of England; it closed in 1914 and is now a bingo hall.

George Street, former Maltings (SK 803543). This street is lined with maltings; on the south side a two-storey six-bay block is now a boys' club and further along is a three-storey block with three kilns. On the opposite side a three- and four-storey block has five kilns.

Lovers Lane, former Maltings (SK 801543) have three storeys and two kilns.

Northgate (SK 799543). Number 35, the Old Brewery next to the *Malt Shovel* inn, is one of the oldest surviving breweries with its buildings grouped around a courtyard. They date from the late 18th or early 19th century and comprise a house, brewhouse, three-storey maltings and a kiln. Nearby at SK 798543 are some floor maltings with a detached pair of kilns with conical cowls, which have been listed. *Warwick and Richardson's Brewery* (SK 798499) has Queen Anne-style offices at the front, a brewhouse of 1882 and bottling stores of 1920 to the rear. Brewing ceased here in 1966.

Riverside, BWB Kiln Warehouses (SK 797544), on the north bank, consist of two three-storey concrete-built blocks erected around 1890 as maltings. The 18-bay by 9- and 12-bay blocks each have kilns at the NW and SW corners and both had loading hoists over the river.

Trent Lane (SK 802547). Formerly Peach's (Gough's) Maltsters, these were malting until recently; originally supplies were brought in across a railway bridge over the Trent. The brick-built malthouse with slate roof has five kilns. The adjacent Baird's maltings, originally built for James Hole, were the last to be built in Newark in 1904/5. They have high hipped slate roofs with dormers, but malting ceased in 1975, and the buildings have recently been damaged by fire.

175. Castle Brewery on Albert Street.

176. Warwick and Richardson Brewery in Newark.

Transport

Castle Station, Newark (SK 796543) was built by the Midland Railway in 1846. It is in the Italian style with elaborate architectural embellishment. North of the station, the line to Lincoln is crossed on the level at SK 802555 by the Great Northern east coast route which opened in 1852.

Trent Bridge (SK 796541). The earliest bridge on this site dates back to 1135, but the present seven-arched brick structure with stone dressings was erected in 1775; the railings and footways were added in 1848 and a two-storey toll house survives. The Great North Road (now the A6065) continued north over the Trent flood plain on the *Causeway* (SK 790555) which incorporated a series of brick flood arches; this was built by John Smeaton in 1770 and was widened on the west side in 1930. The Castle, slighted after the Civil War, commands the river crossing.

Trent Navigation. Of the *Town Locks* (SK 795539), the eastern one was built 1772/3 and is now a dry dock. The larger western lock and adjacent dry dock date from 1952. Slightly to the south, by *Mill Lane* (SK 794537), is a former oil and cake mill erected in 1870 which later became a warehouse for the Navigation Company and has a classic river frontage with loading doors. The building now houses the Millgate Folk Museum with displays portraying social and industrial life from the Victorian age to 1940. Adjacent company workers' houses in *Mill Lane* have been restored.

On the opposite side of the river to the south, the seven-arch stone *Longstone Bridge* (SK 792537) was built by the Navigation Company in 1819 across a weir and arm of the river to carry a towpath. This arm of the river served a large corn mill which was burnt down in 1965 but there are remains of three wheel pits and control sluices.

Newark Air Museum, Winthorpe (SK 827565) on a former airfield displays over thirty aeroplanes, mainly post World War Two. (Enquiries tel.0636 707170.)

Manufacturing Industry: Engineering

Trent Iron Works (SK 796542) are conveniently located by river, road and railway. They were built in 1860 for agricultural engineers who also provided ironwork for the brewing and malting industry of the town. The workshop frontage and a decorative office block survive.

3: Derby

The earliest settlement in the present city of Derby was the Roman Derventio at Little Chester to the north which remained as a hamlet until absorbed into the borough. The town itself was a Saxon foundation of *c*.920 situated at the lowest crossing point of the Derwent near its confluence with the Markeaton Brook. The main rivers, the Trent south of the city and the Derwent, offered communications to east and west and to north and south respectively. The early burh was built on either side of a spinal road, now Queen Street and Irongate, and it became one of the five boroughs of the Danelaw which controlled the East Midlands. Derby remained small until the 12th century; indeed its development may have been restricted by a charter granted by Henry II between 1155 and 1160 which favoured Nottingham as far as trade was concerned. From the Lay Subsidy roll of 1377, the population has been estimated at 3,500

177. One of the many former maltings beside the River Trent.

178. The two Town Locks on the Trent Navigation.

179. Trent Navigation warehouses, indicating the importance of Newark as a transhipment point.

and the community was dominated by various religious foundations; not until after the Reformation did lay families begin to exert influence.

Even by the beginning of the 17th century the population was still only around 4,000. The Speed map of 1610 shows the limit of development south of St Mary's bridge on the west bank of the Derwent. In 1693, a trades list recorded 455 businesses in the town which then had 4,164 people living in 694 houses; the main occupations were concerned with leather, textiles and metalworking. Three thousand loads of coal were being brought into the town annually from pits at Denby and Smalley. Coal was also going down into Leicestershire and Northamptonshire where it was being exchanged for barley. This was brought back for malting and brewing which became an important trade in the town and was later located beside the canal and railway.

Daniel Defoe, following his visit in 1725, described Derby as 'a town of gentry rather than trade', and also stated:

> Here is a curiosity in trade worth observing, as being the only one of the kind in England, namely, a throwing or throwster's mill, which performs by a wheel turn'd by the water; and though it cannot perform the doubling part of a throwster's work, which can only be done by a handwheel, yet it turns the other work, and performs the labour of many hands.

Defoe was of course referring to the Derby Silk Mill. The first mill was erected in 1702 on the west bank of the Derwent for Thomas Cotchett, and was the precursor of the water-powered textile factory system. The engineer was George Sorocold, who had already established his reputation in Derby with the construction of a pumped public water supply system from the Derwent in 1692; thereafter he erected similar works elsewhere and in 1701 reconstructed the waterworks on the Thames at London Bridge. The selection of Derby for this silk mill can only be explained by the presence of local entrepreneurs, an ample source of water power and of course a demand for thread for the local domestic hosiery industry. Cotchett's first mill failed, but the idea was taken up by a London silk merchant, Thomas Lombe, whose half-brother John had been an apprentice in Cotchett's mill and had visited Italy to study silk-throwing machinery there. Nottingham was the main centre for silk hosiery at the time rather than Derby, but the Derwent was more suitable as a source of power than the Trent. Lombe patented his water-powered silk-throwing machinery and his mill was built in 1718, the wheel also being designed by Sorocold. By the time his patent expired in 1732, the mill employed 300 people. The original mill was followed by others in the town and by 1789 there were an estimated 1,200 silk workers. The expansion of the silk trade was further assisted by the sale of Nuns Green, adjoining the Markeaton Brook, which provided further water-powered sites. The surrounding area was laid out with streets and poor quality workers' housing erected.

By 1801, although Derbyshire had the largest population of the four counties of the East Midlands, Derby itself had only the third largest population of the county towns at around 12,500, compared with Leicester's of nearly 20,000 and Nottingham's nearly 29,000. The borough boundaries were extended first in 1877 with the inclusion of Little Chester, Litchurch and New Normanton and again in November 1901 to absorb Alvaston, Boulton, Normanton, Osmaston, Chaddesden and Spondon. At this date, the population of Derby was still smaller than Nottingham or Leicester but that of its county grew at a much faster rate. By 1901 there were 59 places in Derbyshire with a population greater than 2,500 compared with 29 in Nottinghamshire and 21 in Leicestershire.

Derby therefore lagged behind the rest of the county in its development, yet it did not suffer from the chronic land shortage of Nottingham. Poor communications did not hamper development either, since river crossings of the Derwent and the Trent, at Shardlow, had been established since the late 13th century and 1761 respectively. Sorocold had also been responsible for improving the River Derwent for navigation in 1721, including making a new cut through The Holmes water meadows; this enabled goods to be shipped out along the Trent to Gainsborough for transhipment to London and elsewhere. The improvements provided the impetus for other industrial developments which included copper and iron rolling and slitting mills, potteries, clockmaking, plaster grinding and lead works. A further benefit was received with the opening in 1796 of the Derby Canal from the town to the Trent near Swarkestone bridge, via a junction with the Trent and Mersey Canal. There were also canal links to the Erewash Canal at Sandiacre and from the Derby basin to higher up the Derwent above the silk mill weir which enabled boats to reach Darley Abbey. A further branch was built to Little Eaton and a waggonway from there connected to the Drury-Lowe coal mines, ironworks and potteries at Denby; this was closed in 1908. The link from the Trent and Mersey to the River Trent at Swarkestone was abandoned by 1837. Derby was therefore extremely well placed with regard to waterway communication and became an important distribution centre. Unfortunately there are few traces left of the Derby Canal and its extensive network of basins in the city centre due to infilling and much of the routes to Sandiacre and Little Eaton have disappeared beneath recent road construction.

Derby as a market town supported the surrounding area with the usual service industries associated with agriculture and the coaching trade, including two iron foundries by 1800. The silk industry continued to develop and by 1833 there were 11 mills, eight making hose and three weaving, some of them using steam power. However, silk was an expensive commodity and with changes in fashion, silk hosiery declined faster than other branches of the trade. Many Derby firms changed from silk throwing and weaving to the manufacture of narrow tapes, braids and webbings, the first in 1806. By 1850 the silk industry had contracted, although Derby remains a centre for narrow fabrics. Powered machine lace and hosiery manufacture were introduced in the later 19th century.

The second and most influential phase of Derby's industrialisation began with railways and, although they came first to the eastern outskirts of the town, the railway became a physical barrier and had profound effects on its development. Three railways were constructed almost simultaneously; the Midland Counties Railway to Nottingham and Leicester was opened in 1839; the Birmingham and Derby Junction Railway followed in the same year and the North Midland Railway between Derby and Leeds (via Masborough) was opened in 1840. All three lines used a common station sited on The Holmes, a low-lying area to the east of the town centre. The three companies amalgamated in 1844 as the Midland Railway and Derby was chosen as headquarters. Locomotive, carriage and wagon building and signal works began to proliferate and their impact was most noticeable in the parish of Litchurch to the south east of Derby. It grew from a hamlet of 30 people in 1801 to a township of 6,562 in 1861 with its own local board. By 1877, when it was absorbed into the borough, there were over 18,500 in Litchurch, a large proportion of them being railway employees. A later arrival on the railway scene was the Great Northern line from Nottingham to Burton-on-Trent (via Egginton). Primarily aimed at coal transport, it was opened in 1878 and closed in 1968. This line, with its bridges, viaducts and cuttings, had a greater impact on the old town than the others in 1840. The railways provided a demand for the products of existing and new foundries and engineering works and also other service industries such as printing and clothing manufacture.

Derby's lack of other industrial growth was due to railway dominance, and this was recognised by the Chamber of Commerce who in 1906 established a Borough Development Committee with the express intention of attracting new industries to the town. They succeeded with the opening in 1907 of the Aiton works making steam and hydraulic pipe installations on Stores Road and in 1908 of the Rolls Royce works on Nightingale Road. Derby provided attractive sites with good transport communications, an experienced work force and an established foundry industry for other companies. Engineering is still a major employer in the city.

Water supplies for the town, initially provided by the Sorocold scheme of 1692, continued to be taken from the Derwent with the construction in 1848 of a new pumping and filtration plant from springs and the river at Little Eaton. Developments there met requirements until Derby became a partner with a 25 per cent share in the Upper Derwent Valley scheme, begun in 1912. Effluent disposal was less satisfactory. The local board at Litchurch installed a scheme in the 1880s but the borough scheme was not operational until 1900 and not completed until 1910. The town showed lack of foresight in the construction of its Cavendish gas works in 1820, away from the river wharf; further expansion on the site was impossible after 1840 and new works were built at Litchurch in 1859, this time with both canal and rail access. The Derby Gas Light and Coke Company later bought gas supplies from steelworks coke ovens at Blackwell, Clay Cross and Stanton.

The electricity generating station, established in Full Street in 1892, whilst it could use river water for cooling, was on a cramped site and again without rail access. Power generation here ceased in 1969 and the site is now partly occupied by a transformer station from the grid. Public transport in the town was initially provided privately by horse buses in 1877 and these continued until 1917. Horse trams began service in 1880 and lasted until 1907. Electrification had begun in 1904 and electric trams were entirely superseded by motor buses and trolley buses by 1934.

The industrial heritage of Derby has suffered considerably with the vast redevelopment in the town centre and new road construction. The planned regeneration of industrial areas which can be seen in Nottingham is absent, although the Midland Railway village is a notable exception. Some refurbishment of isolated factories is taking place as can be seen at Britannia Mill on the Markeaton Brook and at other mills on Lynton Street, Boyer Street and Drewry Lane. The Upper Derwentside Development Area is proposed around a nucleus of listed buildings in the St Mary's railway goods yard.

The Gazetteer which follows is therefore not a comprehensive one for the city. The sites included are grouped into two sections; firstly, the former Midland Railway lands and adjacent areas and secondly, the sector along the Markeaton Brook, Friargate and Uttoxeter Road on the west side.

GAZETTEER
(OS sheet 128)

SECTION I
Extractive Industry

The *Osmaston Road, Royal Crown Derby Porcelain Works* (SK 356352) are located in the former workhouse, erected in 1832. China manufacture began in Derby in 1750 on Nottingham Road. The porcelain works began on this site in 1877, becoming the Royal Crown Derby Porcelain Co in 1890. The front elevation has been modified but the original cupola tower has been retained. There is a Museum on the site and factory tours can be arranged.

180. An old illustration of the Royal Crown Derby Porcelain Works, where the office block survives.

181. Part of the village built by the North Midland Railway, now a Conservation Area.

Transport

Large areas of the city were developed for railway use, for tracks, sidings, stations, workshops and other buildings which reflected Derby's position as the Midland headquarters prior to 1923. These buildings are located in the sectors between London Road and the river: between Osmaston Road and London Road to the south of Litchurch Lane: the Chaddesden sidings north of the river and south of Nottingham Road: and the St Mary's goods yards on the east side of Mansfield Road. The earliest developments were centred around Derby station.

Derby Midland Station (SK 362356) was originally designed by Francis Thompson as a single platform tri-junct station. In 1891 it was re-fronted and the platform layout changed. During a total rebuild in 1986 the pediment and Midland Railway crest of the 1891 frontage was retained as a feature on the south end of the office block further north along Railway Terrace.

The Railway Village (SK 361356) is now a Conservation area and includes most of the 57 terraced cottages built 1841/2 for the North Midland Railway which represent some of the earliest examples of railway housing. They were restored by the Derbyshire Historic Buildings Trust after demolition was averted in 1978. A sympathetic modern housing scheme may be seen on the western side. The area also includes the *Brunswick Inn* of 1843 and the *Club and Institute*; the latter was erected by the Midland for the welfare of its

182. The Midland Railway crest from the former station of 1891.

employees and families in 1894 and has multiple pediments and a corner tower liberally decorated with terracotta. Nearby on the north side of Siddalls Road is the former *Enginemen's Barracks* (SK 361359) of 1872. Opposite the station, adjacent to the railway offices is the *Midland Hotel* (SK 362354), originally privately built in 1840, and one of the first station hotels; it was bought by the Midland in 1860 and subsequently enlarged.

The Locomotive Works (SK 364356) may be seen from the far platform of the station. The original single storey block fronting the polygonal round house was built for the North Midland in 1839 and additional storeys were later added, the top one in 1893 when the clock was raised. The roundhouse, the first of three, could accommodate 32 locomotives on 16 tracks and was used for storage and repair until after the amalgamation in 1844. Then locomotive standardisation and manufacture was introduced by Matthew Kirtley and the first Derby-built locomotive emerged in 1851, some 30 being completed by 1855. Subsequent additions included engineering shops, foundries, sawmills, gasworks and an electricity generating station.

A Railway Overbridge (SK 362358) over the access road to the railway works formerly spanned the Derby Canal which ran parallel to the river at this point; marks made by towing lines may be seen on the bridge abutments. A canal branch went under Siddalls Road which served a wharf and extended under Park Street into the basement of Bemrose's printing works.

The *Railway Carriage and Wagon Works* (SK 366345), now BREL, were originally located behind the station with the locomotive works and soon outgrew their capacity. In 1864 new works were added at *Etches Park* (SK 367347), beside London Road, and a further 50 acres added in 1873 with the rest of the Osmaston Park estate, some 235 acres, being purchased in 1888. The works, occupying nearly 130 acres, are characterised by large single

183. St Mary's railway goods yard.

184. One of Derby's best known companies: the Rolls Royce engineering factory in Nightingale Road.

storey brick buildings with floor areas of 120,000 sq ft (large for the 1880s), arranged within a grid of lines and accessed by traversers; they had high roof clearance to allow for travelling cranes to lift rolling stock. Later, pressure on storage requirements led to sidings and sheds being opened beside the goods sidings at *Chaddesden* (SK 375359) in 1899.

St Mary's Goods Yard (SK 357370) was opened in 1855 to relieve the congestion in goods and minerals handling facilities at the main yard near the Midland Station. The area has now been abandoned for railway use and is the subject of a redevelopment scheme, the Upper Derwentside Local Plan, which hopes to find new uses for the remaining buildings on the site. These include double-decked horse stables, fruit stores, a goods shed and a granary, both with handling gear powered from the adjacent hydraulic power house which were all erected around 1862. The *Sundries Shed* (SK 357368) dates from 1940 and was built on the site of the former Britannia Bridge and Girder Works of Andrew Handyside & Co which had closed in 1911. The former *Bonded Stores* (SK 358369), beside the main line, have been converted to the Derwent Business Centre. The sidings once extended south across Fox Street, where they served several large maltings; this industry had been long established in this area which also bordered the Derby Canal but there are few remains now visible.

Manufacturing Industry: Textiles

Canal Street (SK 361357). A former silk mill backs on to the dry arm of the Derby Canal, of which traces remain in banks of sleepers. The 19-bay four-storey block has small windows with stone lintels and has been converted to office accommodation.

Osmaston Road (SK 361347). The Osmaston Works were built in the 1880s as a machine lace factory. The original T-shaped block with pediment has three storeys; four more bays, with cart access, were added at a later date.

Manufacturing Industry: Engineering

Litchurch Lane (SK 363347). The Masson Works were begun in 1860 by George Fletcher for the manufacture of steam engines and sugar processing machinery. The business was relocated from Southwark.

Nightingale Road, Rolls Royce (SK 363335). The original 1908 building remains behind the office block which has a portico entrance; other blocks are dated 1910, 1912 and 1920. The company transferred its car production here from Manchester for a planned output of 200 units per year until it was transferred to Crewe in 1945. Rolls Royce remain a large employer in Derby, both here and on the outskirts at Sinfin.

Osmaston Road (SK 361345). Former foundries remain on either side of the railway, to which they originally had direct access. That on the north side was the Wellington Foundry, now largely cleared, whilst behind more remains of the Vulcan Iron Works opened by Ley in 1874 for the manufacture of malleable iron castings. On the south side of the bridge were the Victoria and the Railway Iron Works which amalgamated to become Eastwood and Swingler. They supplied the ironwork for the GNR Bennerley viaduct across the River Erewash. The large buildings near to the road were subsequently used as a trolley bus depot and are now occupied by Rolls Royce. Further south, along *Cotton Lane* (SK 360340), is the non-ferrous foundry of John Smith which moved here around 1900 from the town centre.

Miscellaneous

Osmaston Road Arboretum (SK 356350). This is the first specially designed urban public park in England and was given in 1840 by Joseph Strutt, a member of the local textile manufacturing family. The 11-acre park was landscaped by J. C. Loudon and provided open space for the rapidly developing Litchurch parish.

Park Street, Bemrose Printing Works (SK 360356) are a massive island block of four- and five-storey buildings erected over several decades. The original works of William Bemrose, official printers to the Midland Railway, were established in 1854 adjacent to the Canal Street Ironworks which had begun in 1846 manufacturing railway wheels, buffers and forgings. Other buildings on the site were originally silk mills. The vacant buildings pose an interesting problem of re-use.

Liversage Walk (Park Street) Works (SK 359358). This site has been occupied by timber merchants and wood workers since before 1880. The front block has houses on either side of the central entrance and behind are extensive two-storey workshops of timber construction.

SECTION II
Agriculture-based Industries

Abbey Street Maltings (SK 349354) are now a printing works but the kiln remains behind the 13-bay two-storey block.

Ashbourne Road Maltings (SK 344366) with three floors and an internal kiln, have small diamond pattern cast iron windows. By 1891 they were occupied by a corn factor.

Curzon Street (SK 349362). The white stuccoed building is the former corn warehouse built by George Sowter in 1819 with loading doors in the north wall.

Forman Street Maltings (SK 348361) were established on this site in the 1830s by Robert Forman. There are three kilns remaining, although the buildings were converted to cardboard box manufacture by 1899. The houses on the east side of Forman Street were built by the maltsters.

Lodge Lane Steam Corn Mill (SK 349357) was built in the 1880s with rail access from the newly opened Great Northern Railway. The four-storey main building has a high infilled central cart access and has been converted to office use. Adjacent on the north side is a small warehouse and on the south side two- and five-storey warehouses which have also been converted to office accommodation.

Surrey Street Maltings (SK 338368). This complex was established by Strettons, who had a large number of local tied houses. The polychromatic brick maltings at the east end have ornamental tie bar ends, and three of the four kilns retain their cowls. Their Manchester Brewery, next to the nearby school, has been demolished. A contrast in brewing scale can be seen on the opposite side of Ashbourne Road, behind the *Gallant Hussar* public house, where a small brewhouse remains with its vented roof and slatted windows.

185. The former steam corn mill in Lodge Lane.

186. Maltings in Surrey Street, once part of the Manchester Brewery.

187. One of Derby's best known landmarks, Handyside's Great Northern Railway bridge over Friargate.

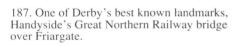

188. The stark outlines of the former Great Northern Railway goods warehouse.

Transport

GNR bridge over the Derwent (SK 352372). This grade II listed bridge was erected by Handysides in 1877; it is an arched skew bridge designed so that the rail deck was partly suspended from and partly supported by the arch. Following railway closure, the bridge has been retained as a footpath, and the original footbridge attached to the south side has been removed. On the west side there is a tunnel under the embankment through which the Duke Street siding passed. This was reached by a reversing spur along the river bank and gave access to Bath Street mills, corn mill and Handyside's Britannia Foundry and Engineering Works located on the west bank of the river.

Friargate Bridge (SK 347364). This is probably the most impressive of the GNR remains, dated 1878 and built by Handysides. There are actually two converging bridges, with ornamental cast iron parapets and spandrels incorporating the town's buck motif, supported by dressed stone abutments. The northern access viaduct arches at one time served as stables for the horse tramways. Proposals have been made to carry a ring road over the bridge.

St Mary's Bridge (SK 354368). The present bridge, with three stone arches over the Derwent, was rebuilt between 1788 and 1793. Now called 'Causey Bridge', it is overshadowed by St Alkmund's Way.

Stafford Street, GNR Goods Warehouse and Hydraulic Station (SK 346362). This impressive multi-storey red brick goods and grain warehouse is listed Grade II but is now largely disused and awaiting re-development. The basement is reached by a tunnel from Great Northern Road and rail access was by four tracks from the west end. Subsidiary buildings have been demolished, with the exception of a four-road locomotive shed (SK 338362) and the hydraulic power house with accumulator; this was steam powered but was electrified in 1922, when the chimney stack was felled. Behind the warehouse are the high level platforms of Friargate Station to which access was gained from Friargate by a subway; the planned access from Stafford Street was never built and only the centre platform was provided with any shelter.

Manufacturing Industry: Textiles

Agard Street, Brook Mill (SK 347366). The nine-bay building with stepped glazed roofline, beside the Markeaton Brook, was built in 1879 for the Derby Smallware Co. who manufactured braids, laces and elastic web. The L-shaped block on the street frontage, also dating from the 1870s, was occupied by Longdens, manufacturers of surgical bandages. Along Searle Street is an eight-bay two-storey factory, retaining its engine house and chimney which also manufactured smallwares; the street was once linked with Brook Walk by a footbridge.

Bath Street Mills (SK 354371) is a large range of buildings, with a three-storey pedimented frontage and single storey sheds behind. The works were established by George Holme in 1848 to make silk and woollen fabrics. They were the first in Derby to make elastic webs; the range is now in multiple occupation.

Boyer Street (SK 346353). Vale Mill was erected for tape weaving. The older buildings and the adjacent Brookside silk mill have been demolished, but the 1905 building has been converted to living accommodation and new housing built carrying the legend 'Vale Mills 1990'.

Bridge Street (SK 347367). Rykneld Mill consists of two stark five- and seven-storey brick blocks with small windows but most of the ancillary buildings have been cleared. The mills, listed Grade II, with cast iron columns and beams with brick arched floors, were begun in 1823 for weaving silk ribbon and trimming, later switching to the weaving of cotton tapes and bindings. They are now mostly empty.

Bridge Street Mill (SK 346367). This five-storey L-shaped corner block has 11 bays to Brook Street and in the angle the former engine house with reduced chimney stack can be seen. The mill was occupied by silk throwsters until about 1900.

Cheapside/Bold Lane Corner (SK 350363). This four-storey brick block is one of the few buildings remaining from the domestic textile industry in the City. Long top floor windows have been bricked up, and even larger windows infilled on the centre floors.

189. Brook Mill, Agard Street, built for the Derby Smallware Company in 1879 (from *Derby Illustrated*, 1892).

190. The Union Foundry in City Road, another example of Derby's important engineering industry (from *Derby Illustrated*, 1892).

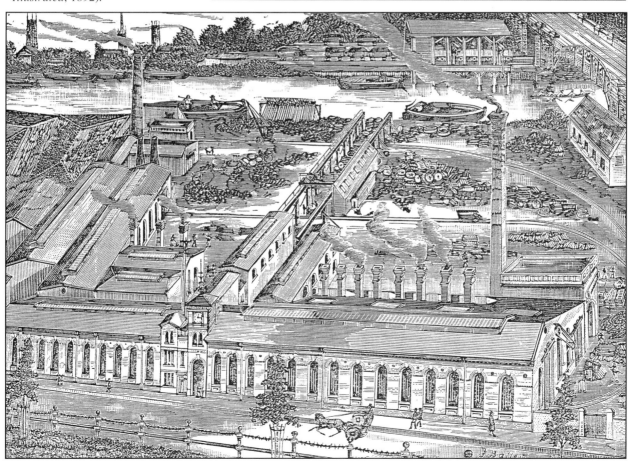

191. The gaunt Ryknèld Mills built for silk ribbon manufacture.

192. The Britannia hosiery factory on Markeaton Lane.

Drewry Lane Works (SK 346360). These works closed in 1987, having been occupied by James Smith & Co, who were established in 1856 as clothing contractors to the Midland Railway manufacturing serge cloth uniforms. The buildings are now being converted to residential use.

Full Street, Old Silk Mill (SK 354365). Located behind the fortress-like structure of the transformer station, which replaced the electricity generating station, is the site of the Old Silk Mill. The present building is a 1910 rebuild on the arched foundations of the original Lombe silk mill of 1721. The bell tower has been retained and also the wrought iron gates by Robert Bakewell, which once guarded the causeway across the mill race, now infilled. The Derby Industrial Museum, with displays on county industries including the Rolls Royce aero engine collection, is open daily.

Lynton Street Mill (SK 344357) consists of three phases, two identical nine-bay three-storey blocks, with single and two-storey blocks adjoining. They were built around 1890 for Joseph Bonas, a Fazeley (Warwickshire) manufacturer of narrow tapes, and have recently been refurbished as business units.

Markeaton Street (SK 341369). Britannia Mill is built on the site of the Ellam's Paint and Colour Works, powered from the Markeaton Brook. The present building, of red brick, four storeys with basement and attic, is dated 1912 and was built for hosiery manufacture by Moore Eady and Murcott Goode; this company was a prominent Leicestershire manufacturer.

Great Northern Road, Alexandra Mill (SK 345361). The road, originally Dog Kennel Lane, gave access to several brickyards which have now been built over. The grey brick mill with stone quoins was built in 1863 by William Higginbottom for silk and elastic web manufacture. By 1904 it was occupied by R. Rowley & Co, hosiery manufacturers, who also built the later four-storey factory which is adjacent on *Uttoxeter New Road*.

Parliament Street Mill (SK 343357). Grim brick three-storey buildings with segmental headed windows, dating from the 1870s, were constructed for elastic web, tape and small ware manufacturers; at the west end of the site are remains of the former Sun Foundry. On Peet Street and Olive Street are contemporary houses, a school and *Olive Mill*, dated 1900, built for H. Lilley and Sons, dyers and smallware manufacturers, whose name can be seen on the 12-bay block in Parliament Street.

Manufacturing Industry: Engineering

City Road (SK 356372). Union Foundry on the east bank of the Derwent has a 33-bay frontage with tall round headed windows. The area between the river and Mansfield Road was developed by 1852, with several foundries, timber yards and housing. Peach's Union Foundry was acquired in 1868 by A. Seale Haslam who had worked for Armstrongs; he established The Haslam Foundry and Engineering Co. Ltd. and erected the present buildings. Hydraulic machinery was made and by 1891 over 500 hands were employed. Haslam patented in 1880 a dry air refrigeration plant for shipping which received its successful trial on a meat-carrying vessel from Australia in 1881.

193. Street furniture: an electricity distribution box in Friargate.

Public Utilities

Friargate (SK 346364). On the south side pavement, by the kerb, can be seen one of the cast iron distribution boxes, bearing the town crest and dated 1893, which was built to supply electrical power to the fine Georgian residences along Friargate, many of which remain unaltered. The only survivor of the associated 1893 lamp standards by Handysides is preserved in Museum Square (SK 351363).

Jury Street (SK 349365). A two-storey building dated 1879 constructed of polychrome brick has six gables with access doors and lifting gear to two of them. This was built as a council depot.

Litchurch Gasworks (SK 370350). Some buildings and two gas holders remain of the works which opened in 1859.

4 : Leicester

Leicester, the Roman *Ratae Coritanorum* was founded on the site of a late Iron Age settlement situated on a gravel terrace on the east bank of the River Soar. The river valley to the north was marshy and so the Fosse Way crossed the river in Leicester. Two other Roman roads westwards and south-eastwards ensured that the town developed into an important market centre. It became a cathedral town within Mercia and was one of the Five Boroughs recognised by the Danes at the partition of Mercia in 877. Its medieval prosperity rested, like other East Midland towns, on the wool trade and the Guildhall of Corpus Christi survives to indicate this. Although its woolcombers were important, much of the town's worsted was sent to Norwich or Yorkshire for weaving, but an important handknitting industry developed from the 15th century onwards. When the framework knitting industry migrated from London to the East Midlands in the late 17th century, Leicester became such an important centre that Daniel Defoe could say in 1720: 'one would scarce think it possible so small an article of trade could employ such multitudes of people as it does'. The town continued to be an important hand worsted spinning centre, providing yarn for the hosiery trade, but experiments in powered worsted spinning in the 1780s came to an abrupt halt because of riots led by woolcombers and jersey spinners against what they saw as a threat to their livelihood. The progenitors moved away, and it was not until the 1820s that mechanised spinning mills returned. By the middle of the century a new industrial landscape had been created in Leicester which was well described by Dr John Barclay, the town's medical officer, in 1857: 'On all sides vast blocks of warehouses have arisen, while the development of new manufactures, or the substitution of steam machinery for hand labour, has raised a forest of long factory chimneys'.

The depression in the hosiery industry in the mid-19th century was alleviated by the introduction of large scale boot and shoe manufacture from Northamptonshire. In 1851 10.1 per cent of the working population were employed in hosiery and only 2.3 per cent in boots and shoes, but by 1881 boot and shoe manufacture had overtaken hosiery with 10.6 per cent engaged in their production compared with 6.8 per cent in hosiery. At the same time the population had more than doubled from 60,584 to 122,376, representing a real growth in the numbers employed in both industries. Leicester did not attempt to duplicate the heavy footwear of Northampton but specialised in the production of children's and ladies' shoes. As an industry new to the town, mechanisation was more readily adopted than in Northampton. The production of knitting and boot and shoe machinery became an industry in itself, which diversified into more general engineering, employing nearly 6,500 in 1911, the third largest employment group.

The original Roman grid pattern of streets within the walled town has been retained within its subsequent expansion. Major development followed the enclosure of the South Fields in the first decade of the 19th century. This was followed by expansion to the north and east and it was not until the 1880s that much building took place west of the river. The introduction of horse tramways in the 1870s enabled development of the surrounding villages to take place and in 1888 Aylestone, Belgrave, Evington, Humberstone and Knighton were absorbed into the County Borough. Suburban growth continued following the electrification of the tramways in 1904. A particularly interesting turn of the century project was the creation of North Evington as a purpose-built town community by the architect and entrepreneur Arthur Wakerley: his town centre, comprising shops, market hall, police and fire stations, may still be seen.

Leicester was at the centre of a network of turnpike roads from the early 18th century, but coal had to be brought by packhorse trains or carts from Swannington and Whitwick. The improvement of the River Soar from the Trent to Loughborough in 1778, with its reduction in coal prices, excited the jealousy of Leicester manufacturers, but it was not until 1794 that the Soar was made navigable as far as Leicester. This enabled Erewash Valley coals to reach the town, a vital factor in the mechanisation of the worsted spinning industry. The west Leicestershire coal owners sought to protect their market in Leicester, following the failure of the Charnwood Forest Canal. The opening of the Leicester and Swannington Railway in 1832/3, the country's third locomotive railway, finally enabled them to compete with the Derbyshire coals. Only seven years later the Midland Counties Railway, promoted by the Erewash coal owners, opened through Leicester, connecting it to London via Rugby. Communications to the capital were further improved by the opening of the line to Kettering and Bedford in 1857 which reached King's Cross via the Great Northern Line. Only in 1868 was a direct Midland Railway line opened to a new terminus at St Pancras. The final link to London at Marylebone came with the Great Central Railway which reached Leicester in 1899. The construction of this line on a blue brick viaduct over a mile long just to the west of the city centre entailed the demolition of nearly five hundred houses, factories and other buildings. People were re-located in railway company-built houses in Newfoundpool and elsewhere. East-west communications were also improved by lines eastward to Peterborough via Melton Mowbray and Oakham (1846), westward to Birmingham (1864) and finally with the construction of a line from Belgrave Road station to link with the Great Northern's route to the east coast (1883).

Until the advent of a public water supply following provisions made in the Public Health Act of 1848, Leicester's water was obtained from wells which were often polluted by sewage due to the low-lying land. The Leicester Waterworks Company was established in 1851 and constructed a storage reservoir at Thornton, from which water was fed by gravity to the town in 1853. Further reservoirs followed at Cropston in 1870 and Swithland in 1896 which entailed building steam pumping stations; these were sufficient to meet demand until the opening of the Derwent Valley joint scheme in 1912.

The only means of sewage disposal until the 1850s was by way of the natural watercourses in the town with serious pollution problems in the Soar valley. Wicksteed conceived a piped scheme in 1849 which was operational by 1855. His scheme involved the treatment of effluent with lime for sale as fertiliser, but sales fell short of output. The system was also inadequate in times of flood and as an expedient a night soil bucket system was introduced in 1872, effluent being removed along the canal to the north of the town. A new pumped land irrigation system came into service in 1891 at Beaumont Leys and operated until 1964, but the Abbey Pumping Station with its four beam engines has been preserved by Leicestershire Museums.

Leicester's first gas works were opened in 1821 on a site in Belgrave beside the canal; a second works was opened in 1878 at Aylestone, by both navigable river and railway. The first works closed in 1954 and in 1969 gas production ceased in the town with the change to North Sea natural gas; some of the original buildings at Aylestone now house the John Doran Gas Museum. The first public electricity supply was also generated at the Aylestone gas works in 1894 and continued there until 1928. A second generating station was built in 1904, initially to supply DC power for the tramway system, but later extended for public supply. In 1922 a new power station at Aylestone was commissioned which was ultimately connected to the National Grid. The cooling towers using river water have now been demolished and the only generating equipment remaining is stand-by gas turbine plant.

More of the 19th-century industrial landscape survives in Leicester than in the other East Midland county towns. The buildings are notable for their high quality brickwork, with cornices and string courses incorporating moulded brick and terracotta ornamentation. The flat facades of many of the factories have been relieved by the use of pointed gables, and bay windows overlook the main entrances, presumably to enable management supervision. The most ornamental buildings are, as in Nottingham, the warehouses which are grouped in certain streets and were meant to impress the customer. Industrial buildings have survived in Leicester because of their interchangeability between its two staple industries, which both remained prosperous until recently. Their high quality makes them worthy of re-use and the lack of car parking space has been solved by selective demolition and the adaptation of ground floors. Private sector initiative has been responsible for specific developments and the local authority has confined itself to an urban renewal programme which has included the cleaning of many of Leicester's best buildings.

194. Master hosier's house in Darker Street with attached workshops.

195. Wooden storage warehouse in Butt Close Lane, in which long timbers could be stored on end.

196. The front elevation of British Steam Specialities' works in Lee Circle, indicating the high standard of brick building in Leicester in the late 19th century.

197. Raven's hosiery factory in Wheat Street, one of the canyon-like streets which were created by the replacement of earlier terraced housing by factories.

GAZETTEER
(OS sheet 140)

Several sites of interest in the city of Leicester which are within easy reach of the canal are included within the Gazetteer for Chapter Three, Section Four .

The following Gazetteer is in two sections, the first in the form of a trail in a clockwise direction around the city centre. The second section deals with the North Evington suburb, a 'green field' development begun in the late 19th century as the creation of a local architect and property speculator, Arthur Wakerley.

SECTION I

Darker Street (SK 586048), probably the only remaining example in Leicester of a three-storey master hosier's house with attached single and two-storey workshops and consequently listed. The earliest section dates from 1852, making the complex one of the last of its kind to be built in the town.

Butt Close Lane (SK 586048). Behind 66 Churchgate is a tall timber-framed and clap-boarded warehouse. The shallow roof has wide projecting eaves. This Listed building was used to season timber lengths on-end and dates from the first half of the 19th century.

74/6 Churchgate (SK 586048), at the corner of Butt Close Lane, is a four-storey factory with elaborate cornice and ornamental brickwork. The earliest section is dated 1877 and the almost identical adjoining block was added in 1896. It belonged to E. Jennings & Co, shoe manufacturers, who by 1891 were employing over 200 people. On the opposite side, only numbers 77/9 Churchgate remain as an example of paired houses with central cart entrance to back yard workshops.

Short Street (SK 587049) reflects the canyon-like appearance which must have been a feature of much of Leicester's townscape in the second half of the 19th century before street widening destroyed much of it. The domestic-style building on the east corner was part of a sewing cotton factory and probably dates from the 1830s. Adjacent on Mansfield Street are two recently cleaned buildings, the first a glove factory and the other for cigar manufacture, both originally operated by the same family.

Mansfield Street (SK 588049). On the south side is the back wall of a large factory complex extending through from Langton Street, which has now become a private courtyard. In contrast to the plain red brick rear of the building, the frontage to Langton Street boasts an elaborate doorway; there is also a water tower. The factory was originally built for shoe manufacture but is now Mansfield Knitwear.

Jubilee Road (SK 590050). Jubilee Buildings, dated 1887, are an elaborate development featuring Dutch-style pediments and first-floor bay windows. They have always been in commercial use.

Fleet Street/Lee Circle (SK 595049). An elaborately fenestrated brick building with three gables and stone ornamentation. The central archway gives access to other buildings around a quadrangle, each with separate porch entrances. The complex dates from around 1900 and one of the original occupants, British Steam Specialities, still operate there.

Wheat Street (SK 591049), another canyon-like street, was formerly lined by terraced houses which were demolished to make way for powered hosiery factories after 1870. The original blocks were extended as business boomed in the late 19th century. One company, Ravens, occupied premises on either side of the street and steam pipes were tunnelled beneath it. The buildings have been renovated as a business centre which incorporates in *Crafton Street* the Sparkenhoe Works, another relic of domestic-style hosiery workshops.

On *Erskine/Clyde Street* corner (SK 592047) is an impressive range of buildings, dating from 1888, with elaborate carved and moulded brickwork. They were erected for B. Ellis & Co., ladies' shoe manufacturers, established in 1870, who were the first to adopt a 48-hour working week in the industry. In 1891 they were employing between 400 and 500 hands, which probably included out-workers. The adjoining building on Clyde Street was added in 1889 for hosiery manufacture.

66 Humberstone Gate (SK 591047). On the corner of St James Street is a five-storey shoe factory with elaborate doorway, corner tower and dormer windows in the attic. Further along St James Street is a later steel framed building with large windows which adjoins the Boot and Shoe Trades Hall of 1902. This boasts a very elaborate facade reflecting the prosperity of this industry at the time.

44 Humberstone Gate (SK 589046), at the corner of Clarence Street, has an elaborate two-storey facade in the Renaissance manner. This fronts a plain brick three-storey block where infilled windows indicate its origin as the malt floors of the former Midland Distillery, established in 1864.

The open area down the centre of *Humberstone Gate* was originally the hay market for the town; the carts could not pass through the narrow East gate into the town itself. The market was discontinued in 1865 but the house for the former public weighbridge keeper (SK 592047), built of local granite and slate, remains near the junction with *Rutland Street*. Here, a purpose built hosiery warehouse, dated 1881, has large windows with pointed gables, a common feature of late Victorian buildings in Leicester. It forms the end of a row of small warehouses on the west side of Rutland Street which continue into the adjacent streets.

198. Wholesale clothing factories in Southampton Street, which developed to supply retail outlets.

HART & LEVY LTD.,

Wimbledon Works, LEICESTER;

AND 91, WOOD STREET, LONDON, E.C.

Manufacturers of all Classes of

CLOTHING for Men, Youths & Boys.

199. Shoe mercery warehouse in Rutland Street, Leicester.

Where *Wimbledon Street* joins *Humberstone Road* (SK 592047) is St George's Mill, a factory and warehouse which belonged to Faire Brothers, manufacturers of shoe mercery. This 28-bay long five-storey building was begun in 1887, extended in 1906 and the pedimented front to Humberstone Road was later rebuilt following a fire. The side of the mill to Morledge Street is much plainer and the engine house and private gas plant were located there.

19 Humberstone Rd (SK 592047) on the corner of Morledge Street, dated 1900, was a wholesale clothing factory. It is an example of the successful re-use of a factory building with a new facade added on the east side.

From *St George's Way* some of the surviving buildings associated with the Midland Railway may be seen. The two adjoining three and five-storey brick warehouses on *Sussex Street* (SK 596048) had both road and rail access and date from the turn of the century. Further south in *Samuel Street* (SK 595046) is the 1875 engine house and small accumulator tower for the hydraulic power system in the railway goods yard. Other warehouses have been converted for retail use.

Southampton Street boasts a fine range of buildings in street corner positions. Three of those on the north side (SK 593046) were the Wimbledon Works of Hart and Levy, wholesale clothing manufacturers. The four-storey block on the east corner of Wimbledon Street is particularly fine, with a parapet which was originally topped with ornamental urns. The factories-cum-warehouses date from the last two decades of the 19th century.

47 Rutland Street (SK 592046) at the corner of Southampton St, Alexandra House, is one of the finest of the city's warehouses. This was built for Faire Brothers, shoe mercers, in 1897 and has a buff terracotta facade, marble plinth, elaborate parapet and corner tower, which was once topped by a dome. The semi-circular windows in the top storey are echoed by those of the adjoining warehouse extension in Rutland Street and those of St George's Mills, all belonging to the same firm and all designed by Edward Burgess.

78/80 Rutland Street (SK 592046) on the west side is a contrasting building showing strong vertical motifs. The four-storey building with basement was built as a leather warehouse in 1922/3 and is said to be a replica of the original owner's headquarters in the USA.

Queen Street (SK 592045). On the north side is the former Hide Market where the raw materials for the leather industry were collected. A two-storey block fronts open sheds supported on cast iron pillars surrounding a stone paved yard. On the opposite side is a large four-storey hosiery factory, now belonging to Courtaulds, which consists of two blocks linked at either end.

Rutland Street. On the south corner by the church (SK 592045) is a former shoe warehouse, built 1897, which supplied retail shops. Like other warehouses in this area, there is a top storey with semi-circular windows and parapet, here topped by pointed gables and tower. On the other side of the churchyard are Carron Buildings, built in 1899 as a leather warehouse. Adjacent is the original exchange building erected by the National Telephone Company in 1898. On the corner of *Colton Street* is a very elaborate buff brick shoe warehouse, built *c*.1875. On either side of the corner doorway are two medallions, probably Minerva and Mercury, but holding modern transport emblems in the form of a railway engine and a sailing ship.

Charles Street was widened in 1932 and largely rebuilt. The Cherub hosiery factory (SK 591044) reflects the architecture of this period. It is significant that even at this date large factories, employing mainly female labour, were still being built in the city centre. Opposite at the corner of *Northampton Street* (SK 591042) is a dark red brick hosiery factory of four storeys plus basement, with water tower for a fire sprinkler system.

London Road Station (SK 593040). The second station constructed on this site by the former Midland Railway, it was designed by Charles Trubshaw and built between 1885 and 1902. There is extensive terracotta ornamentation both on the station building and on the bridge parapet on the opposite side of the road. Recent modernisation has preserved the facade, unlike some other stations on the London line.

In *Nelson Street*, opposite the station (SK 593039), is an interesting Art Deco factory built in 1932 for the manufacture by Goddards of their well-known silver plate powder and polish.

200 & 201. Shoe warehouses in Rutland Street, elaborately decorated to impress buyers.

York Street. At the corner of *Granby Street* (SK 590042) is a former shoe factory, probably dating from the 1860s, with elaborate tiled cornice which has been cleaned to good effect. Adjacent extensions were built in the 1880s for the same shoe manufacturer. Number 16, with brick arcading, is dated 1888 and was designed by Wakerley for a wholesale manufacturing confectioner.

45 Chatham Street (SK 589041), on the corner of *Stamford Street*, was built in 1868 for a shoe manufacturer in classic Victorian style. Adjoining, in Stamford Street, are the plainer but tasteful Stamford Buildings, dated 1901 and 1902. These were originally warehouses but, like the corner block, were later used for hosiery manufacture. In the same street is a much earlier pedimented building with a wall mounted crane serving side loading doors. This was built in 1851 for a wool stapler.

Belvoir Street is now lined with retail shops, many of them inserted into former leather and yarn warehouses. The upper two storeys are largely unaltered and have elaborate cornices and pillared windows. On the corner of *Albion Street* (SK 588042), the building with an impressive terracotta facade was a leather warehouse purpose-built in 1887 to include ground floor shops.

Bowling Green Street (SK 588042). On the east side are the former offices of the Leicester Waterworks Company, built in 1865 in Gothic style. On the opposite corner a hosiery warehouse now forms part of a multiple store.

Wellington Street (SK 588041). A range of warehouses once lined both sides of this street which was laid out in the second decade of the 19th century. The earlier ones remaining nearer Belvoir Street are in plain domestic style in contrast to the Italianate style of numbers 11-13, built *c*.1865. On the opposite side, at the corner of *Dover Street*, is Pick's hosiery factory *c*.1913 with characteristic decorated corner entrance block. Its curtain wall construction contrasts with that of the earlier warehouses.

Running parallel to Wellington Street is *New Walk*, a promenade laid out by the Corporation in 1785 and once lined with genteel houses, many of which have been converted for office use or replaced by new office blocks.

35 King Street (SK 588040), at the corner of Marlborough Street, dates from 1851. Originally a hosiery factory, it is built around an interior courtyard with plain domestic-style windows and an elaborate cornice. There are later curtain wall extensions along King Street. On the opposite side of King Street is *Cramant's Yard*, a restored row of court housing, a type which was once common in Leicester. Some of the cottages date from the 1820s and at least one housed a knitting frame.

Duke Street (SK 588039), parallel to King Street, has several adjoining late 19th- and early 20th-century four- and five-storey hosiery factories. One has a white tiled wall, presumably to reflect light into the opposite factory. Nearby, *39/41 Welford Road* (SK 587039) is one of the few surviving hosiery factories on this street, dating from the 1860s. It is typical of the period with domestic-style windows and an elaborate cornice.

Lower Brown Street (SK 586039) is another canyon-like street lined with textile factories. On the west side is a five-storey red brick hosiery factory of 1892 with an elaborate central cart entrance. This originally gave access to a courtyard around which were small workshops dating from the 1850s. The buildings have recently been refurbished. Continuing into *Upper Brown Street*, Jubilee Buildings (SK 586041), dated 1887, was a shoe factory while the taller adjacent block was built for corset manufacture.

Newarke Street has been widened, leaving only the north building line intact. At the west corner of *Marble Street* (SK 586042), the original plain domestic-style factory made fancy hosiery, while on the opposite corner the more decorative Enfield Buildings were built for a yarn merchant. Beyond the public house, on Newarke Street, the three-storey plus basement hosiery factory of the 1880s has a variety of window styles and gabled main entrance.

Oxford Street (SK 585040). Now the Clephan Building of the De Montfort University, this fine factory was built for I. & R. Morley, the prominent hosiery manufacturers, in 1888. The central entrance block has a large oriel window below a flattened dome. Adjacent, on *Bonners Lane* corner, the University has also taken over a former early 20th-century shoe factory which has a prominent corner domed feature. The contrast between the public facade and the utilitarian rear of these buildings can be seen from Bonners Lane.

202. The present Leicester railway station on London Road, with elaborate buff terracotta decoration.

203. Court housing at Cramant's Yard, typical of much of Leicester's 19th-century townscape.

204. The fine hosiery factory on Oxford Street built for I. & R. Morley in 1888.

On *Southgates* (SK 584042), a former hosiery factory has recently been converted to office use; the site had been used by Strettons for nearly 200 years. The present corner building with four pointed gables dates from the 1890s whilst the adjoining section down Castle Street with its functionless chateau-like corner tower dates from 1913.

At the corner of *St Nicholas Place* and *Guildhall Lane*, another narrow original street, the curved three-storey block (SK 584045) was formerly a cigar factory with elaborate shop facades at street level. The adjacent rendered building with tile inserts was a cheese warehouse which dates from the 1860s.

SECTION II

The North Evington Suburb

The area which became known as North Evington lies to the south east of Leicester and was later described thus:

> much of the lower area consisted of disused clay-pits, full of water. On the eastern slope of the spinney was a series of escarpments, oozing with mud ... the only tracks of any kind were two agricultural sloughs ... and one or two footpaths.

This unprepossessing land belonged to three principal landlords in the 1870s, who saw potential in the eastward expansion of Leicester beyond the Midland Railway. A young architect, Arthur Wakerley, employed in planning the original layout of the new development, began purchasing parcels of land on his own account in 1885. Wakerley envisaged the building of a suburb complete in itself with services that would make it independent of the adjoining town and create a coherent community. By 1907 North Evington was advertised as 'The Most Rapidly Developed and Prosperous Manufacturing District in England ... with Roads made paved and sewered' with 'double electric car service' (trams). The layout and construction of streets and services and the erection of good quality terraced and larger houses, as well as factories and workshops, proceeded apace. The first factory was complete, awaiting a tenant, in 1888 and by 1900 eleven more had been completed. By the beginning of the First World War there were 28 factories, employing 5,170 people in 31 different trades. Since the suburb was developed after Leicester had diversified from its staple hosiery industry, many of these were involved in boot and shoe manufacture and engineering.

The developer's ambitions were perhaps not entirely fulfilled, although the nucleus of a town centre with indoor and outdoor markets, police and fire stations, shops, post office and banks, was completed. The more prestigious housing, such as that in Wood Hill, and most of the retail shops were built by Wakerley himself. Much of the ordinary terraced housing was left to local speculative builders, whose different identities can be determined from the patterns used for lintels, sills and door cases. This can be particularly well seen in Asfordby and Baggrave Streets and Prospect Hill. Even at this late date, many of the houses were built with cart access arches to back yard workshops. The increased mobility of the 20th century meant that the inhabitants could travel elsewhere both to work and shop, and so the independent community was never fully realised. However much remains, comparatively unaltered, of the infrastructure, houses, workshops and factories, the latter still accommodating a variety of industries. In the following gazetteer, the factories are listed under their original industry type, but now fulfil a variety of purposes.

205. Asfordby Street works, one of several in North Evington intermingled with terraced housing.

206. Terraced housing by Arthur Woodcock in Asfordby Street, showing his trademark in the patterned lintels.

Manufacturing Industry: Boots and Shoes

Asfordby Street. Number 20, the Asfordby Street Works (SK 606046), is a three-storey factory with basement and stepped front gable. Numbers 92 and 100 (SK 606048) are also three storey with basement, one of 1891 with three pointed gables and first-floor bay window and the other of later date with much larger windows and round gable. Between here and Green Lane Road is a row of terraced houses with distinctive lintels by the local builder Arthur Woodcock, more of whose houses can be seen in Baggrave Street. At the corner of *Atkinson Street* (SK 606047) are the former premises of the Anchor Boot and Shoe Company, erected in 1895. This was a workers' co-operative organisation from which emerged the Garden Suburb at Humberstone, a co-partnership housing project which commenced building on a 17-acre site in 1907.

Baggrave Street (SK 607049). This street contains examples of shoe manufacture carried on in both back yard workshops and factories. Number 108, typical of many houses in the area, has an arch giving cart access to back yard workshops. Number 49/51, a typical three-storey plus basement factory, has round window heads and decorative tile work. Nearly opposite, number 88 is a smaller two-storey factory.

Granby Avenue (SK 605046). Numbers 16 and 18 are two-storey small workshops built on either side of an access passage to other workshops which utilise the space behind terraced houses.

Halstead Street (SK 605048). The Wood Hill end of this street is closed off by Wakerley's first factory, which was completed in 1888 but remained empty until 1890 when a shoe manufacturer was found to occupy it. It is a well-designed building with elaborate windows. There is cart access from *Wood Hill*, where the tenant occupied one of the substantial Wakerley-designed houses on this street. A series of steps from Halstead Street gives access to Wakerley's second factory on Wood Hill with its distinctive square tower.

Linden Street (SK 609042). A large shoe factory occupying the entire street frontage between Dorothy and Constance Roads, with a gable end to each of the latter. It was built in 1912 for F. J. Palfreyman and Company, whose name appears on a stone lintel.

207. One of the functional factories built for the developing boot and shoe industry in Linden Street, Leicester.

208. Housing in Baggrave Street with cart access to workshops at rear.

209. Elaborate terraced housing in North Evington.

210. The police and fire station on Asfordby Street, part of Arthur Wakerley's projected town centre.

211. A shop in the Wakerley-designed shopping area of North Evington.

212. Framework knitters' cottages in Lower Bond Street, Hinckley.

Prospect Road (SK 605049). Factories and houses are built on the steep hill down to Green Lane Road. The factory on the south corner of Sylvan Avenue, with semi-circular top floor windows, contrasts with the smaller two-storey building opposite. The houses, built in pairs on Burnaby Avenue, are an early development whilst those on Prospect Hill have shared front porches and have been the subject of a regeneration programme.

99/101 Rolleston Street (SK· 607047). Two houses, dated 1882, with cart access arch to a rear workshop.

St Saviour's Road was mainly developed after 1900 and is lined with larger factories, shops and some housing. The earlier buildings were designed by Arthur Wakerley. On the north side, Park Vale Works (SK 610044) were built in the late 1890s as an integrated shoe factory, with large ranges of single storey north light workshops to the rear of the elaborate street frontage. Cart access was under the distinctive tower. Just to the east at the corner of Benson Street is a second smaller factory with gabled ends.

Manufacturing Industry: Engineering

St Saviour's Road (SK 609044). The Corona Machine Tool Works with tiled pediment and porch were built in 1911 for Frederick Pollard. Nearer East Park Road are some substantial semi-detached houses of Wakerley design. Further along St Saviour's Road at the corner of Temple Road (SK 613042) are the former Faraday Works built for Gent's electrical engineering firm, complete with clock of their manufacture. In *Temple Road* itself (SK 614042) is the Art-Deco factory built *c.*1920 for Steels and Busks, suppliers of corset stiffeners for local elastic web manufacturers.

Public Utilities

Asfordby and Baggrave Streets (SK 606047) form the centre of Wakerley's North Evington. The Market Hall, now a club, stands in a central position and market stalls once occupied the adjacent open space. Other public buildings are situated on Asfordby Street, such as the fire and police stations. Retail shops, which originally included a bank, cafe and coffee palace, stretch down Wood Hill.

Gedding Road (SK 611041). Wakerley not only built large private houses but assisted the Corporation's attempts to alleviate the shortage of housing after the First World War with his £299 house. There are several pairs of these semi-detached residences, some in an unaltered state.

Gwendolen Road/St Margaret Road (SK 610041). Wakerley's charitable activities are commemorated in the Blind Institution erected on land donated by him during his mayoralty in 1897-8. Substantial workshops are included where basket manufacture is still carried on.

5: The Leicestershire Market Towns

HINCKLEY, in the south-west corner of the county near the Warwickshire border, is known as 'the cradle and home of the hosiery trade' because of a claim that the first stocking frame outside London was recorded here in 1640. The industry grew rapidly, making the town the most important hosiery centre in the county: in 1778 the trade occupied nearly half the total population who worked 864 stocking frames. By 1844 the number of frames in Hinckley and the surrounding villages of Barwell, Burbage, Earl Shilton, Stoke Golding and Dadlington had risen to 3,500. Unlike Loughborough, no spinning was carried out and yarn was obtained from Leicester and the West Midlands. Hinckley remained a one-industry town until the end of the century when shoe manufacture was introduced.

There is little archaeological evidence for its 17th-century industry apart from the important timber-framed cottages in Lower Bond Street. The buildings remaining represent the transition to powered machines in the last three decades of the 19th century, with small utilitarian factory buildings. From these several large firms, such as Atkins, emerged to dominate the 20th-century industry. The scale of change can be appreciated by comparing their cottages and factory facing each other across Lower Bond Street. Like Leicester, the prosperity of the hosiery industry has ensured the survival of factories but recent trade recession has put many of its buildings at risk.

Hinckley's two major satellite villages of Barwell and Earl Shilton were both also important framework knitting centres, but diversified even more than Hinckley into boot and shoe manufacture towards the end of the 19th century.

GAZETTEER
(OS sheet 140)

Manufacturing Industries: Textiles

Lower Bond Street (SP 425941). On the west side of the street are two timber framed thatched cottages which probably date from the end of the 17th century although they were heavily restored in the 1920s. The street elevation is more heavily fenestrated than was normal for cottages of this date, while at the rear are two long first-floor windows characteristic of framework knitting. The cottages are preserved by the hosiery firm of Atkins and contain several early knitting machines. On the opposite side of the road are the four-storey blocks of their present factory, mostly built between 1877 and 1910. There are later extensions to the side and rear, the latter including workshops built to accommodate the large and heavy fully-fashioned hose machines introduced in the 1930s. The premises overshadow the domestic-style Unitarian chapel of 1722 at the back with which the Atkins family, like other hosiers, were connected.

Upper Bond Street (SP 426943). On the west side of the street are two large factories, one of them with only two storeys remaining from the original four. These buildings, with segmental headed windows, extend through to Factory Road at the rear. The adjacent property is of later date, steel framed and concrete faced, with an ornamental rounded corner which contrasts with the plain 'Workpeople' entrance at the other end of the building.

Castle Street (SP 431940). Some of the three-storey houses on the north side, now shops, were originally used for framework knitting as can be seen from the rear second-storey long windows which are visible from Wood Street.

Druid Street. A number of factories of different styles may be seen on the corners of Albert Road and Spencer Street; these range from the 1930s Art Deco factory at the corner of Albert Street to the plainer red brick two-and three-storey structures dating from *c*.1900 (SP 427943). On the opposite side adjacent to Neale's Yard are the former 'Unique' works of William Puffer, dated 1911, where the first experimental knitting of rayon stockings was first carried out (SP 428945). Adjoining is an interesting survival of the earlier framework knitting trade, with the former works of Tanseys, makers of needles and sinkers.

Factory Road, formerly Back Lane, was developed for industrial purposes at the end of the 19th century. On the west side are several small two-storey factories, including one on *Gopsall Road* (SP 426945) with blind arcading and cast iron windows. The works on the opposite side of Factory Road are mostly linked to premises fronting on to Upper Bond Street.

Hill Street (SP 430939). An elegant buff brick factory with unusual gothic windows picked out in white brick. The acute angle at the south end conforms to the building plot adjacent to a narrow alley, a common feature in Hinckley.

213. Hosiery factory on Hill Street, Hinckley, with unusual gothic windows.

214. Framework knitters' top shop on Wood Street, Earl Shilton.

215. A functional hosiery factory on Upper Bond Street, Hinckley.

216. Hinckley's most elegant industrial structure, built in 1891 to store water.

John Street (SP 431945). A two-storey domestic-style factory with north light workshops at the rear.

Queens Road/Southfields Road (SP 433935). This two-storey 15-bay factory has cast iron windows and, when built for the Manchester Hosiery Manufacturing Company, was situated in open countryside.

Trinity Lane (SP 425941) A large factory, formerly Botts as marked on the roof, with pedimented facade and large cart entrance. There are several phases of building, the earliest *c*.1900 with one extension marked 'GB 1912'.

Manufacturing Industry: Boot and Shoes

Upper Bond Street (SK 427944). A turn of the century four-storey brick factory used for shoe manufacture by Finns until very recently.

45 Factory Road (SP 426944). A two-storey ornamental brick factory, dated 1896, originally built for J. Harris & Co, Boot Manufacturer.

John Street (SP 431945) The former Highfields Works were built for shoe manufacture around 1900. The central tower carried a clock as well as serving for water storage.

Public Utilities

Water Tower, behind Highfields Road (SP 431944). This is probably Hinckley's most elegant industrial structure, built to store water from Snarestone pumping station 14 miles to the north. The cast iron tank with its iron railings rests on a brick tower built in 1891.

BARWELL was a framework knitting village, but since all its 400 frames which Felkin noted in 1844 were narrow ones employed on fashioned hose, poverty was rife. Its population remained static until the 1880s, when the boot and shoe industry became predominant. The village development is disjointed but remnants of several phases of the boot and shoe industry can be detected. The second edition of the 25-inch OS map indicates the existence of several rows of garden wall workshops, similar to many in Northamptonshire villages. Remnants of such a row can be found behind *34/42 High Street* houses (SP 443967), near the Barracks. The earlier factory phase can be seen on *King Street* and *George Street* (SP 446969), also the Mill Street/Goose Lane corner (SP 441964), where there are two-storey brick factories with loading doors and wall mounted cranes. Particularly interesting is the early 20th-century development of elaborate office blocks fronting extensive north light workshops. This is well shown on *Arthur Street* (SP 447970) and *Kirkby Road* (SP 445972), where the front blocks are single storey. On *Hill Street* (SP 448968) and *Stapleton Lane* (SP 443971) there are two-storey blocks with elaborate brickwork and stone ornamentation.

EARL SHILTON is a long straggling village in which framework knitting again predominated in the first half of the 19th century. Felkin's survey indicates that in 1844 there were 600 narrow frames at work; there were no wide frames, which as in Barwell may account for the fall in population between 1851 and 1881. There are few remains of domestic framework knitting in the village, but there is a pair of topshop houses at *100 Wood Street* (SP 462977) and some long windows on the ground floor of a terrace of houses at *9/21 Hinckley Road* (SK 460976). Across the yard here are small heated single storey workshops which were probably built for basket work in the boot and shoe industry. This penetrated the village towards the end of the century and several factories were established, largely for ladies' shoes and slippers. In *New Street* (SP 460976) are several three-storey brick factories with cast iron windows while at number 94 is a single storey factory with extensive north light sheds, representing the later phases of the industry. In 1896 there were 12 boot and shoe factories, most of which have been altered or demolished.

LOUGHBOROUGH lies on a gravel terrace above the flood level of the River Soar near the important crossing at Cotes, where the 13th-century bridge and causeway still form part of the present Nottingham Road. The elaborate 15th-century parish church bears witness to its importance in the medieval wool trade. Its geographical position between the wilderness of Charnwood Forest and the flood plain of the Soar hindered town growth, and it was not until the sale of the manorial estates in the first decades of the 19th century that the town outgrew its medieval plan. The release of land, coupled with the availability of cheap coal following the opening of the Loughborough Navigation in 1778, paved the way for industrial growth during the 19th century. It was already an important centre for worsted spinning, putting out yarn to both its own framework knitters and those of the surrounding villages. Machine lace manufacture was introduced from Nottingham, resulting in the town's first population boom in the 1820s. Once hosiery production was mechanised in the 1870s, the town underwent its major expansion, growing from 11,710 in 1871 to 21,508 by 1901.

Loughborough's position astride the main Leicester to Derby road, turnpiked in 1726, made it an important coaching centre. The canalisation of the Soar was extended from Loughborough to Leicester in 1794, eventually connecting the town to the national waterway system to the south. Connection to the Leicestershire coalfield via the Charnwood Forest Canal was less successful. However, Loughborough's situation in the Soar valley ensured its place on the first main line railway to be built in the region, with a station on the Midland Counties in 1840. This maintained cheap supplies of Erewash valley coal for the town's growing industries, but it was not until 1883 that a direct rail link was established to the west Leicestershire coalfield across Charnwood Forest. Loughborough's excellent communications were further improved by the opening of the Great Central Railway in 1899, parts of which still survive as a working steam railway.

New industries moved into the town, attracted by its good communications, development land and a skilled male labour force made available by the mechanisation of hosiery and consequent employment of women. Engineering became of great importance, with Brush Electrical Engineering being established in 1889 and Herbert Morris' crane works in 1897. Loughborough is a classic example of the growth of a small market town through industrialisation, and much of its 19th-century landscape survives. The quality of brickwork and terracotta decoration, both in the factories and terraced housing, is testimony to the products of Tucker's brickworks, who also provided the bricks for St Pancras station and the London Airport terminals. Nothing remains of their works beside the Great Central Railway south of the town except the flooded brick pit now known as Charnwood Water.

GAZETTEER
(OS sheet 129)

Sites of interest within easy reach of the canal are included within the Gazetteer for Chapter Three: Section 4.

Transport

Great Central Station (SK 543193). The station, inscribed 'GCR 1898', is now the headquarters of the Great Central Railway and steam-hauled trains run to the outskirts of Leicester at Birstall. The engine sheds are open to visitors.

217. Hosiery factory in Duke Street, Loughborough, *above left*, which has a blank rear wall.

218. Needle factory in Albert Street, Loughborough, *above right*, one of many which supplied the hosiery industry.

219. Great Central Railway station, Loughborough, still functioning on a preserved steam-hauled railway.

220. Cartwright and Warner's woollen spinning mill on Queen's Road, Loughborough.

221. Taylor's bell foundry on Cobden Street, Loughborough, one of the only two surviving bell foundries in Britain.

222. The former I. & R. Morley hosiery factory on Nottingham Road, Loughborough.

223. Housing for textile machinery factory workers in Pinfold Gate, Loughborough.

224. Herbert Morris' engineering works on Empress Road, Loughborough, which back on to the canal.

225. The Brush Company's Falcon works on Nottingham Road, Loughborough, with direct access to the Midland Railway.

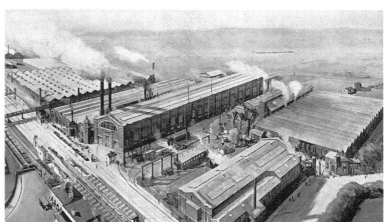

226. Nottingham Manufacturing Company's hosiery factory in Moor Lane, Loughborough (from *Leicester Chamber of Commerce Yearbook*, 1921).

Midland Station, Nottingham Road (SK 544204). This is the second Midland Station, opened in 1872, which still retains decorative canopy supports. The original station was on the opposite side of Nottingham Road, where the stationmaster's house is heavily disguised by factory units. It was to this station that Thomas Cook brought his first railway excursion in 1841.

Manufacturing Industries: Textiles

Albert Street (SK 535192). A small factory with large windows which belonged to the Grudgings family of knitting machine needle makers who also had premises in School Street.

Clarence Street (SK 541201). On the south side a three-storey grey brick factory with elaborate lintels and cornice which was built in the 1870s. The attic mending windows are reminiscent of Nottingham lace factories.

Duke Street (SK 539200). An interesting two-storey brick factory with segmental headed windows, dating from the 1870s. There are no windows in the rear wall which overlooked the town workhouse.

Great Central Road (SK 544192). A lace factory, whose domestic style belies its date of 1921.

Off *Meadow Lane* (SK 539101). A small two-storey workshop, dating from the 1880s, which produced knitting machine needles. It has windows in all four walls. On *Meadow Lane* itself (SK 539200) are two factories opposite one another which catered for hosiery finishing and packaging. The 16-bay factory on the west side was a dyeworks, while that on the east produced cardboard boxes.

Moor Lane (SK 541194). This large factory, founded by the Nottingham Manufacturing Company, dates from 1888, a rebuild following fires in 1881 and 1887. The firm acquired the rights to use the Cotton patent knitting machines. The ornamental corner tower disguises a sprinkler system storage tank.

Nottingham Road (SK 543202). Another factory built for a Nottingham firm, I. & R. Morley, in 1889. The elegant pedimented facade is best seen from the canal towpath, but the canal basin underneath has been infilled.

Pinfold Gate (SK 539196). The only surviving purpose-built domestic framework knitters' houses in the town, with large windows lighting top floor workshops. Opposite is an example of a different type of industrial housing, built by William Cotton to house employees of his adjacent hosiery machine factory. They have intricate cast iron windows and a cart entrance to the works, of which no trace now remains.

Queen's Road (SK 542206). The extensive premises of the important firm of Cartwright and Warner were begun in 1794 alongside the Leicester Navigation. The firm were originally worsted spinners but pioneered steam-powered hosiery manufacture and the production of shrink-proof woollen yarns. Some of the surviving buildings date from the 1830s and there are pedimented three-storey buildings facing both Queen's Road and the canal.

Manufacturing Industry: Engineering

Cobden Street (SK 542198). Taylor's Bell Foundry was established in Loughborough in 1839 and moved here in 1859, as shown by a datestone. Along with Whitechapel in London, Taylor's continue their traditional craft and have created a Museum. Visitors can also see the foundry where bells are still cast and tuned (tel. 0509 212241). The corner tower contains a small carillon but Taylor's also made the 47-bell carillon in *Queens Park* (SK 533194), erected as a war memorial in 1923.

Empress Road (SK 546195). The former East Works of Herbert Morris were built alongside the canal in 1897 for the manufacture of pulley blocks and lifting machinery. Subsequently the West Works were added in 1902 opposite and the South Works beside *Windmill Road* were completed in 1917. The firm became important manufacturers of overhead cranes and continue to trade as Davy-Morris at the North Works on *Meadow Lane* (SK 539029).

Falcon Works, Nottingham Road (SK 543206). Development on this greenfield site, adjacent to the Midland Railway, began when Henry Hughes purchased seven acres for the manufacture of steam locomotives and tramcars in 1865. Later known as the Falcon Engineering and Car Works, it was taken over by the Anglo-American Brush Electric Light Corporation in 1889, who were seeking premises outside London. The business continues as part of the Hawker Siddeley Group and some of the original buildings remain on the now vast site.

6: The Northamptonshire Shoe Towns

NORTHAMPTON's medieval prosperity was derived from an extensive wool and cloth trade, making it in the 14th century one of the six wealthiest towns in England. In the late Middle Ages the cloth industry declined because of guild pressure and was slowly replaced by the leather industry for which the town is internationally renowned. In the early 16th century over 20 per cent of the town's taxpayers were involved in leather trades but this was not significantly higher than in comparable towns. Yet a century later it was in Northampton that Cromwell placed his order for boots for the army in Ireland. Further wars in the 17th and 18th centuries stimulated this aspect of the leather industry so that by the time of the Napoleonic wars Northampton was producing between 10,000 and 20,000 pairs of army boots a week. The town continued to specialise in men's footwear, although its shoemakers were notoriously resistant to the introduction of machinery, a factor which may have contributed to the rapid mechanisation of the industry in the other shoe towns.

The carriage of boots and shoes from Northampton to its principal market, London, was restricted to road transport until the second decade of the 19th century. The River Nene was improved for navigation to Northampton by 1761 but only provided an eastward connection. The town was by-passed by the main canal system when the projected link from Market Harborough was abandoned and it was not until 1815 that Northampton was linked to the Grand Junction Canal at Gayton. Northampton was equally unfortunate with railways as all the main north-south lines to London passed it by. The town's first railway station in Bridge Street was on the cross country line between Peterborough and the London and Birmingham Railway at Blisworth, opened in 1845. Castle Station, the second, was built on the line to Market Harborough, opened in 1859. A third station, St John's, was erected in 1872 as a terminus of a line to Bedford. The town only lost its branch line status in 1881/2, when a loop line was built between Rugby and Roade, giving the town a direct link to the capital. This is the only line now working and uses the rebuilt Castle station. Northampton, compared with the other three East Midland county towns, was at a tremendous disadvantage in both its canal and rail transport, upon which it relied for fuel supplies as there were no coal seams in the county.

A private waterworks company was established in 1837 which built the Ravensthorpe reservoir to supply the town. This was enlarged in 1884 following its purchase by the corporation; a second reservoir was constructed in the nearby Hollowell valley in 1917. The gas works, established in 1823, remained a private company right through to nationalisation in 1949. Their works were on the Mill Holme, by the Nene and the canal link to facilitate coal supplies. Electricity was available in 1891 following the opening of a generating plant in Angel Street, later augmented by the Nunn's Mill power station by the River Nene.

Northampton borough extended its boundaries in 1900, nearly trebling the town area, when the Kingsthorpe, St James and Far Cotton parishes were included. The population in 1901 was 87,000 (39 per cent of the county total) and then increased very slowly for the next three decades to 92,000 in 1931. Transport within the town was improved by the private provision of horse tramcars in 1881, the private company being purchased by the Corporation in 1902. The system was electrified two years later when a separate generating station was built in Castle Street. This used steam from a refuse destructor plant until closure in 1934, by which date the trams had all been replaced by motor buses.

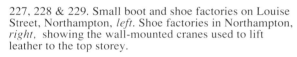

227, 228 & 229. Small boot and shoe factories on Louise Street, Northampton, *left*. Shoe factories in Northampton, *right*, showing the wall-mounted cranes used to lift leather to the top storey.

230. Shoe factories on
Dunster Street, Northampton.

The historic industrial landscape of the town is still dominated by the boot and shoe industry. This was organised on a putting-out or basket work basis, with much of the lighter work being carried out in garden or back yard workshops; fewer of these survive in Northampton than in the other shoe towns. Those which do remain are two-storey, sometimes attached to the house, rather than the detached rows of single storey workshops found elsewhere. The terraced housing fronting these workshops is of good quality and unusually the party walls were extended above roof height to prevent fire spreading, following an Improvement Act of 1846. Many of these houses were built by the Freehold Land Society, which by 1893 had provided around 25 per cent of the town's housing. Multi-storey boot and shoe factories developed in Northampton from the 1870s. Most of the early factories were small and it is only at the turn of the 20th century that big firms like Manfields built large scale factory complexes with single storey north light workshops. Compared with Nottingham or Leicester, the town centre has been redeveloped on a much larger scale but significant industrial buildings still survive around the periphery. The skyline of Northampton is now characterised by two modern industrial buildings, the heavily glazed Carlsberg Brewery beside the river and the 127m-high concrete Express lift testing tower in the western part of the town.

GAZETTEER
(OS sheet 152)

*(arranged in **approximate** clockwise order, starting in the northern part of the town)*

St George's Street (SP 753612). The Phoenix Boot Works, built for J. Marlow and Sons in 1890, on a corner site with a prominent tower and dome. The four-storey extension was added in 1895 especially to accommodate machine welting plant on the Goodyear system, the first British firm to do so.

Kingsthorpe Road (SP 752620), the Footshape Boot Works, a magnificent edifice with buff terracotta

ornamentation. This was built in 1913 by the Scottish
architect A. E. Anderson for Barratt's as a centre for
their new bespoke mail order footwear system,
whereby customers sent in an outline pattern of their
feet and received custom-made shoes by return. The
firm also operated a chain of retail shoe shops.

Louise Street (SP 757613), shows a typical piecemeal
development of the 1880s with two-storey houses
intermingled among two- and three-storey plus
basement factories. This is echoed in adjoining
Lorne Road, where a well-built shoe factory has been
re-windowed for office use. Upper class houses of
contemporary date can be seen on *Watkin Terrace*,
their balconied bay windows facing the old
racecourse.

Oakley Street (SP 758613) has a good example of the
two-storey back yard workshops which were a feature
of Northampton. This modest street contrasts with
Duke Street which was lined with larger multi-
storeyed factories on both sides, some with wall
mounted cranes. A proportion survive but others
have been replaced by new houses and featureless
industrial units.

Earl Street (SP 760611). On the corner of Clare
Street the classic three-storey plus basement factory
with fully glazed roof was formerly Allinson's Crispin
Works.

Gray Street (SP 761613). On the north side a classic
factory with an ornamental centre pediment and wall
mounted crane. Maximum use of the site is made by
plainly constructed side wings off the main spine of
the building. In adjacent *Shakespeare Road*, the
street corners have been utilised for factory
development: at *Hood Street* the rendered factory
has a polychrome brick decorative cornice and a wall

231. Marlow's Shoe Factory on St George's Street,
Northampton, with an elaborate corner tower.

crane, while that on *Cowper Street*, inscribed 'Cowper Works', was built in several stages and also has a wall
crane. At the south end of Shakespeare Road is *Carey Street* with a red brick L-shaped factory with cast iron
segmental headed windows.

Clare Street (SP 761612). The factory of G. M. Tebbutt & Sons, on the corner of Grove Road, was founded in
1872 and shoes were made there until 1968. It demonstrates both phases of machine-made shoe manufacture, the
earlier multi-storey factory and the later single storey building with glazed roof lights fronting Clare Street.

Overstone Road (SP 760609) contains several factories but most interesting are the tall Dutch-style buildings at
the corner of *Dunster Street*, where the top windows have wooden louvres indicating their use by leather dressers.
On the corner of *St Michael's Road* (SP 758608) is the important factory of G. T. Hawkins which was established
in 1886. On the north side of St Michael's Road, many of the terraced houses have two-storey workshops at the
rear, some of which back on to single storey factories in Dunster Street itself. On the south side of St Michael's
Road are a number of shoe factories and leather works, some with cast iron windows and loading cranes: the latest
seems to be R. E. Tricker Ltd., built in 1903 with a brown glazed tiled exterior.

232. The former shoe mercery warehouse on Derngate in Northampton, now a theatre.

233. Corn warehouse by the River Nene in Bridge Street, Northampton.

234. Manfield's factory on Wellingborough Road, Northampton, an elaborate office frontage to single storey workshops.

Henry Street and *Talbot Road* are two parallel streets running into *Artizan Road*, the southern half of which was laid out by 1884. On Talbot Road (SP 765611) two classic shoe factories face one another; on the north side is the 'Normal Boot and Shoe Factory' of 1889, ornamented with ironstone lintels and a central pediment. Opposite is the complex factory which once belonged to Norvic where electricity was generated by gas engine. This has single storey sheds behind the multi-storey front block. Five smaller works may be found in Henry Street, number 52 being dated 1890. *Artizan Road* has some good quality two-storey terraced houses and on the corner of *Billington Street* a three-storey factory with pedimented corner porch.

Adnitt Street (SP 768614) possesses an elegant three-storey factory, dated 1913, which was formerly the Trueform works. It is now re-windowed and converted into flats. In nearby *Magee Street* (SP 766614) is the large factory of Crockett and Jones, the older section with stone pediment and cornices and a later curtain walled section extending into Perry Street.

Wellingborough Road (SP 772614) was in open country in 1892, when Manfields opened their new factory near Abington Park. First established in Northampton in 1844, the firm had a superb Italianate warehouse in Campbell Square which was regrettably demolished in the 1980s. Their new factory was of revolutionary design in that all processes were accommodated on one level behind a 400-feet street frontage. In 1908 the firm employed 1,000 people and made 400,000 pairs of shoes. The exterior of the building has the appearance of a public institution, but fronts north light sheds. Adjacent is a splendid Victorian public house, the *Abington Hotel*, which still has its own small brewery. Nearer the town, south of Wellingborough Road, on *Christchurch Road* is a two-storey dark red brick factory, with north light sheds to the rear: this was built in the 1920s for the Co-operative Wholesale Society for shoe manufacture.

Between Wellingborough Road and the more elegant Billing Road, a large area of factories and housing was developed in the last quarter of the 19th century. Much of this has been demolished but a representative selection remains, the factories being nearly all three storey with wall mounted cranes. In *Stockley Street* (SP 767607) are three factories, all with cast iron windows. The factory in *Palmerston Road* (SP 765608) is ornamented with Gothic arches and buff brick pilasters. On *Woodford Street* is an interesting complex, consisting of two-storey workshops, a factory with Gothic cast iron windows and another of 1875 date which has now been converted into 'The Works' warehouse apartments. On *Victoria Road* is a whole range of small factories, one opposite Harold Street dated 1873.

The more elaborate buildings remaining in *Derngate* (SP 758604) and *Fish Street* (SP 759605) reflect their function as trading rather than manufacturing establishments. The Derngate Theatre incorporates the preserved facade of Phipps' shoe mercery warehouse, while on Fish Street, the City Buildings were designed in 1901 by A. E. Anderson as a warehouse for the Glasgow firm of Malcolm Inglis, leather factors. Also in Derngate is the *Central Museum*, with a good local history display and the largest collection in the country of historic boots and shoes, together with shoe machinery. In *Bridge Street* (SP 754603) is the Museum of Leathercraft, with displays illustrating the use of leather on a world-wide basis.

On *Bridge Street* (SP 755598), near to the South Bridge, it is possible to appreciate the value of navigable waterways to the town. Wheat and barley from East Anglia were brought up the River Nene, indicated by the four-storey brick corn warehouse with wooden lucams to both river and road, which belonged to Latimer and Crick. Further west along the north river bank are two maltings, one now converted to a restaurant. The Carlsberg Brewery is the modern successor to the six breweries of late 19th-century Northampton. A railway goods and grain warehouse remains south of the river at SP 755596.

KETTERING was transformed in the last four decades of the 19th century from a small market town into a thriving industrial centre. Its earlier worsted weaving trade had declined by the early 19th century and the development of the town was hampered by poor communications: the Midland Railway's Leicester to Hitchin line was finally opened through the town in 1857. The large footwear firm of Thomas Gotch was founded in 1778 but remained the only one in the town until the 1860s. The population in this decade was 6,000. The footwear industry was

235. Housing and garden workshops in Princes Street, Kettering. (1:500 Ordnance Survey Map Sheet XXV.10.17, 1886.)

stimulated by large government orders at the time of the Franco-Prussian War, and the mechanisation of the industry resulted in many factories and associated housing being built in the 1870s. During this decade the population of the town grew by 55 per cent and the number of factories increased to 20. In the following decade the population expansion was even greater, reaching 75 per cent, and the number of factories doubled. By 1901, the population had risen to 29,000, a fourfold increase in as many decades.

Manufacturers like Meadows and Bryan and J. T. S. Stockburn built estates to accommodate this growing workforce to the north and east of the town centre, where the classic landscape of interspersed terraced rows with garden workshops and factories remains largely intact. Ancillary industries developed, including leather dressing and the manufacture of heels and lasts. The production of shoe machinery diversified into the more general engineering which still functions in the town. Kettering was an important centre for the Co-operative Movement, founded in the town in 1866, which both entered manufacture and provided housing. Further industrial development took place alongside the railway on the northern outskirts of the town where a large ironworks was built in 1878. This continued in production until 1959, although the quarries were worked until 1962, the ore being processed at Corby.

236. The decorative wholesale clothing factory on Field Street, Kettering.

237. The distinctive outline of the Crown brewery and maltings on Lower Street, Kettering.

GAZETTEER
(OS sheets 141 and 153)

Agriculture-based Industries

Bakery, Crown Street (SP 868792). The elaborate Co-operative Model Bakery of 1900, with a grocery warehouse alongside. The intricate tie bar plates bear the initials 'KICS' for Kettering Industrial Co-operative Society.

Lower Street (SP 866789). An impressive four-storey brewery of six bays, bearing the monogram 'JE, 1885' for John Elworthy. The kiln at the rear has an elaborate cowl and a slated roof, while a loading door backs on to Tanners Lane. The former Crown Brewery ceased operation in 1930 but the buildings, including several water tanks, survive despite nearby development. On the south side of Lower Street is a five- bay three-storey brick factory inscribed 'T H Geary, Leather Dresser'. The range of buildings to the rear has the louvred windows necessary for the storage of leather.

Transport

Midland Station (SP 863780) is typical of others on the Midland Railway extension to Hitchin, retaining good terracotta work and decorative cast iron platform canopy supports. Threatened by demolition in the 1970s, the local Civic Society spear-headed a successful campaign for its retention.

Manufacturing Industries: Textiles

Dryden Street (SP 866792), west of the Rockingham Road, comprises a complex of factories, multi-storey to the road and single storey behind. The office block has an elaborate Venetian-style porch. On the Field Street corner is the impressive building of the Kettering Clothing Manufacturing Co-operative Society, established in 1893: this has flat brick pilasters between the windows and ornate tie bar plates.

Northall Street (SP 866790). Number 55 is a complex of factory buildings, faced with ironstone on the street and brick behind with a central stone tower. The occupancy of J. T. Stockburn, stay manufacturer, is indicated by the letter 'S' over the central porch.

Manufacturing Industry: Engineering

Bath Road (SP 872791). The Perfecta Works of Timson were established in 1896 to manufacture shoe machinery; the present complex stretches back to Catesby Street and the main building has an interesting mansard roof.

Scotland Street (SP 874791). The works of Wicksteed Leisure were founded in the 1870s by Charles Wicksteed as a small engineering firm. He equipped Wicksteed Park to the south of the town and came to specialise in playground and leisure equipment.

Manufacturing Industry: Boots and Shoes

Bath Road, North Park (SP 872800). A massive multi-storey factory complex built in 1923 for William Timpson, who was established in another part of the town by 1865. The works is now Burlington Shoes, part of the British Shoe Corporation. This steel-framed building is a good example of the entry into the shoe trade of a manufacturer producing goods for his own multiple outlet retail chain.

Digby Street (SP 871792) contains several factories, in particular that at the corner of Bath Road. This has ornamental gables with alternate brick and stone banding fronting single storey workshops. It carries the monogram 'THB 1891' denoting T. H. Bird and a wall crane on the rear gable in Digby Street. The adjacent housing is contemporary and was erected by the shoe manufacturer.

Ebenezer Place (SP 868788). A narrow four-storey brick factory, dated 1873, belonged to Meadows and Bryan; a plaque depicts shoe making and leather working tools and the motto 'Nisi Dominus Frustra', recalling the firm's original premises in a converted chapel.

Field Street (SP 865792), particularly on the Cobden Street corner, contains an interesting variety of factories of different dates. J. Avon Ltd, built in 1878, has polychrome brickwork and round headed windows, while opposite are later steel-framed buildings of the 1920s and 1930s.

Green Lane (SP 869686). A fine three-storey factory with stone quoins, stringers and lintels above round headed windows and an elaborate corbel table. Originally built for Abbot and Bird in 1873, with later additions in 1885 and 1891. The factory used the first bricks made by the Kettering Brick and Tile Company.

Manor House Museum, Sheep Street (SP 868783) contains displays on Kettering industries.

Morley Street (SP 872798). An elaborate double-gabled office block, built in 1901 of stone and brick in Tudor style, fronting extensive single storey north light workshops.

Newman Street (SP 871786). The factory begun for N. Newman and Sons in the 1870s has several sections of three-storey and single storey north light workshops.

Princes Street, Crown Street and King Street (SP 870792) have identical terraced houses dated 1883/4, some bearing the motif 'Union in Strength'. These were built by a shoe-making co-operative and have workshops in the rear gardens.

Regent Street (SP 870794). A symmetrical 10-bay three-storey factory, dated 1890 with cast iron windows and four gables; an adjoining smaller building is dated 1891.

Regent Street, Havelock Street and Wood Street (SP 8779) are three parallel streets of terraced houses, developed in the 1880s and 1890s with small factories at street and alley corners; the houses are built of quality brick with terracotta ornamentation. Many of the houses have single storey garden workshops backing on to an access alley. One factory carries the motto 'Hand in Hand, Justice to All, 1890' over the door, an indication of the Co-operative movement. This area forms part of the development by the shoe manufacturers Meadows and Bryan.

Tresham Street (SP 871792). An uncompromising three-storey factory, 13 bays long and three bays wide, with a wall mounted crane on one gable end.

238. An unusually ornate shoe factory on Green Lane, Kettering, built in 1873.

239. Street corner factory, part of integrated development by J. T. S. Stockburn on Victoria and Alfred Streets, Kettering.

Victoria Street Much of the development by J. T. S. Stockburn leading east from this street has been demolished but early factories remain at the corners of *School Lane* (SP 870789), *Albert Street, Carrington Street* (SP 870788) and *Alfred Street* (SP 870789). The latter, of plain brick three-storey construction, is 16 bays long with gable mounted wall crane.

Wellington Street (SP 870792) Two three-storey factories, both dated 1887, stand at the corners of Princes Street and Montagu Street.

Wood Street (SP 870796). A two-storey factory with Dutch gables, built in 1894 for Loake Brothers, who are still in occupation. The front block fronts single storey north light workshops behind.

240. The converted railway station at Desborough, in typical Midland Railway style.

241. One of several surviving shoe factories: Victoria Street in Desborough.

242. Several boot and shoe garden workshops survive in Rothwell.

243. Small two-storey workshops on Well Lane in Rothwell.

DESBOROUGH

At first sight an uninspiring town on the A6, but a number of sites of interest remain to the east of the main road. As elsewhere, the leather industry was superimposed on an earlier centre. In the late 19th century, many leather and shoe factories were built, with associated terraced housing still provided with garden workshops. Much has been cleared, but workshops survive behind houses in *New Street* (SP 803834). At the top of this street, on *Gladstone Street*, is a three-storey 18-bay factory with cast iron windows. This was built as a shoe factory and still functions as a leather cutting warehouse. Further along Gladstone Street is the former *Railway Station* and adjoining house, built of ironstone in typical Midland Railway style with steep gables, barge boarding and twin round headed windows with leaded lights. In *Victoria Street* (SP 803832) two almost identical factories survive, two-storey plus cellar, each of nine bays with a centre gable. The earlier is dated 1896 and inscribed 'Co-operation', indicating the importance of the Co-operative Movement here as elsewhere in the shoe towns. This theme is continued in the large works on the A6, *Rothwell Road* (SP 801828), inscribed with white tiles 'Co-operative Wholesale Society Ltd, Corset Factory', an outlier of the elastic web industry established in Kettering and Leicestershire. Alongside are streets recalling the factory's designation, Federation Avenue, Pioneer Avenue and Unity Street.

ROTHWELL

Proud of its early town status, Rothwell was granted a market charter in 1204. It has some interesting buildings, including an almshouse and elaborate market hall, but interspersed with these are the remnants of its industrial development. Once a centre for the manufacture of silk plush for hats, it developed an extensive leather industry in the late 19th century. While the larger factories have been demolished, there are many garden workshops behind terraced housing which can still be seen, particularly to the north-west of the market square off the *Rushton Road* (SP 820813) and in *New Street* (SP 817814). From the dates on the terraces, many of these workshops date from the last two decades of the 19th and even into the 20th century, indicating the persistence of the outwork system in the shoe trade. At the market place end of Rushton Road (SP 819812) is a very functional T-shaped three-storey factory, once the Stanley Works of Taylor's Footwear. Evidence of the importance of the Co-operative Movement is, as in Rothwell, shown in the 'Co-operative Villas' and retail outlets. At the southern end of Market Hill, in *Well Lane* (SP 817811), near the almshouses, is a complex of industrial buildings including a bakery, a row of houses converted to workshops and several small two-storey workshop blocks in both brick and ironstone, one dated 1877.

Bibliography

General

P. H. ANDERSON, *Forgotten Railways of the East Midlands* (David & Charles, 1985)

P. Howard ANDERSON, *Regional Railway Handbooks: The East Midlands* (David & Charles, 1986)

J. V. BECKETT, *The East Midlands from AD.1000* (Longman, 1988)

British Regional Geology: Central England (HMSO, 1969)

British Regional Geology: Pennines and adjacent areas (HMSO, 1954)

S. D. CHAPMAN, *Early Factory Masters* (David & Charles, 1967)

C. R. CLINKER and Charles HADFIELD *The Ashby de la Zouch Canal and its Railways* (Avon Anglia, 1978)

G. H. DURY, *East Midlands and the Peak* (Nelson, 1963)

John GREENWOOD, *The Industrial Archaeology and Industrial History of the English Midlands: A Bibliography* (Kewdale Press, 1987)

Charles HADFIELD, *The Canals of the East Midlands* (David & Charles, 1970)

W. G. HOSKINS, *The Midland Peasant* (Macmillan, 1957)

Robin LELEUX, *A Regional History of the Railways of Great Britain: Vol 9, The East Midlands* (D St J Thomas, 1984)

Jean LINDSAY, *The Trent and Mersey Canal* (David & Charles, 1979)

Colin OWEN, *The Leicestershire and South Derbyshire Coalfield, 1200-1900* (Moorland, 1984)

Marilyn PALMER, *Framework Knitting* (Shire, 1984)

Marilyn PALMER and Peter NEAVERSON *A Guide to the Industrial Archaeology of the East Midlands* (AIA, 1986)

L. T. C. ROLT, *Navigable Waterways* (Penguin, 1985)

Ronald RUSSELL, *Lost Canals and Waterways of Britain* (Sphere Books, 1983)

David M. SMITH, *The Industrial Archaeology of the East Midlands* (David & Charles, 1965)

P. S. STEVENSON ed., *The Midland Counties Railway* (RCHS, 1989)

P. C. SYLVESTER-BRADLEY and T. D. FORD eds., *The Geology of the East Midlands* (Leicester UP, 1968)

Eric TONKS, *The Ironstone Quarries of the Midlands: Part 1: Introduction* (Runpast Publishing, 1988)

F. A. WELLS, *The British Hosiery and Knitwear Industry: its History and Organisation* (David & Charles, 1972)

Derbyshire

S. D. CHAPMAN, *Stanton and Staveley: A Business History* (Woodhead-Faulkner, 1981)

Joy CHILDS, *A History of Derbyshire* (Phillimore, 1987)

Brian COOPER, *Transformation of a Valley: The Derbyshire Derwent* (Heinemann, 1983)

Maxwell CRAVEN, *Derby, An Illustrated History* (Breedon Books, 1990)

Maxwell CRAVEN, *Bygone Derby* (Phillimore, 1989)

Trevor D. FORD and J. H. RIEUWERTS ed., *Lead Mining in the Peak District* (Peak District Mines Historical Society, 1983)

Dudley FOWKES ed., *Derbyshire Industrial Archaeology: A Gazetteer of Sites, Part I: Borough of High Peak* (Derbyshire Archaeological Society, 1984) and *Part II: Borough of Erewash* (1986)

Helen HARRIS, *Industrial Archaeology of the Peak District* (David & Charles, 1971)

John HEATH, *The Illustrated History of Derbyshire* (Barracuda, 1982)

John HEATH and Roy CHRISTIAN, *Yesterday's Town: Derby* (Barracuda, 1985)

John MARSHALL, *The Cromford and High Peak Railway* (David & Charles, 1982)

Frank NIXON, *Industrial Archaeology of Derbyshire* (David & Charles, 1969)

Don PETERS, *Darley Abbey: from monastery to industrial community* (Moorland, 1974)

Brian RADFORD, *Rail Centres: Derby* (Ian Allan, 1986)

P. RIDEN, *The Butterley Company, 1790-1830* (Derbyshire Record Society, 1990)

Peter STEVENSON, *The Nutbrook Canal* (David & Charles, 1970)

Leicestershire

John ANDERSON, *Leicestershire Canals: Bygones in Camera* (Author, 1976)

Norman ASHTON, *Leicestershire Watermills* (Sycamore Press, 1977)

Denis BAKER, *Coalville: the first seventy five years* (Leicestershire Libraries, 1983)

C. R. CLINKER, *The Leicester and Swannington Railway* (Avon Anglia, 1977)

David CRANSTONE ed., *The Moira Furnace* (NW Leicestershire DC, 1985)

Malcolm ELLIOTT, *Victorian Leicester* (Phillimore, 1979)

The Forest Line: an exploration of the Charnwood Forest Canal (Loughborough WEA, 1974)

Foxton Locks and Inclined Plane: A Detailed History (Leicestershire CC nd)

Richard GILL, *The Book of Leicester* (Barracuda, 1985)

Dave GOODWIN, *Foxton Locks and the Grand Junction Canal Company* (Leicestershire CC, 1988)

David HENRY, *Wind and Watermills of Rutland* (Spiegl Press, 1988)

W. G. HOSKINS, *The Making of the English Landscape: Leicestershire* (Hodder & Stoughton, 1957)

Wallace HUMPHREY *et al*, *Loughborough 1888-1988* (Charnwood BC, 1985)

The Leicester and Swannington Railway: A Car Trail (Leicestershire Museums, 1982)

Leicestershire Industrial Heritage (Leicestershire CC, 1983)

M. G. MILLER and S. FLETCHER, *The Melton Mowbray Navigation* (RCHS, 1984)

Roy MILLWARD, *A History of Leicestershire and Rutland* (Phillimore, 1985)

Nigel MOON, *Leicestershire and Rutland Windmills* (Sycamore Press, 1981)

Marilyn PALMER ed., *Leicestershire Archaeology Volume 3: Industrial Archaeology* (Leicestershire Museums, 1983)

N. PYE ed., *Leicester and its Region* (British Association, 1972)

D. A. RAMSEY, *Groby and its Railways* (Tee Publishing, 1982)

Jack SIMMONS, *Leicester Past and Present: Volume One: Ancient Borough and Volume Two: Modern City* (Eyre Methuen, 1974)

Philip A. STEVENS, *The Leicester Line, a History of the Old Union and Grand Union Canals* (David & Charles, 1972)

David TEW, *The Melton to Oakham Canal* (Sycamore Press, 1984)

Eric TONKS, *The Ironstone Quarries of the Midlands, Part VIII: Rutland* (Runpast Publishing, 1989)

Northamptonshire

The Boot and Shoe Industry in Northampton (Northampton Museums, 1976)

John BOYES and Ronald RUSSELL, *The Canals of Eastern England* (David & Charles, 1977)

Cynthia BROWN, *Northampton 1835-1985: Shoe Town, New Town* (Phillimore, 1990)

R. L. GREENALL, *A History of Northamptonshire and the Soke of Peterborough* (Phillimore, 1979)

Eric TONKS, *The Ironstone Quarries of the Midlands, Part III: The Northampton Area* (Runpast Publishing, 1989)

Nottinghamshire

John BECKETT, *The Book of Nottingham* (Barracuda, 1990)

Ian BROWN, *Nottinghamshire's Industrial Heritage* (Nottinghamshire County Council Leisure Services, 1989)

K. C. EDWARDS ed., *Nottingham and its Region* (British Association, 1966)

A. R. GRIFFIN, *The Nottinghamshire Coalfield 1881-1981* (Moorland, 1981)

Zillah HALLS, *Machine Made Lace in Nottingham* (City of Nottingham Leisure Services Committee, 1985)

David KAYE, *A History of Nottinghamshire* (Phillimore, 1987)

J. P. WILSON, *The Development of Nottingham's Railways* (Nottingham Civic Society, nd)

Subject Index

206